Fanfare for Brazil

by the same author

SUMMER SAGA
DANISH EPISODE
(*published by Faber and Faber*)

GATEWAY TO THE KHYBER
MADEIRA: PEARL OF THE ATLANTIC
(*published by Robert Hale*)

Fanfare for Brazil

ROBIN BRYANS

FABER AND FABER
24 Russell Square
London

First published in mcmlxii
by Faber and Faber Limited
24 Russell Square London WC 1
Printed in Great Britain by
W. & J. Mackay & Co Ltd Chatham
All rights reserved

For
JOSÉ AND REGIS

Contents

Illustrations

ILLUSTRATIONS

Obbligato

Obrigado is the way to say 'thank you' in Portuguese.
The reply is *de nada*, 'it's nothing'.
For me it was always something in Brazil. *Obrigado* was always
on my lips—meagre thanks for the astonishing Brazilian generosity,
in things, no less than in things of the spirit.

Obrigado is no way to thank Wladimir do Amaral Murtinho,
Chief of the Cultural Division of the Brazilian Foreign Office, and
his staff, for their heroic patience and endless kindness to a hungry
author who devoured their time, consumed photographs and books,
and tried to digest masses of information provided by the no less
patient staff of the Foreign Office library.

Nor is *obrigado* any way to thank Herbert and Hilda Konen of
Brasilia. Herbert was more than manager in the Bank of London &
South America. He was friend, savant, and a naturalist who saw
beauty where none might be thought to exist. Hilda was more than
a hostess, she was Brazilian hospitality personified. Nothing was
too much trouble for them.

Obrigado is hardly thanks enough to Baron Jesco von Puttkamer,
whose love and knowledge of the Araguaia and Xingu river Indians
was the great inspirer of his photographs, which he so freely put
at my disposal.

Obrigado says little to Dr. Raul de Oliveira, Secretary General of
the Fundaçao Brazil Central, nor to the members of the Brazilian
Air Force who gave generously of their services to fly me hither and
thither, always cheerfully.

And *obrigado* betrays nothing of my debt to Oscar Niemeyer,
whose genius and whose architecture are so Brazilian because they
are human and warm, as Oscar himself was during the times when
he talked to me of his art . . . and of Brazil.

My book could be filled with *obrigado* obbligatos for the known

15

OBBLIGATO

and unknown people who gave me lifts in their cars or boats, who played music for me or gave me gifts, and who went out of their way to be generous.

De nada, they would all say, 'it's nothing'.

But it was everything.

ROBIN BRYANS

São Francisco do Sul,
State of Santa Catarina
1961

Profile of young Brazil—
serious with the long
hope and the long me-
mory

Serenity and a straw hat
for the sun of Bahia

Sertanista—the backwoodsman fights at the frontiers of starvation

Shy boy with skull—his skin will shine like polished mahogany

1

An Independent Air

I felt guilty about slipping away like that. It wasn't as though even the summer in England had been good. But to leave the country in early December, when the terrible autumn floods had given way to the first fogs, traffic jams and ice-bound roads, was treason. So I thought it only just to suffer right up to the actual moment when the ship left. To expiate my sin of leaving for the south and the sun, I had to face an excruciating railway journey from Nottingham. It started late because of fog. We had to 'all change' into a bus because the floods had washed a railway bridge away.

But at each new infliction I rejoiced. When a porter at Swansea station pointed out a commercial hotel across the road, I could have leapt. For my boat to Brazil was leaving from Swansea in the morning and I thought that a night of discomfort would completely purge my soul by 8 a.m. Then I could join the ship with a clear conscience, having borne my share of the pains which the Briton endures in the winter. This done I could cheerfully send sunny, palmy postcards from Las Palmas to my friends—*Wish you were here. Wonderful food and drink.*

However, weakness of the flesh prevented my night of discomfort. The hotel asked for my money before I saw the room. The woman explained that some of their customers fled before morning without paying their bill. So I handed over my cash. But that room! Of course, I had roughed it years before in seamen's dolly-dives. But all my good intentions vanished when I saw the damp walls and the bedclothes unchanged from at least three previous occupants. I wanted my money back—and got it after the police had called out the chief public health inspector. He came up, took one look at the room and immediately banned it. The ex-champion boxer who owned the place was almost in tears.

'I didn't know, see?' he kept repeating. He paid my premium back gladly.

I spent one of the most comfortable nights of my life in the voluptuous bed of a nearby boarding-house. The last thing I saw on the sitting-room TV was Lady Violet Bonham Carter in the Brains Trust. She was talking about discomfort and morality. She didn't believe in punishing the body for the good of the soul. She thought it best to be unaware of one's body—which I certainly was until next morning.

Walking through Swansea's grey streets towards the docks, I was feeling superior. All *these* wretches, I said to myself, these poor Joneses and Lewises and Llewellans and Griffiithses, were going to spend a miserable, rainy Christmas round smoky fires filled with soft coal from Swansea's mountain valley hinterland. Whereas I would spend Christmas in Rio de Janeiro, basking on Copacabana beach, watching slim brown figures from behind my sunglasses.

I passed a chapel with a notice outside, *To all who enter God's blessing be upon you. To those who pass by may the same blessing go with you.* Excitement about boarding the m.v. *Rubens*, lying now out in King's Dock, would not let me linger. I continued my dockland walk, for I only had light hand-luggage. Besides, the *Rubens* was a cargo boat, so there would be no swanking about with other passengers, making up fours for bridge as if in a Somerset Maugham festival. The *Rubens* came from Liverpool and put in to Swansea to collect neither sandalwood nor sweet white wine, nor a cargo of cheap tin trays, but pressed tin for Brazil. It is impossible to be romantic about pressed tin.

The dock area was like something conceived by Dylan Thomas. I walked past Wards the shipping butchers and Crimes the ship fumigators, Tom Smith for chain slings and then, so surprisingly and absurdly out of context, white and trim among an atmosphere of sad decay, a little church—the Norwegian Seamen's Church. It was built quite close to a low railway bridge whose stones were corroded by time, grime and sea-atmosphere to a crumbly, Gruyèreish texture which, together with some magnificent nineteenth-century brick warehouses not far away, would have made a nice day out for John Betjeman or John Piper. The Norwegian church however was irresistible, too. By its crisp whiteness it seemed to bring the peerless Scandinavian atmosphere to the Swansea haze.

The docks and quaysides and sheds were threaded by a tangle of railway lines. They moved and merged on the ground like aeroplane trails high up in a blue sky. Their meeting and parting and vanishing to some unknown destination was a symbol of my journey to Brazil. Also the railway lines made me think of ruined temples in jungles. In view of my respect for personal comfort, it was extremely unlikely that I would emulate Colonel Fawcett in Brazil. Yet, with luck, I might stumble over some fallen masonry whose carved mouldings looked exactly like the rails' cleats. This connection of ideas amused me—Swansea docks on a grey drizzly day and Brazil's hothouse jungles. Yet it was not all drollery, for the link from Swansea to Rio was real and direct—or would be if I could find the *Rubens*. Some dockers ambling along in the afternoon light like Daumier characters told me where the ship was berthed. Round the corner of one of the huge sheds, sweeping iron architecture of the *Rubens's* bows loomed over my head.

Castles had always fascinated me, and so had ships. I learnt in school that ships had a forecastle, and in one school book I saw an engraving of a mediaeval ship complete with little round towers and battlements and a man about to shoot a crossbow through a slit. I thought castles and ships a wonderful combination. Both, I used to think, had a fine solidity and bigness about them. Mere houses or rowing-boats were not to be compared. Most childhood magic evaporates, but this spell had never been broken for me. So when I saw the boat for Brazil, the image of a castle sprang into my mind. Like a defensive outer wall, the *Rubens's* black-painted plated sides rose sheer from the quayside. As in a castle wall, there were only a few openings, portholes small as arrow slots. High above me was the anchor drawn up like a portcullis. Instead of a barbican there was a bridge and in place of a keep the strangely keep-like funnel. I knew the ship would have decks at different levels, connected by

19

steep stairs, like a castle's inner defences. When we sailed the gangway would be pulled up like a drawbridge and we would be alone, inside the walls, listening to sounds of attack from our enemy, the sea.

The sea, in fact, was not to attack too furiously. December gales and storms had dropped. When I boarded the *Rubens* not a breath of wind disturbed Swansea's murky waters. But in any case, even if there had been a gale, I should have wanted no delay. Nothing ought to stop us now before we came in sight of Las Palmas in the bland islands of the sun. But, of course, ships cannot just be driven off like cars, though in this respect ships are better than castles which cannot be moved at all. So there was a lot of coming and going and this included a Customs official who gave me clearance. He apparently decided, contrary to usual practice, that I was telling the truth when I declared that I had nothing to declare. Night came down drawing a veil over Swansea's architectural indecency. Clad in darkness, decked with strings of sodium lamps and ropes of pearl bulbs for matching jewellery, Swansea looked almost attractive. Beautiful or not, that was how I was to see Britain vanish, a chain of lights strung out like dew on a spider's web.

Las Palmas was four days away, though this was a problem in relativity. Time signified nothing. All I cared was that the Canary Islands would be different. Not only would the sun shine and be hot, but it would also carry the manufacturer's guarantee of quality and permanency. During that summer, the English sun had been an inferior product, unreliable and without spare parts for break-downs. But there was none of that sort of nonsense about the Canaries. Meanwhile I prepared for the four days' siege in the castle. A full-scale attack from the enemy could reasonably be expected in the Bay of Biscay. The only effective weapon was aptly described to me once by an American woman—'If you've got plenty down, you've got plenty to come up.' So I began to get plenty down. This was an easy task in the *Rubens's* officers' dining-room. The menu looked like a French Dada poem—though the food it represented made a good deal more sense, as did the ship's rum, gin and whisky at ninepence a go.

We left the Channel, entered and left a Biscay Bay as smooth as a Buddha's belly. We exchanged, as it were, the monotony of hymns in Swansea's chapels for the subtleties of Debussy's *La Mer*. And when I walked out of my cabin to the upper deck on the fifth morning the blunt, bow-headed, whale-backed mountains of Wales were exchanged for the sharp, arrow-pointed, shark-finned ridges of Las Palmas. The acquaintance was brief, because the *Rubens*'s principal business there was simply to bunker for the run down to Brazil. This run itself intrigued me, for in error I had supposed we would follow the African coast and then go *across* the Atlantic to Brazil. But Mercator's projection, however adequate for the technical points of navigation, does not reveal the world's curvature and the Atlantic's immensity and anonymity to the inexpert eye. Our course was a straight one. Las Palmas—Salvador (Bahia), on the *Rubens*'s chartroom table, was at 208 degrees.

Barbeiro, barber, officer on the ship said, is the Brazilian favourite term of abuse. In the Argentine, apparently, they said 'shoemaker' instead. After we left Las Palmas and its long mole, I was expecting somebody to call me *barbeiro*. In a three-hour session I cut the junior officers' hair. Most of them needed a barber, and did not get ashore at Las Palmas. Others did not need a barber, but fell nevertheless victim to my scissors, clippers and comb. My qualification was that I had learnt to cut hair when I went to sea as a boy. My clients included one cadet on his maiden voyage. Some of the officers had a go at the cadet's hair and left me to repair their damage. He took it very well. Captain Williams behaved well also at dinner that night when most of his officers trooped in looking like Japanese wrestlers. I had given them a cross between a crew cut and an American college-boy cut. They called it the *Rubens* skullcap. But for the hot weather we were running into the skullcap was ideal.

I was very pleased when the birds came. They started before we even got to the Canaries. They tumbled and flitted erratically about the waves, running as it were with dangling black feet from crest to crest. They were storm petrels and followed us for many days. Quite a number of them landed on the deck in an exhausted condition and were rescued by the crew. The storm petrels seemed to like human company and had no objection to being made a fuss of in the crew's quarters, where they were treated as pets. Other sorts of birds came aboard also. Whenever Captain Williams spied a specimen from the bridge he would send word to me. The one I least expected to see was the little stint, the smallest and most dainty of waders. But unlike the storm petrels the little stint did not take to cabin captivity. He died overnight much to the sorrow of the dining-room steward, who was the most enthusiastic of the bird collectors.

Birds, of course, were not the only things which flew in that part of the world. Schools of flying fish flung themselves out of the sea. They hurtled across the blue water like squadrons of jet fighters. The fish flashed in the sun as they turned on their fin-wings. Then they vanished beneath the surface again. More than for their appearance and the shoals' excellent imitation of a splattering Halloween sparklet, flying fish were coveted for their taste. The crew was sorry that the sea was not rougher. Flying fish would then crash-land on the deck and be collected, gasping, carried below and converted, in a trice of the cook's knife, into excellent trout-like eating. We also had a following of porpoises, the sea's most graceful and beautiful creatures. They played and dived all round the boat. Their favourite station was at the bows, where they took baths in the bow-wave. To rid themselves of sea-lice the porpoises scraped themselves against the bows and the thud of their bodies could be heard through the plating in the holds.

Sixty miles or so north of the Equator we passed close in to St. Paul Rocks. Not many ships run quite as far in and consequently not many people see them in detail. This is no loss. The rocks are singularly uninteresting. Nobody would bother to look at them at all except that they are the first object resembling dry land which is seen for several days in any direction. They are not large or high and except for sea-birds have no inhabitants—not even a Lorelei. In profile they were not unlike the view of Whitehall's skyline seen from St. James's Park, with a pinnacle of rock like the Albert Memorial.

Such an association of ideas, obviously enough, could not have occurred to the early Portuguese navigators who were cruising about this area of the South Atlantic. However, if they *did* see St. Paul Rocks they may well have thought that another continent was about to be discovered. The disappointment can be imagined. A Portuguese gentleman called Pedro Álvares Cabral had more luck. He was on his way to India in the year A.D. 1500. On the 22nd April he sighted land. It could have been an island, or just more rocks. But he decided it was an island and named it 'Ilha da Vera Cruz'. Then it turned out to be a vast, immeasurable land. Cabral, no doubt feeling pleased with himself, changed the name to 'Terra da Santa Cruz'—Land of the Holy Cross. He claimed it for Dom Manuel, King of Portugal. Eventually the name of Santa Cruz was changed to Brazil.

Portugal took little or no interest in Brazil for nearly half a century. Then the rumour went round—gold! The first governor-general went south like a shot and in March 1549 sailed into a most splendid, immense bay. This was called the Bay of All Saints. He established a settlement and named it St. Saviour. The complete name in Portuguese was a most beautiful euphony—*São Salvador da Bahia de Todos os Santos*. Suitably, the first governor-general arrived with the first Jesuit priests. They were as hot in the pursuit of Indian converts as the governor was for gold. But it was no rumour, for there was gold. The town of Salvador thrived and two centuries later was still the capital of the vast colony. But in 1763 the capital was moved farther south to Rio de Janeiro. Two centuries later still, in April 1960, the capital moved once more, this time to Brasilia in the interior. The new capital was going to be a pilgrimage for me. Meanwhile I was pleased to have the Bay of All Saints as my first sight of Brazil and to first put my foot ashore at Salvador itself, which is still, after four hundred years, the fourth city of Brazil.

Santa Cruz was perhaps not a very inspired name to give such a momentous discovery. But doubtless navigator Cabral was no poet. The new name, however, evolved simply enough. A red wood used for dyeing was exported, and this wood was known as *pau-brasil*, while the exporters were called *Brasileiros*. Quite early on the

English had a finger in the Portuguese trading pie and did business in brazilwood. King Charles II of England fixed this when he married Catherine Braganza. In fact, it was one of the reasons why he married her. They were not in love. His cousin Louis XIV had already refused her. Yet Charles was most anxious to lay hands on her dowry, for it included the exclusive right to trade direct with Brazil—a Portuguese monopoly until then.

From the beginning, Brazil developed its own individual characteristic. At the moment in which Cabral claimed the new country for Portugal, Portugal also lost it. As Brazil grew rich and expanded, as cities appeared on the long Atlantic seaboard, power was germinated. Brazilian problems were never European ones, although Portugal often shipped its problems and problem people, especially criminals, to Brazil. When the strings were pulled in Europe the South American puppet did not always react as expected. When Philip II of Spain added Portugal to his crown he more or less abandoned Brazil to fend for itself. Brazil was extremely vulnerable. Communication from one part of the country to another was difficult. Pirates and Philip's enemies appeared time and again on the green-blue horizon to sail in and sack the coastal cities. The experts at this plundering were England, France, and Holland. Brazil at that time was going as a prize for anybody who could bag it. Even when Portugal was again independent of Spain in 1640, the Dutch still held great tracts of Brazilian territory.

Meanwhile, Brazil continued to grow. Before long the European immigrants outnumbered the indigenous Indians. And this, perhaps, was the fulcrum on which the fate of Brazil turned. The native Indians were insufficient in number to man the vast estates developed by the Portuguese. The possibilities of expansion were limitless, yet not enough labour could be found. And so the African slave was brought to sweat and die in the sugar-fields. He multiplied and continued to sweat and die in slavery for many generations. His descendants are today born free. The smiling negro face, happy as only negroes can be, has become the richest feature of the Brazilian face.

Mass slavery on the scale that was necessary to maintain the European colonies is now difficult to envisage. The sheer size of the shipping operation, the accommodation, feeding and setting to work of the thousands of slaves is staggering. Jungle was cleared, states established, sugar planted, cut in season and shipped to Europe. Docks and harbours were built. Towns, roads, bridges and every kind of building were constructed. The slave was the indispensable member of this society, yet totally devoid of rights in it. Miraculous indeed is not that it ever started, but that, once wound up and running, it was ever stopped. Portugal dealt in slaves from as early as 1444 and by 1530 some towns had more negroes than whites. Evora was one of them. The saintly and scholarly Henry the Navigator had some of the earliest slaves shipped from Lagos. At that time the Moors were being ejected from the Iberian peninsula and the attack against Islam carried to neighbouring African shores. Henry's own brother Fernando was held captive at Fez after a battle. The Moors treated him savagely. When slavery began, no love was lost between Christian Europe and non-Christian Africa.

The slave trade was big business. Even Charles II and his queen held shares in the Company of Royal Adventurers of England into Africa, whose accounts for 1673 show the profits on 15,585 slaves given in exchange for 3,500 tons of sugar and other bills of commerce. Because the shippers knew that only half of each cargo would get to Brazil alive, they packed their ships as full as possible with the unfortunate Africans. Conditions below the deck cannot be imagined. Slavers could easily be recognized at sea, even from great distances away, by the fearful stench borne on the wind. Apart from mental disturbances arising from captivity, or the effects of being branded with hot irons for recognition purposes, the negroes contracted a disease called *maculo*. They caught it from each other, and having no natural resistance went down by the thousand. The principal symptom was a terrible diarrhoea, worse than the kind politely suffered today by Europeans on moving to the tropics. Nobody cared about the sick slaves. There was no herbal tea or chemists' preparations. They simply died.

The half which did not die must have considered arrival in Brazil as a comparative paradise, at least until they reached the slave market and went to forced labour on the plantations. Here they found themselves in a curious situation occupying a place between their Portuguese masters and the native Indians. The negroes' performance as slaves was altogether better than the Indians. Some of the negroes were, in fact, more cultured than their European masters, many of whom could neither read nor write.

The most sinned against in Brazil was the negro, whether he was given as a plaything to the master's vicious children or to the sadistic whim of the master himself. Jesuits themselves at one time banned the negro from their mission schools. The Society presumably foresaw considerable losses to its own treasury should its own slaves learn the arts of freedom. The Jesuit record in Brazil is far from blameless, however much culture and catechism they may have brought. They were much involved in slave traffic and often their missions were nothing better than export warehouses trading in drugs and sugar.

Only one person succeeded in facing up to the Jesuits. This was the great Portuguese minister of the mid-eighteenth century, Pombal. He banished the Jesuits from the mother country and declared the Brazilian Indians free men and granted them the land and villages taken over by the Jesuits. Pombal also abolished the Inquisition, just in time before he became inflicted with a horrible disease which prevented him from putting his feet to the ground without pain and continuous diarrhoea.

The thousands of tormented negroes had to wait longer for liberation. The nineteenth-century abolition of slavery is usually ascribed to the Nonconformist conscience. But possibly this conscience was propelled by deeper, more widespread feeling in man that the time for less inhumanity to man was more than ripe. Some such deep undercurrent allied to mass feeling may have lain behind the Church's possession and use of slaves in Brazil. It would hardly be likely to do otherwise when even a pope had issued an edict 'to attack, subject, and reduce to slavery the Saracens, Pagans and other enemies of Christ'. The Brazilian possessions of the Church were immense and wealthy. Its estates were well organized. There appears to have been less brutality than on secular estates, and sick or aged slaves were cared for.

Such a situation, to modern eyes, is nevertheless anomalous. Yet the lot of the slave on Brazilian sugar plantations was probably not a great deal worse than that of the peasant in the mother country, Portugal. And it is often supposed that the negro slave was snatched from a paradise in West Africa and sent to a hell in South America. In fact, the negro was often betrayed to the slave-trader by enemy tribes, or worse, by his own tribal chief who received a cut on the profits. Subject to fear of the witch-doctor, a prey to disease, subject at all times to sudden death or deprivation by attack, the West African was far from free even in his own country. Although wrong in principle, it is not impossible that on Brazilian Jesuit estates many of the slaves lived longer and more peaceably than they would have done in Africa. In Brazil, as elsewhere, the whip and the leg-irons were always there. In Africa there was the poisoned arrow and bondage to tribal custom and superstition.

Slavery in Brazil, for better or worse, grew to tremendous proportions. On the foundation of profits from slave labour, Brazil began to find itself. It could think and act without reference to Portugal. And tables were completely turned when the Portuguese Court moved to Brazil. And this was perhaps the most significant point in the country's history. Unlike other South American countries final independence was achieved without the services of a liberator. And from the first days of independence Brazil had none of the backwater colonialism about it, due in part to the Court's presence.

This important royal move to Brazil took place early in the nineteenth century when Napoleonic France invaded Portugal. The decision was taken by the Prince Regent. As in Britain at the time, the Portuguese sovereign was mad. But Queen Maria I was probably worse than our George III, as no doubt Dr. Willis would have told you, for he attended them both in his capacity as expert in royal insanity. She had much to madden her, and after the Paris Revolution she spent her time screaming about imaginary flames of hell. The Portuguese Prince Regent, like his opposite number in England, moved the Court to Brazil, as Prinny carried his to Brighton. Safe from the French, Dom João set to and did what he could to improve

Rio de Janeiro. The city became a famous centre for commercial and artistic activities. He didn't want to go home when poor Maria died and when Portugal was freed from French occupation in 1815. So he stayed on, now as King João VI, and for five years ruled Portugal from Rio de Janeiro—Brazil itself now being a kingdom of its own under the Portuguese crown.

In 1821 King João went home, leaving his own son, Dom Pedro, as Regent of Brazil. Dom Pedro, however, was a man of ideas. In 1822, on 7th September, he declared Brazil totally independent of Portugal and was himself made constitutional Emperor. Dom Pedro I may not have been altogether altruistic in his motives. Perhaps he preferred to remain in the hot, sensuous south, since his special love was for young negro girls. But a decade later he was forced to abdicate in favour of his son, Pedro II, who began to govern personally at the age of fifteen. And it was during the fifty years of this reign that modern Brazil emerged—a system of government, opening up of the country by railways and industry, with cotton, rubber and, of course, coffee as the basis of wealth.

So, painlessly, Brazil survived intrigue and without bloodshed achieved stature as a nation. It remained for Dom Pedro's reign also to end slavery. The first law prohibiting slavery had been made in 1831 (thirty years before the American Civil War!), though the law was not enforced. The planters still needed vast quantities of cheap labour to tame and cultivate the wild hinterlands behind the coastal cities. But Emperor Pedro II was bent on complete abolition. By 1850 this was almost achieved and by 1888, completely so, with all Brazilian slaves declared free. The act itself was signed on the 13th May by Princess Isabel, then Regent of the Empire, on her father's behalf. There was, of course, much rejoicing. But there were also rumblings of rebellion among the aristocracy and the planters, whose wealth depended on slavery. To the poor, the princess was Isabel the Redeemer, but her noble gesture made the rich her enemies. On signing the edict Isabel said to the President of the Cabinet, 'You see, my dear Councillor, I have won the game.' He replied prophetically, 'Your Royal Highness has won this game, but have lost your throne.' Nevertheless, Isabel still remains a favourite with Brazilian people. I was told with delight how the Emperor had asked his daughter what she would like for a birthday gift. For months she had been going incognito among the city's slave quarters, moved to distress by what she saw. To have the people freed was not only her birthday wish but the desire of her life.

In 1889 Pedro II was forced to leave the country to the Republicans. But his principal objects were achieved. Unlike so many other countries, the newly liberated Brazil did not turn and rend its royalty. With fond irony the heads of kings and emperors and Princess Isabel still appear on Brazilian banknotes. And the Government even went to the trouble of bringing Dom Pedro II's body back to Brazil to inter it in state at Petropolis Cathedral.

From then on Brazil has been governed by elected presidents, although it was by a revolution that the great Getulio Vargas first got to power in 1930. His is possibly one of the great names in this century—his permanent monument is Brazil's modern architecture. Vargas committed suicide in 1954 rather than allow the armed forces to overthrow him. Then Juscelino Kubitschek won the 1955 presidential elections. His achievement was to bring to fruition the long-conceived idea of moving the Brazilian capital into the interior and in opening the interior itself. This was the first major move of civilization from the coastal belt. The inception and construction of Brasilia within five years was the most audacious project ever undertaken in Brazil or perhaps anywhere.

Much has been and will be said about Brasilia. According to their lights the prophets foretell its early failure or long rise to success. But this much is clear, the creation of Brasilia has a familiar air of boldness about it—familiar because the early Portuguese navigators of unknown seas, who discovered Brazil, had the same boldness. Even in our modern world, the human being can still do the rash, crazy, inspired thing. Or perhaps it takes a Brazilian to bring it off. But I was on my way to Brazil to see for myself.

29

2

Black Magic

A myriad impressions of Salvador could have come to me as the *Rubens* came alongside. Yet one ousted all the others. We could see her long before the ship tied up. She stood on the quayside, a little apart from the stevedores and hangers-on, a lone figure beside a gantry. As the *Rubens* drew silently nearer, I could see that the woman was probably in her late twenties. One hand was held in an imploring gesture to all of us on board who lined the rails. The other stroked the head of her young son. It was a blonde head.

Salvador vibrated with heat. In the shallow shadow cast by a long line of warehouses the dockers lounged. Many were negroes. I could not see how anybody in Salvador could overcome the midday torpor in order to work. Yet our cargo had to be unloaded. Before nightfall the *Rubens* would be out to sea again. But the young woman stood in the sun. She called to the crew that the boy's father had been an English sailor. A sailor from England, she said over and over again. Her voice conveyed pride, accusation, and the melancholy of things past.

For the present moment, however, the woman had no hope of establishing further relations with English sailors, because the *Rubens* crew had no shore leave in Salvador. So she contented herself by asking for food to fill the boy's white stomach. She lifted his ragged shirt to prove that it *was* white. She also wanted empty beer cans. I thought of all the beer cans which left a trail across the bed of the Atlantic as we had thrown them through the ship's portholes. I wondered why she wanted empty cans. But later I saw her sitting at the roadside near the dock gates with a pair of scissors, very cleverly making lampshades from old tins.

But I was aware simultaneously of a thousand other impressions —fleeting glimpses of Salvador's cliff-top skyline, of ships in the bay, of football being played in a cloud of dust, of vultures circling above the town, of green slimy water between the *Rubens*'s side and the quay, of traveller's tree windmill arms somewhere above roof-tops, of heat and of light so intense that it washed the blueness from the bluest of skies. Men on the quayside ambled in that loose-limbed easy way which comes from an African ancestry, and from movement in heat. It was too hot for them to walk in the stiff-muscled, military way of the European. Because of the heat they wore hats with wide brims, and their shirts open at the front to show brown torsos. Most of the men were barefoot or had the frailest of slipper-soles. I could hear them flap-flapping along the quay.

Not all the modern clutter of dockside machinery, gantries and rails, the great steel ships, nor the tangle of electric cables, nor the hum of traffic beyond the dock could destroy my illusion of a romantic Salvador. This was the city I had dreamed of, the colourful, hot-blooded Salvador of the ancient air. Without closing my eyes I could see the place as it was when sailing ships came in, stinking with their loads of new slaves, and when the quaysides thronged with crowds of negroes and their masters.

I was not indulging entirely in romantic fancies, but also in facts. For Salvador had been flamboyant with unbridled life. I could sense that this lingered still. The woman and her English sailor's son was the continuing story of the old Salvador. The golden little boy was not the first Brazilian to be born of sailor-love. Here, where the *Rubens* hovered waiting to tie-up, had come the slave ships. To meet them had come the Portuguese planters wanting to buy the strongest or most beautiful negro men and women; here had waited the German merchants and Jewish jewellers to look over the Queen's Orphans shipped out from Portugal.

It was like catching a fever. My temperature went up, my pulse increased, and I looked at my first sight of Brazil with delirious eyes. But no better way of arriving in Brazil could be imagined. This snatching of a few hours was tantalizing and only sharpened my appetite. But I would have to wait for Rio de Janeiro before going ashore permanently. Fortunately I was to have other, longer visits to Salvador. Even distantly, from the sea, Salvador was bewitching, for it was a city of skylines. The modern city, too, which sprawled crabwise out from the old centre, seemed perched along the cliff-top. And the old town itself was studded with the towers of many churches. I doubted whether there really were enough for the faithful to use a different one on every day of the year without repeating themselves. But true or false, from the *Rubens*'s rails I could see already a dozen or more, ranged along Salvador's escarpment. The eighteenth-century city must have been choked with churches, for it was much smaller than the modern town. This has half a million people and a large percentage of them are negroes.

To get ashore I had to fight my way through the traders. They invaded the ship as soon as the gangway was down. Parrots and monkeys, wild cats and marmosets, clay water pots and dope were amongst their wares, though I suspected the last of not being the genuine article. The traders preferred to be paid in cigarettes rather than money. And the only English they spoke was to quote the prices. 'Eight hundred ciggies', one said when I asked about his parrot. We both understood that if I really wanted it he would let the bird go for five hundred Players. In true sea fashion, four of the galley crew bought parrots to keep company with the orphan storm petrels still on board. However, not having cigarettes or Scotch whisky or Cadbury's chocolate to barter for love herbs or toucans, I escaped to the gangway and the dock gates, although outside there were more vendors. There were also coffee booths in shacks with a complement of parrots on chains and more marmosets hopping about in their filthy cages.

As soon as I left the docks, Salvador's extraordinary skyline became even more dramatic. But this closer view showed that the tall, narrow houses, perched at the escarpment's top, were old and crumbling. No less crumbly were many of the baroque churches set among them. Below, on the steep-sided cliffs, stood rougher huts, half-hidden by the large, fleshy leaves of banana trees. There was dust in the air and pungent smells of which sanitary inspectors would rightly not approve. There was the atmosphere of broken-

Let's dress up and dance . . .

. . . or eat at the Bahian sweetmeat stall

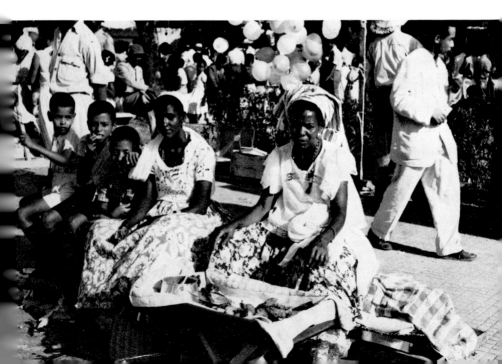

Feathers for a *festa*—her beads and bangles jangle in the sambas

Tiles and transport—*azulejos* on the wall, farmer on the bullock

down pavements, peeling paint, cracked windows, fouled-up drains which is common to South America. But in no less measure there was the indefinable tropical allure which had brought me to Brazil. I was not less sceptical than other Europeans about the filth and poverty, not unaware of the indifference which bred it. But an elusive magnificence remained none-the-less, the same magnificence that clung to those gilded baroque wonders up in the town, despite age, despite the Church's decline in power since slaving days. So walking into Salvador's heat and dirt I was glad of its glory, glad of its sun and the burning reds of its flamboyant trees.

The city's escarpment must always have been a handicap. It divided Salvador into upper and lower towns. A precarious-looking car was hauled up rails by a cable. I found that this installation, the *Plano Inclinado*, had been made in 1915. How Salvador managed to commute between its two parts before then, I had no idea. Perhaps the problem had been solved by slave labour, as most problems seemed to have been before steam and emancipation. I decided to leave the *Plano Inclinado* alone until the afternoon and concentrate on the lower town, although 'concentrate' hardly describes the way I wandered aimlessly about. I probably missed important master-pieces of architecture and vital links with Brazil's past, but I was more than content to take things as they came.

They came, in fact, in fairly rapid succession, especially the first car which almost ran into me. If Salvador had a speed limit it must have been at least 80 m.p.h. Without knowing exactly how, I got across the lower town's main thoroughfare and went into a side street. Everywhere there was decay. Even new buildings, or those still under construction, looked worn out already. Yet there was the charm of narrow streets glowing with reflected light, and between tall buildings sudden open places where Brazilians lounged, talking in their energetic way, hands moving expressively, like dancers of Bali. Glimpses of tropical plants, luxuriant, succulent, could be got as they climbed the escarpment over a tiled roof, or hung over high garden walls. Salvador throbbed with life. Nobody was still. In the stultifying heat, half-naked negroes staggered in and out of a ware-house with gigantic sacks of grain on their shining backs. In another place more negroes attacked a mountain of gravel with shovels. Few passers-by took any notice of the pavement cook-shops and their sizzling beans, nor of the negro women selling their strange African-Salvadorian dishes, such as *acaragé* beans served as a cake, or the same beans served with shrimps and oil and wrapped up in banana leaves and called *abará*. Women, too, threaded their way along the crowded pavements, balancing impossible bundles on their heads. To the dust and traffic fumes was added the smell of spices and the stench of hides being loaded on to a lorry.

Lorries charged dangerously along the main roads. Labourers were standing up in the back, shirts open, cooling off in the flow of air. There were mule carts, too, a reminder that in Salvador the old Brazil is not extinct. Some of the carts carried loads of razor-grass. Mango-sellers went by, astride their asses, their mangoes in two panniers each side of the beast. Brazil takes first place in the world for the breeding of asses. This, together with other curious facts, is part of a Brazilian tendency to indulge in the art of world comparison. Besides the ass production, there was a new, all-time record of Brazilian-produced motor-cars. Nearly every one of three hundred pages in a book about Brazil claimed the largest this or that. For instance, the book said that Brazil has the world's largest football stadium, the largest refrigerated slaughter-house in South America, Brazil occupies the first place in world production of tantalum, and that the country is also first in the production of castor oil. And not to be outdone, Salvador had its record number of churches.

One advantage of Salvador's churches was that they offered frequent cool shelter from the heat. Keeping in the shadow of a wall, I walked to the Pillar Church. The exquisite, florid carving of its stonework astonished me. It was far too expert, its inventiveness too rich for those broken-down surroundings. The main façade stood on a little raised square. Wide steps led up to it. Its windows and doors, elaborate, delicate and dignified, were closed. I pushed the heavily panelled west door, but it, too, was locked. The whole place was silent in the sun.

A vast wall flanked one side of the square. On its top stood a great colonnade like a squat Greek temple. But behind the columns only a tangle of lush plants and banana leaves flourished, translucent in the glancing sunlight. Through an archway I found a courtyard beside the church. It was filled with the tinkling sound of water which flowed from a shrine at one end. And there, too, I found the *sala dos milagres*. This room of miracles was also shut. But only wire-netting covered the windows and I could see the miraculous objects hanging inside. These *ex-votos* were a link with African witchcraft brought to Salvador by slaves. The offerings, hung on the little chapel's walls and from its ceiling, took the form of human members and were cast in wax. Their purpose was connected with the miraculous cure of illness. Such offerings are not uncommon in certain Catholic countries, particularly those which once had slaves. But the Brazilian *ex-votos* were different. Most of the waxen votive images, of eyes like castanets, of heads and pairs of legs in all shapes and sizes, feet and arms, kidneys and bladders, ears and noses and tongues, were not thanks for miracles done, as in other countries. They were images on to which the sufferer hoped to transfer his own sickness as in witchcraft's similar process. So thin was the veil of Catholicism drawn across this practice that many Brazilians regarded it as pagan. Some priests banned *ex-votos* from their churches. The poor people used *ex-votos* more than anybody. And who could blame them? These people were likely to get scant medical attention otherwise.

Originally, *ex-votos* were carved in wood. But modern mass production was adopted so that eyes and heads could be cast in the moulds. There were shops selling these things, even in Rio de Janeiro. The *ex-votos* must have brought profit to somebody, even if not the sufferers. There was something not only pathetic about the *sala dos milagres* but gruesome, too. The wax dolls were offerings from pregnant women hoping for a safe confinement. Locks of real hair hung there. These were cut from the heads of children in the best Catholic families when the youngsters' ringlets had to come off. Their parents then brought them to the *sala* to present them to the slain Saviour or favourite saint. And this practice, too, was redolent of old Brazilian Indian lore.

BLACK MAGIC

For the Indians, children's teeth and hair were essential ingredients of magic. To keep all the little Joãos and Marias (Maria of the Cross, Maria of the Sorrows, Maria of the Resurrection, Maria of the Rock, Maria of the Pleasures, Maria of the Snows, as Brazilian girls are called) safe by giving their locks of hair into the charge of God himself was not a difficult step to take from paganism. For centuries Brazilian children had need of special protection. Worse things than European bogeymen and witches waited for them. There was the monster-with-seven-sets-of-teeth and also the man-of-the-sea, *homem-marinho*, who lived at the beach, feeding chiefly on children's fingers and genitals. Numerous Brazilian legends feature some threat of castration and this, not without reason, seems to have been an obsessive fear. *Mão-de-cabelo*, a goblin with hair instead of hands, specialized in knifing bed-wetters. The Old Negro carried out a complete operation on boys who masturbated.

However, in this matter of hobgoblins and things that went bump in the night, Brazilian children merely kept their parents company, for they, too, had their horrors. The whole of Brazil was populated with little negroes who haunted forest travellers. The country was full of she-mules without heads, men with feet turned backwards. (This perhaps was not impossible—at least in Rio I saw men with their feet turned completely inwards, begging in the streets.) Brazilian nightfall brought a terrible train of souls-in-torment. Salvador needed all of its three hundred churches if the horrors were to be kept at bay. Strangely, with the decline of Catholic power, the power of the goblins seemed to decline also. But, like others, Brazilians still liked to frighten themselves, and to do it with horror films. Dracula was appearing at a number of cinemas.

I left the silent church and courtyard and the mausoleum-like chapel of miracles. Out in the fierce sun again I felt as though my own face was smeared with *mingau das almas*. This was the 'ghost soup' which many of the uncanny creatures could smear on children's faces unless they washed. I went back to the ship for a shower and had lunch on board. Afterwards I began my invasion of the upper town. I paid one cruzeiro (less than a halfpenny) to go up the two hundred feet of cliff in the cable railway, past the perched shacks and the banana groves and over-heavy melon trees. The journey was short, but long enough to unfold slowly the Bay of All Saints. It was like a great map being unrolled: wide, liquid with light, studded with islands, ringed with mountains which faded in the afternoon heat. In its early days the capital of colonial Brazil must have been easily defended from the sea approach. At any rate, the inhabitants would have had good warning of any approaching ships. For Salvador's slaves, any threats of invasion could not have meant much more to them than a change of masters. French and Dutch expeditions were attracted by Salvador's riches. And, besides preaching, perhaps it was for prayers for preservation against the fortunes of war that the public oratory was used. This phallic-shaped object in a small *praça* confronts the cable-railway passenger when he walks out at the top of the cliff. I thought this *Oratóbid da Cruz do Pascoal* quite unworthy of the fame heaped on it. Except for the blue and yellow *azulejos* which smothered it, the oratory was quite undistinguished. Many a village war memorial in England is superior.

The remarkable thing, however, was the street where the oratory stood. It had the unreality of a dream. The narrow houses were ochre-coloured and brick-red, and some were green or blue, and all had elaborate iron balconies to the windows. The plastered walls were richly decorated in relief and there were fretted pediments and balustrading along the top. There was something of Spain and Portugal there, but also more than a touch of Muslim art, and a dash of African wall decoration. The houses looked as though the builder was driven by memories of long, long ago, memories of the ways of life brought by Salvador's generations of masters and slaves. Behind the turned wooden grilles in windows or doors, I saw figures looking out from dark rooms into the brilliant street. There were white eyes in dark, voluptuous faces, and black eyes in pale faces full of sensuality. The eyes followed me as I passed. Friendly people in doorways watched me until a bend in the street took me out of sight.

In that part of Salvador it was impossible to go the length of one street without encountering at least one church. But I was now faced with two. There is nothing solemn or self-righteous about Brazilian colonial churches. Indeed, there was sometimes little that was even righteous, particularly in the *azulejos*. These tiles are amongst the most beautiful things to be seen in Portugal and its former overseas possessions. Usually the pictures painted on and then fired into the tile had some religious or historical association. Whole murals executed in the six-inch square tiles would be framed with acanthus scrolls and other baroque decorative forms. Yet the sacred was sometimes replaced by the profane, as in one of Salvador's São Francisco churches. This building also contained wonderful wood carvings. But the visitor is liable to miss these in his anxiety to get permission to see the cloister and patio *azulejos* with their fun and games. Only men are allowed in. The Salvadorians were nearly as modest about their unrestricted past as are the Neapolitans at Pompeii.

This relic of eighteenth-century Salvador gives a clue to the city's unbridled life in those days. The church authorities were broad in outlook and allowed *azulejos* craftsmen to record in pictures what went on, in fact, even inside conventual walls. But a better idea of those wild days can be had from a Frenchman who visited Brazil in the eighteenth century. He wrote of what he saw in *Nouveau Voyage Autour du monde*. La Gentil de la Barbinais had his eyes open. In 1717 he was in Salvador and at the convent of Santa Clara for the feast of São Goncalo do Amarante. The nuns put up quite a show. And it was unquestionably more pagan than Christian. There were licentious dances round the saint's image. The aged Viceroy, who was present, hopped around with friars and strumpets, freed slaves and planters. The company wreaked all sorts of untold outrages on poor São Goncalo's image before the holy sisters put on a special comedy of love. And this was all fairly normal in Salvador. Life was, in any case, a non-stop carnival.

The blame must rest with São Goncalo, for he was a most earthy saint. St. Peter might well have had the power to find lovers for Brazilian widows, but the faithful turned to Goncalo for almost any kind of sexual need. Strictly, in theology, his job was confined to being the patron of the older women, for whom he found hus-

bands or lovers. But younger girls cashed in on his benevolence and
turned him into a sort of marriage bureau, singing,

> *São Goncalo of Armarante,*
> *You heard the old one's plea,*
> *So why not marry the young girls, too,*
> *What harm have we done to you?*

The noisiest scenes always took place on São Goncalo's feast day.
It is highly likely that he was a mere superficial replacement of
ancient fertility gods. Certainly, Brazilian churches were more
rowdy with dancing on his day than on any other. The rudest of
comedies were often performed by the religious orders as well as the
laity. These particular outrageous goings-on cannot be blamed on
climate and Latin temperament. They happened in Ireland, too, at
wakes. I doubt whether the sisters of Salvador went to the extremes
that the good Catholic housewives of Ireland did. The Irish honoured
their dead with obscene games, such as 'Bout'. This ended with the
representation of laying a ship's keel. A woman would erect the
mast with gestures that could only come from pagan fertility rites.
Another Irish wake game 'Holding the Light', was generally
accepted as profaning Christ's own sufferings. I can remember from
my own boyhood the straw-boys who went mumming. They acted
in a way that the Lord Chamberlain would certainly never allow
on an English stage. But ours is a too-modest age. It is difficult to
imagine the Brazilian women who, on failing to get any response
from the statue of a pregnant Our Lady of Expectation, actually
threw off their clothes and embraced the legs of the Saviour's image
in public. In their urgent desire to conceive children, they had no
shame.

With such highly excitable congregations and clergy and such
hair's-breadth division between Christianity and paganism, it was
no wonder the church buildings themselves were so voluptuous.
But only the churches and statues and the gilding and the carving
survived for me to see. The rest had all passed away, as had the
author of the *Nouveau Voyage Autour du Monde* himself. The
churches I peeped into had an air of piety and respectability about

them. I could not imagine that nowadays noblemen would ride on their horses into church and make their mounts genuflect during mass. Dancing in the churches continued well into the nineteenth century, when it was finally banned by the bishops of Brazil. The taking of sherbets and courting, however, still went on, and could hardly do otherwise when even the Emperor in his palace chapel was known to let his eyes wander critically over the young women present.

Vicious and violent the eighteenth century may well have been, but it is doubtful whether life was improved by the heavy hand of the nineteenth century. Without the wild excesses of the people, the wild excesses of the architecture have little meaning. Now that Brazilian Catholic bishops must fight a new menace, militant Protestantism, the gay paganism of the past could be a weapon in their rivals' hands. Around Brasilia I was to see the hold which Protestant churches were getting. This was going to be more trouble to modern Catholic priests than even the pagan *ex-votos* were.

But on that scorching day in Salvador I was not concerned with the Church's modern Goliath. The fabulous churches were still there to be seen. But the wizardry of their architecture was made richer still by knowing something of the feverish life and belief which caused them to be built. On the slightest pretext—or none at all—a church, with or without convent, was built in Salvador. It seemed that the houses and the people were installed to serve the churches, rather than the reverse. Each of the buildings had some special characteristic. Exiled Portuguese gypsies were associated with the Chapel of Santo Antonio. Another, the Church da Graca, contained the tomb of Catherine Paraguacú, an Indian woman who saw the Virgin Mary. Most people go to see another tomb, that of Júlia Feital, who was shot in a fit of jealousy by her ex-fiancé. He used a golden bullet. Churches often had sculpture by the amazing Herculino Duarte, who suddenly became disgusted with his art and spent the rest of his life as a water-seller. I looked into many buildings of whose names I had no idea. But there was no mistaking the Convent do Carmo, because a plaque outside the great door announced its name and date of foundation.

Here again there were two churches side by side, each a further variation on the stereotyped pattern: five bays to the façade, with the height divided into two parts, plus a central pediment and flanking bell turrets. Like all the baroque churches of Portugal and the colonies, these buildings had a distinct domestic appearance, more like a palace than a church. This effect, due largely to the rows of windows and the absence of giant columns, also persisted in the interior, where houselike windows with balustrades overlooked the naves. The Carmo convent was no exception, but it was having its siesta when I rang the bell in an outer vestibule. In spite of his disturbed sleep, the porter was most affable when I explained my mission. He produced an iron ring loaded with big keys and closed the door behind me. We were in a spacious, high cloister. A prolific garden of trees and flowering bushes grew in the sun which fell into the cloister. The stillness was perfect. In that place, in 1625, the surrender of the Dutch occupiers of Salvador had been signed and sealed. My guide held open a tall door and I went into the church. Apart from a certain impressiveness because of its size, the building had nothing to commend it. But the high altar was an astonishing object of beaten silver and gold. Its thickness and solidity was proudly pointed out by my guide, who tapped the metal with his fingernail. By weight of silver and gold alone it must have been worth many thousands of pounds. I could well understand how Captain Kidd felt when faced with the silver and gold of Peru's churches.

As a corrective to such impiety, however, there was the Madonna. She was set high; completely inaccessible in an apse behind the altar. She was a typical Madonna, overdressed and of a pallid, film-star beauty, floating among a series of theatrical flats, representing waves or clouds. In fact, the apse looked like a stage with movable scenery. I wondered if the whole thing did work like a stage, with the Virgin ascending into heaven, and perhaps a resurrecting Christ, and a descending Holy Ghost, all in their proper season. Such contraptions were commonly used in baroque Italian churches. But I could not convey to my guide what I wanted to know. He kept patting the silver altar and grinning.

41

There is a curious paradox concerning images. The Roman Church is primarily concerned with mystical truths, yet it uses means of the utmost realism and emotion to convey them—crucified, thorn-torn Christs as gruesome as Grünewald's, and bleeding martyrs and glorified saints. Yet the Protestant Church, which preaches a cold set of facts, disdains any kind of visual stimulus to belief. But perhaps the Roman Church can be understood in its use of lifelike and deathlike images and statues, and even a certain amount of dramatic representation in the mass itself. For the Church had, from its first days in Brazil, serious rivals in the pagan gods. And although so much of the Church's lively existence has now passed, that rivalry has by no means gone. *Candombles* are as much alive today as when the negro slaves brought to Brazil the fetishes of African sorcery.

The word 'fetish' itself is linked with pagan practices and was first coined by the Portuguese navigators in connection with West African gods. These gods came to Brazil with the negroes, who wore talismans round their necks. Because by law the slaves had to be baptized and converted to Christianity within six months of arriving in Brazil, confusion was only to be expected. The slaves would doubtless rather bow to the strange god Jesus Christ and His fetish the cross than be flogged for not doing so. Yet the negro's own gods remained with him. Officially Christian, in the slave hut or cane-field he could think as he wished. *Candombles* was the resultant compromise, and it still flourishes. This cult had powerful appeal because if offers so many qualities absent from Christianity.

Candomble's devotees take part directly in the ceremonies, and these include the excitements of dressing-up, singing, and dancing wildly into a state of exhaustion and trance. During this trance the gods of *Candomble* enter the body of the dancer. There are various weird results, including states like epilepsy. Though given other names, the *Candomble* deities, in type and hierarchy, resemble Christianity so closely that Catholic priests are divided among themselves about it. Father of the Gods and the Creator is called Olorum. He has two children, Obatala the Sky, and Odudua the Earth. There is Oxala the Good Spirit, and he is the figure in

Candombles most easily identified with Jesus. Correspondingly, Exú is the Evil Spirit.

In Brazil Exú was driven off by offerings of black hens. And this intrigued me, for in the mountain villages of Madeira a few years earlier I found a similar idea. Nobody would stop the black hens which were wandering freely about, because, they said, the birds were possessed of the evil eye. And there might still be a few places left in Ireland where black chickens are buried alive to cure epileptics.

But in *Candombles* Exú does not have things all his own way, for the religion has its equivalents of the Christian saints, too. Xanapan is the God of Smallpox, and he may be regarded as St. Lazarus. The Thunder God is Xango and corresponds to St. Peter, while Ogun the War God might be St. Anthony. There is even an opposite number to the Virgin Mary, and it was this dusky Mother of the Waters, Yemanja, with whom I was to have most contact. Yemanja even has her own temple in the dark waters of the Laguna of Abaeté at Itapoan, eighteen miles from old Salvador, for she is perhaps the most popular amongst the gods.

Far from being a hangover from more primitive times, and from Salvador's wild seventeenth and eighteenth centuries, *Candomble* is still active. The Catholic priests' dilemma is difficult. Some condemn *Candomble*. They cannot bear with the negro priests of the cult who have their own hierarchy and holy places and religious calendar, who dance themselves into violence and epilepsy. In Rio de Janeiro growing numbers of white people were attaching themselves to *Candombles*. And perhaps in this the Roman priests smelt the presence of Spiritualism as well as a pagan distortion of their own Church. But other fathers of the Roman faith take a gentler view. They realize that during the days of slavery the negroes were forced into conversion and that the fusion and confusion of ideas was inevitable. In any case, the African cult is very closely related to Catholicism and its saints are similar except in name. The Roman Church certainly needed to provide strong counter-attraction if it was to loosen *Candomble's* hold on the Brazilian people. It was an old problem. Perhaps the Madonna floating on her scenery clouds in the Convent do Carmo was meant to challenge the attraction of the *Mãe d'Agua*, the Mother of the Waters, as Yemanja was called.

Next to the convent church was a most fabulously decorated room. This was the sacristy, proportioned approximately on a double cube. Its ceiling shocked me with the profligacy of its decoration, its ribs and deep, moulded coffers, painted panels and gilding. The room's extravagance again belonged more to a palace than a male convent. Though prepared to a certain extent for what Brazilian baroque would offer, I had no idea that such a creation as the Carmo sacristy existed, nor that it would be so overwhelming. The arbiters of architectural taste had long excluded Spanish and Portuguese baroque. Such sensuousness was deemed indecent for northern eyes. And since it was only a distant echo of major events in Italy, particularly Vignola's Gesu church, this Iberian development has been frowned upon. Only recently has it become a permissible art. Enthusiastic books have at last been published about it. Yet the orchid might just as well have been excluded from the world of flowers. The Carmo sacristy was an orchid of architecture well suited to the voluptuous life it had once served.

This room was also fitted out with beautiful furniture made of the dark, sultry jacaranda wood. In an eighteen-foot chest were kept gold embroidered vestments from the eighteenth century. In contrast were the cheap, nastily-coloured clothes which constituted the wardrobes of the convent's various saints. And not since the time when I worked with the Fol-de-Rols had I discovered such a collection of wigs as those for the statues. The guide was more proud of these than he was of the room itself, and although the sacristy is one of Brazil's priceless treasures, he did not even look at it.

After a walk round the cloister to admire again the garden in the afternoon's flood of sun, I found my way into the tremendous tunnelling beneath the convent. These spaces were burrowed into the earth and lined with stone vaults. At one place the tunnel opened into a loggia with a view across banana trees and slum shacks. Many of the city's churches stood over such underground spaces. Their original purpose is unknown and has lent itself to controversy. That the church's slaves were chained there at night was one theory.

Another maintained that these numerous, winding passages were hiding-places for the Jesuits' amassed treasures. But the magnitude of physical effort required to hollow the cellars out amazed me more than possible purposes. Salvador's need for a constant supply of slaves was not surprising.

I had to find the church of São Francisco de Assis. Somewhere among old Salvador's precipitous streets and unsuspected squares, somewhere on top of one of its hills was the diadem of Salvador's jewels. I knew that the interior was all of gold and a mass of carving, and that there was no church more ornate to be seen anywhere in Brazil, nor probably in the world. Outside the Carmo convent I asked the whereabouts of St. Francis' gilded cage. There should be no difficulty in finding it, for everyone knew the way. The old quarter of Salvador was a little Switzerland of narrow, mountainous streets. Still more churches were crammed in. One of them cheated the narrow confines that its great façade should have kept. On the opposite side of the street a vast flight of steps dropped down to yet a lower street, so that from there, looking up, the church had grandeur beyond its real size. On the steps a group of boys were playing draughts. Their board was simply chalked on the stones, and the draughts were Coca-Cola bottle tops. This church, too, had a maze of vaulted tunnels and corridors attached to it. There were also some old wrought-iron gates of exquisite design.

Contrasting with these tunnels were the streets. The one was dank, the other blazing in the sun. The tunnels were empty of life, the streets abundant with it. Again nobody could tell whether the stone chamber, where I found a carpenter using an adze, was once used as a rainwater reservoir or as slave quarters. Yet Salvador's ancient streets raised no problems. Here life erupted as it had always done. And those people who were not hurrying up and down the hills, or cutting through slotlike alleyways were spectators from shop doorways and balconies and windows with shutters wide open. All the shops opened without windows directly on to the pavements— where pavements existed. I passed scores of shoemakers and dress-makers working at hand sewing-machines, shuttles flying like a pestilence and hammers going with indefinable rhythms. Many of the craftsmen hard at work were young boys. And each shop had a crowd of people with the important job of simply watching the others and talking. In some shops the proprietor sat on a cane chair by the pavement, his arms folded, his eyes missing nothing.

Quite a number of people turned to stare at me as I twisted in and out of turnings and went up hills, still persisting in the general direction of São Francisco. Wherever I went there were hordes of children, brimming over with energy. Most of them were beautiful. The colour of their skin ranged between the bloom of purple grapes to the tint of pale tea. Because of the heat their clothing was scanty. The very youngest were clad in nothing at all—except some girls who wore earrings. Street games seemed to be much the same as anywhere in the world, except for the noise. But there was one game I had not seen before. This was to drape the overhead telephone wires with strings and ribbons, tied to stones and flung up from the ground. The effect was gay, as though flags and bunting were out. And it occurred to me that in this there lay something very Brazilian.

Festooned telephone wires showed the Brazilians' attitude to technical things. Though fascinated by them the Brazilian was not ruled by them. He believed that, like the Sabbath, they were made for man. When lavatory cisterns in new buildings were broken they often remained so. Cars were smashed and abandoned for new ones. Heating and lighting systems failed without causing disasters. The Brazilian could not bear the chromiumed nudity of industrial products. The drivers of buses and lorries decorated their vehicles with home-made designs and wrote pious or not-so-pious mottoes inside. Blank spaces on walls were covered with huge painted lettering or *graffito* scribblings. Factory products had to be humanized. This putting of technical things in their proper place was also an outlet for the Brazilian sense of humour, with its delight in the ludicrous and the incongruous. Even bald telephone wires could not escape! This desire to elaborate and decorate showed not only in the flowery phrases of the Portuguese language but also in architecture. Portuguese designers took to the decorative aspects of baroque like ducks to water. But even the massive effects of Bernini were too solemn for them. So, like the telephone wires, Salvador's churches had to be loaded, but with profuse carving as well as plaster ribbons.

I came to a large square surrounded by churches (of course!). São Francisco was not far away and I recognized it by the grandeur of its façade. Before I had got half-way down the street—past the melon-seller who belaboured his obdurate jackass—past an old negress asleep in a doorway, oblivious that a bald dog quite covered in sores was licking the peeled fresh pineapple she was selling—past more shops where, despite dust and flies, the fried fish, tomatoes, salamis and bruised-looking meat were hung up outside—past more children scampering about, the boys with heads shaved except for a tuft on top so that they looked like the first of the Mohicans—past more women selling special Salvador cooking with their charcoal stoves burning on the pavements, holding such delicacies as well-seasoned cow's tongue or the popular *vatapá* made of rice flour, ginger and shrimps—past those negresses who took me straight back to the eighteenth century with their walk like a wooden ship rolling under full sail and their costumes of gaudy skirts and short, wide-sleeved blouses—past the thousands of wooden sandals clicking endlessly on the cobbles—past, in fact, the teeming anthill of the street—before I got near to São Francisco I could see that yet another, even more ornate church stood cheek by jowl beside it.

São Francisco de Assis *was* gold. The architectural form was totally obscured by seething decoration. São Francisco was the last word in elaboration. The arches and walls and ceilings, the barley-sugar columns supported a riotous growth of carved foliage entirely sheathed in gold leaf. There were gilded scrolls and volutes, gilded cartouches and coats-of-arms. And hiding among the golden encrustations of this crustaceous gold cave were clumps of cherubs. They peeped from their golden-leafed forest like fat fauns. Besides being fleshy, as they should be, the cherubs managed somehow to look lascivious also, though this may have been because of the example set by some larger carved and painted figures. These were in the church's two shallow transepts. They were hybrid between caryatids and Atlases, these muscle-men-women holding up another vast load of gilded forest, which formed the reredos to the transept chapels. Unfortunately they destroyed any feeling of religion by being buxom, pink-cheeked and looking exactly like waxwork models of Vesta Tilley or Marie Lloyd. As a blow against *Candomble*, as a spectacle to awe the ignorant slave and as a twentieth-century tourist attraction, São Francisco was perfect. As art it was horrifying.

A feeling for human relics is common to countries under strong Roman Catholic influence. But I did not stop to inquire what relics were kept at São Francisco. Judging by the amount of gold, they would have to be something fairly spectacular. What I did not expect to find was that Salvador's most spectacular relics were not in a church at all, but in a museum. The Museu do Instituto Nilla Rodrigues lay in a courtyard off a street near the big square, Praca de 15 Novembro. At first I thought it was a Brazilian Madame Tussaud's. Just inside the small entrance hall a coloured woman in old Salvadorian costume sat sleeping over trays of beans which she was selling. But she was only made of wax.

The first room was dedicated to cut-throat razors. They had been literally cut-throats and consorted with a collection of knives and fire-arms once used in actual murders and suicides—all labelled ARMAS HOMICIDAS. You would be surprised to see what pretty patterns can be made by arranging murderers' knives in glass cases. I liked the case marked FIGAS much better. Only a few hours in Brazil had taught me how important the *figa*, a good-luck amulet, was to the Brazilian. I had noticed the clenched fist, with the thumb protruding between first and second fingers, being worn round many necks. The *figa* was carved from many different materials and wood or semi-precious stones. Originally it hailed from Africa. *Candomble* used its symbolism in ceremonies. Most present-day *figas* which jewellers and souvenir shops throughout Brazil sell are, alas, made from plastic—the same process which had modernized paganism and had mass-produced *ex-votos* in wax. But the museum's collection of the genuine article showed magnificent ones, up to two feet in length, carved from jacaranda. The sign made by the hand in the *figa* would not be thought at all polite in England, yet on some of the rude thumbs, small crosses and monstrances were cut, showing again the mingling of Christian and heathen notions. *Figas*, like *Candomble* itself, were popular and in everyday use. They did not convey good luck to the wearer if bought, but only when presented. And although a plastic *figa* was better than no *figa* at all, the best ones still came from Africa. But the *figas* were by no means the best of what the museum had to show and so I came to the unholy relics. Still unsuspecting, I followed some other visitors into a room which appeared to be full of cowboy equipment, of a variety which would put any western film to shame. There were beautifully worked leather saddles and boots, many revolvers with long bandoliers like the spines of prehistoric fish, and oddly shaped hats with turned-up brims. As though this extraordinary museum were not sinister enough, I was told then that all this accoutrement had belonged to a terrible band of outlaws. They had operated in the wild interior regions for hundreds of miles around Salvador. Then I remembered *O Cangaçeiro*. This famous Brazilian film, *The Bandits*, had been shown in London, and I had seen it long before I had any plans for going to Brazil. The song *O Cangaçeiro* had also captivated me.

The wild and cruel exploits of the bandits were excellent on the screen. But I did not know that the *cangaçeiros* had really existed, really rampaged through village and jungle, raping and marauding. There were a number of gangs operating separately. Some were worse than others. At best, their lives were like Robin Hood's and they robbed the rich to give to the poor. From what I have heard since from those who in their childhood knew the outlaws, the truth is more likely to be that the robbery was indiscriminate, the giving infrequent. The *cangaçeiros* were violent and merciless, terrorizing the population of the primitive areas which they covered. No one dared betray them to the soldiers who came many times to hunt the bandits. The peasant's life was worth less than nothing to the bandits.

The chief among them was called Lampeão. And though he probably had his fill of women taken in raids on farms and villages, Lampeão had a permanent mistress. She shared his roving, plundering life, with all the danger and hardships. This woman was Maria Bonita. The name Lampeão struck more terror into the hearts of the simple people of the northern interior than did the folk-tales of toad-goblins or the men-who-ate-human-livers. Lampeão was himself a myth, but a myth based on a terrible reality. No village he visited with his gang, swooping suddenly on a sleepy unsuspecting community, ever forgot the visitation.

Lampeão was wanted, dead or alive, with a great price on his head. Expeditions went after him and his crew, but for years he slipped through their nets, and was hidden by both poor and rich. No doubt the fear of the *cangaçeiros'* reprisal for betrayal was enough to keep the secret. Or it is not impossible that the ordinary people hated the troops of an unpopular government as much or more than the outlaws. Lampeão then led a reign of terror in northern Brazil. His name was a household word, his exploits in every conversation even in the main cities on the coast, hundreds of miles away. But there came an end to it in June 1938. Lampeão, Maria Bonita, and at least four others were caught and killed.

This might, so far as I was concerned, have been the end of this almost romantic story which gave rise to the fascinating film *O Cangaçeiro*. But I was to come closer to the bandits and the Beautiful Mary: in fact, to make a contact which not many people ever had with Lampeão and his merry men. I touched the flesh of his pickled, severed head.

This happened to me almost by accident. Had I known what I was fingering, I certainly should not have done so. I still had wax-works in mind when a museum attendant showed me six human heads under glass bells on a shelf. They looked like cakes in an English village shop, almost appetizing with the glass cakestand and cover. I never suspected that the heads were more than wax. Something of my disbelief must have showed, for the attendant lifted one of the covers and invited me to touch Lampeão's sagging jaw and the green, glazed-looking flesh of his pudgy face. It seemed that Maria Bonita's ghastly fixed grin from under her glass jar slackened for a moment as Lampeão breathed a little fresh air.

As soon as I realized that it was a real head, and that the matted, straggly hair was not a wig on a wax, I told the attendant that it was more than enough for me. Later, when I learned Lampeão's full story and all about the outlaws, I could not get rid of the horror of having handled his head.

On his capture, together with Maria Bonita and the others, Lampeão had been buried quickly. The events took place in humid country near the Equator, where corpses do not keep. But evidence had to be supplied that Lampeão was dead. He had in his lifetime become a legend, and legends are not easily killed. So, immediately after the bandits' death, their heads were cut off and preserved by immersion in an oil-drum filled with the local brand of alcohol. Then they were taken into the city and the ransom claimed. The fame which Lampeão sought during his life was certainly achieved. And the display of his mummified head, with the death mask on the wall behind, ensures the outlaw's future as a Brazilian romance.

It did not appeal to me, however, as a very romantic way to spend a day in Salvador. Yet perhaps it was not altogether out of key with the city, for Brazilian baroque has a sinister quality. Its carved foliage was of the jungle rather than the sylvan glade. 'Yet', I thought, 'Salvador, I will certainly come back another time to your steep streets and calendar of churches.' But for one day I had reached the limit of absorption. Only the oleanders flowering sweetly outside and the flaming flamboyants could take away the gory but intriguing gloom of the museum of relics. But Salvador's walls had soaked up so much during their hundreds of years that my praise and protest went unnoticed. And anyway, Salvador was changing from afternoon to early evening, a serious business, for night would follow evening and bring its own train of resurrection for those who had slept through the heat, play for those who had been working, and love for lovers.

Salvador's night would bring nothing for me but a twinkle of lights seen from the *Rubens*'s deck, because she was to sail before dinner. Nobody was put off their meal by my tale of Lampeão's head, least of all Captain Williams, who said that I should prepare to be surprised at nothing in Brazil. He told me how he had once worked his ship with a Brazilian crew who fished with lines over the boat's side. Their catches were plentiful until the day when a lady passenger touched the lines. From then on the crew could get not a single fish more. The sailors complained and said it was because the lady was menstruating. (How did they know? This sounded to me like a connection with Zoroastrian scriptures, which almost certainly would have recommended punishment by a thousand stripes with the *Aspahê-astra*.) However, holy water from a Catholic stoup was suggested as a remedy for cleansing the fishing-lines. But this idea was brushed aside. After all, the English officers could not be expected to know that the dusky Yemanja was Mother of the Waters, who, unlike the devil in Ireland, could not be driven off with holy water. And even if they had known that her special offering was of white flowers, from where could such blooms be got while at sea?

But the idea of such offerings ought not to seem so strange, for it was not so long since white may blossom was hung about English doors to keep witches way, and white blossom gathered on Ascension Day was used as a protection against lightning for the rest of the year. Even during my own boyhood I was not allowed to take snowdrops into the house because they made the milk watery. The appeal of magic lies in its whimsical independence of dull facts. Science, after all, is only magic of another sort. I hoped to find a lot more magic in Brazil.

3

Rio Con Brio

That distant night-glow of a great city was from Rio de Janeiro. The tropical darkness had melted sky and sea together. Below there was phosphorescence, and above, the jewel-like stars. Between these two there was a void. The noise of the sea and occasionally the glitter of passing ships filled it. Otherwise there was nothing. Ships gliding by in the darkness are a sad sight. The glimmering, lonely shape appears, goes by on the beam, and then dwindles to nothing again. It is as if one's own ship was reflected in a mirror. The small thing looks so frail, so desperately bright in the inky sea, like a parable of our existence.

It might have been because I was glad to see Rio's warm flood-lighting of the clouds, a more comforting light than that of other ships. Or it might have been because pre-Christmas celebrations had already broken out on the *Rubens* that I was glad my journey was almost over. We caught the Christmas spirit from each other as children catch chicken-pox. Those on the bridge, of course, were excluded. Their watch would take us into Guanabara Bay, where we should have to anchor until Rio's Christmas holidays were over. We might be unable to go alongside and berth for at least two days. I divided my Christmas Eve between craning out of the smoke-room porthole, leaning over the rails, and peering through binoculars from the bridge. The smudge of light did not seem to grow bigger.

In the smoke-room the officers not on duty were laying the foundation of a solid Christmas. Chris Barber was giving us *Sweet Sue* from Birmingham Town Hall on a long-playing record. He had, in fact, been playing *Sweet Sue* all the way from Swansea. The entranced Birmingham audience had also had a vocal number from the Barber boys which had almost become a sea shanty for me,

I'll be glad when you're dead, you rascal you,
I'll be glad when you're dead
With six feet right over your head,
I'll be glad when you're dead, you rascal you.

But I deserted *Sweet Sue* when somebody poked his head in the door and said: 'Come and look at it now.' I dashed up to the bridge and there was Rio, still far away, but clear and sparkling. To the left a chain of lights was strung across the non-visible horizon. That was Copacabana beach, Rio's golden playground by the sea. The two miles of tall luxury hotels and apartment blocks made a haze of light. A red light above the horizon was the summit of the Sugar Loaf rock. And a faint streak of light farther to the right was the gigantic Christ statue on top of the Corcovado—the Hunchback mountain. I had known every feature of the fabulous Rio harbour ever since childhood—from postcards and photographs. But sailing into it at night, guessing at the shapes hidden in shadow until dawn, put a razor edge to my anticipation.

At this first glimpse, Rio was still twelve miles away. But after that we seemed to go in faster. With the ship's brass telescope clapped to my eye I could pick out details. Beyond the vast, looming shape of the sentinel Sugar Loaf, advertisements flashed on and off. I tried to read them, but we were still not close enough. But the outstretched arms of the Corcovado Christ were plain now. Then Rio seemed to rush towards us. With unaccountable speed the Sugar Loaf passed us close by. I saw the red lights of the radio masts on top. The *Rubens*, signalling by lamps to the shore, steamed into Guanabara Bay and the anchorage. Now the city's long waterfront seemed to be within reach. I could see people strolling and cars speeding along. The huge neon signs flashed, and skyscrapers, stacked against the incandescent sky, shone like Hallowe'en lanterns. But though the city was radiant, the soft tropical night cloaked it nevertheless. Like a child with a Christmas stocking, I could hardly wait to see what Christmas morning would bring.

Such subtle changes can occur when expectation becomes realization that it becomes impossible to say whether one is surprised or disappointed. My surprise was when the splendour of Rio harbour and the islands of Guanabara Bay showed themselves in daylight. I knew that Rio and the Bay would look better than I thought they would. The sight was wonderful even in photographs. But in reality it was better still. Mountains and city and anchored ships shimmered in the heat. I basked in the alien fierceness of the colour, the water's green, the mountains' greys and purples. The sky was not a colour but a radiation, too intense to look at even through sunglasses. The heat was a vice which gripped everything. The Bay was sweltering and far hotter than the Equator at sea had been.

My disappointment was over Rio the city as distinct from its Bay. The rows of skyscrapers were less impressive by day. They crowded the waterfront, jammed between the sea and the mountains, and looked anonymous. Copacabana beach, which faced directly on to the Atlantic, was out of sight, because we had anchored far in the Bay. But I wondered whether I would be swimming later at Copacabana—the Christmas present I had promised myself.

The only difference made by the heat to Christmas celebrations was that the captain gave his cocktail party on deck. Even under the awning it was hot. The officers wore their 'whites'. We drank quite a lot to the cool clink of ice in glasses. A heat haze softened the mountains' outlines and drained colour from the sea. The only moving things were occasional ferries crossing the Bay, and the sleek, graceful forms of porpoises scooping and turning lazily near the surface, their moleskin backs gleaming for a moment in the sun. The other ships lay immobile, like models on a sheet of glass. Then the gong rang and in a festive if slightly gyratory manner we went below for the cook's special twelve-course Christmas dinner. It was dinner and not luncheon, because the rest of the day would be needed to recover from it and also because by our normal dinner-time everybody would be well past the eating stage. A prize was offered to anyone who could fight his way through the twelve courses. I gave up the ghost at the seventh and ceded superiority to the third mate, and by the time *he* finished neither he nor anyone else remembered the prize.

Then it was the cook's turn, and the galley crew's and the dining-room stewards'. Christmas Day tradition was that the officers waited as they were themselves waited upon during the year. So from the broiling depths of his galley the first cook emerged with his entourage and took the seats which we had just vacated, and the officers turned-to in the galley and pantry. I could not go to Copacabana beach that afternoon, because there was no means of getting ashore. Before the captain's party on deck the ship had received a *visito*. Officials from Rio came aboard to 'clear' the ship for berthing in two days. This was a somewhat oriental ceremony accompanied by the exchange of cigarettes and whisky, mutual compliments, and the ritual of filling up forms. It included me and meant that I could go ashore whenever I wished except that the customs were closed for the holidays. But by early afternoon a great torpor possessed Rio and not even the ferries seemed to be about. So I went into the galley and cooked the crew's steaks instead of going to Copacabana. If it was heat I wanted, I certainly got it, more than a hundred degrees of it over the galley's oil-burning ovens.

Later, when a little boat did come alongside, the interest in Copacabana had waned. And in any case the boat did not stay long enough to pick up shore passengers. The Brazilian who tied it at the bottom of the gangway ran up to the deck, volubly seeking customers. While the big negro's attention was occupied, the sailors' peggy and a deck-hand stole the boat. With a whirr the outboard motor took them out into the Bay. The outraged boatman shouted after them. In the kind of English used in telegrams he demanded of the officers what they intended to do about it. But what could they do? Meanwhile the outboard motor had stopped and the two sailors were stranded. They had forgotten to turn the petrol on. The boat drifted, but luckily ran to the side of a German ship half a mile away. Two figures could just be seen clambering on to its gangway. Without further words the Brazilian flung off his clothes, plunged into the water and began to swim towards the German ship.

The afternoon's *divertissement* was fast becoming a Christmas pantomime. In a short time the negro had reclaimed his boat and returned with it to the *Rubens*, hoping to get fares to take ashore. He left the two sailors marooned on the German ship as they, in their high spirits, had left him on ours. There did not seem to be any great miscarriage of justice in what he had done. In fact, I imagined our two sailors having a whale of a *gemütlich* Christmas with the Germans and being brought back later that night. The sailors' peggy had a German mother. He had also, just before the trip, been converted to Fascism and delighted to display his black shirt on the *Rubens*. And his political masters had certainly taught the art of hating negroes well. So, on the whole, I felt that if anything the ferryman suffered most. He was still without clothes.

By now the whole of our crew was on the rails, heaping abuse on his head for failing to bring the two youngsters back. 'No sailors, no clothes,' they shouted. But he was adamant. Nothing would induce him to bring them back. The *Rubens*'s first mate gave him a pair of shorts and he took some junior officers ashore. Hours later our two crew came back. Like the negro they had to swim and against the current. The Brazilian, they said, had got the better of them because he had used a spanner on them.

Sammy, the *Rubens*'s seventy-year-old donkeyman, had opened another bottle of brandy. He bet me that he would win a mile race that we were to run when we berthed. But on Boxing Day the shipping company sent a launch with the agent to take me to the quay, so I never ran Sammy's mile. He would probably have won anyway. The launch chugged away to shore. I had enjoyed the journey perhaps more than any I had made and was sorry to leave. Solitude, however, was not likely to be mine in Rio, with three million milling Brazilians around me.

Be surprised at nothing in Brazil, the captain had said, and so I pretended not to be that Rio's main street was like a cross between Fifth Avenue, New York, and the Champs-Elysées. This was the Avenida Rio Branco. The sea was at both ends. Trees lined it and mercifully shaded its tessellated pavements. Those brave leaves also helped to disguise the fact that petrol fumes choked the air. The smoke could not get away, because the Avenida was a chasm between skyscrapers. There would have been even more petrol fumes, presumably, if all the dead cars I saw at the docks had been in use. There was an enormous yard full of once brand-new American cars which had been shipped to Rio. But the purchasers had either failed to get the necessary import permit or could not pay the huge tax, so the cars stayed on the docks. Being Brazil, where red tape is easily cut by a just amount of tactful and necessary bribery, it seemed unbelievable that the cars should remain in the boneyard. Apart from occasionally losing spare wheels or windscreen-wipers and generally suffering from exposure, the cars were untouched by human hand. The Brazilians have a boundless sense of humour. This is probably why the newspapers frequently published pictures of the cars.

Avenida Rio Branco's pretty pavements led me to the most famous and most beautiful of Rio's skyscrapers, where my business of the morning lay. The black and white patterning of the wide pavements reminded me of Funchal in Madeira. But my admiration could hardly be unreserved, for I tripped in a number of dangerous potholes. The patterns were made of separate stones bedded without cement. When they were kicked out, the hole was left and, apparently, never repaired. So what should have been a splendour was merely tawdry, just as the pavements' pattern of sea waves was often obscured by litter. Still, there was no point in cavilling. This was Brazil, part of a continent which, dirty though it may be, has at least not decimated itself with wars twice in fifty years.

I found a similar imperfection marring the Ministry of Education when I got there. This simple building initiated the whole of Brazil's modern architecture. France and the *École des Beaux Arts* were forgotten and young Brazilian architects exulted in the new-found freedom from dead Academism. Le Corbusier was directly responsible for the emancipation. He came to Rio in 1936 to design the new Ministry building and he set the young Brazilian architects' imagination on fire. Among them was Oscar Niemeyer, who more than any other was to win fame for Brazil and for himself. His personality was to be imprinted on the Ministry of Education building, perhaps more than is generally supposed. Limelight which should be Niemeyer's has often fallen on Le Corbusier. Later I spent some days with Sir Howard Robertson in Brasilia. He had been the architect representing Britain at the designing of the New York United Nations' building. He realized how powerfully Niemeyer's suggestions lie behind this famous group of buildings.

There were people who believed that no finer architecture than that of the Ministry of Education existed in Brazil. With great skill the traditional *azulejos* panels were used, designed by the celebrated Candido Portinari. And it was patches of these tiles which I found had fallen off, spoiling the perfection of this beautiful building. The tiles were off and looked as though they would never be replaced. But I chided myself for lack of charity. After all, nobody thinks less of the Parthenon because it is a patched-up ruin.

In more than one way, the Ministry building was the womb of Brazil's new capital. Here was born the kind of architecture which twenty years later made Brasilia possible. And here, too, in a spacious studio, the plan of Brasilia was worked on day after day during the first two momentous years of the new city's construction. I wanted to meet the creator of Brasilia, Lucio Costa. He had been another of Brazil's first generation of modern architects, an urbane, generous-minded man whose genius reached its height in his grand and simple idea for the new capital. In a competition limited to some thirty or so Brazilian architects his design for Brasilia was chosen and miraculously built in its essentials within the two years. The politics which initiated Brasilia might just be called the art of the possible, but Brasilia itself *was* the art of the impossible. It will remain incomprehensible that Lucio Costa's vision became reality in such a short time. It had to, before Kubitschek's term of office expired and the city was built beyond the point of no return, thus committing his successors. Now, where before had been only a green, almost uninhabited plateau, a thriving city sprang up.

I could not see Costa, because he was in Egypt. But I did see the original sheets on which he presented his basic idea for the city. They were historic documents of great value to future Brazilians. When I saw them, five cards pasted with typewritten pages, they were dog-eared and dusty from being kept under piles of papers on top of a cupboard.

Quite by chance, Oscar Niemeyer came into the building. By years of success and experience which earned him international fame he was the man most fitted to make architectural reality out of Costa's initial conception for the whole new capital. He had just come down from Brasilia, motoring the seven hundred odd miles, to spend New Year in Rio. Niemeyer was too nervous to come by plane, unless pressed to do so by Brazil's President. He preferred to drive himself, though this was no safer. He had just had an accident—another one, as people in the planning office said when they heard about it. His car was left smashed somewhere on the road between Brasilia and Rio. Nevertheless he came into the studio to meet me.

Somehow, one does not expect genius to be located in a human form. Perhaps this is the after-effect of looking at Victorian statuary labelled with high-sounding names—Justice, Liberty—or those monstrous contortions which sit on top of the pillars facing Buckingham Palace and are labelled Africa, India, and so on. I can never rid my mind of another statue with a plaque, GENIUS. So I was surprised when a small, slight man came into the room and held out his hand. His eyes were heavy-lidded and their expression far-away. He said he would see me again in Brasilia on the 'five of January'.

Then he went, leaving me to knock down my statue of Genius. Oscar Niemeyer had no time for the observance of polite niceties. Other people's opinion of him counted for nothing. That was why he was unashamedly a Communist and at one time sold Communist literature in the streets of Rio. He himself told me the story of Brasilia's inauguration, when the Government and diplomatic corps were present for the great occasion. So was Oscar Niemeyer, the President's great friend. But because he had no tie, the soldier on guard at the Congress building, not recognizing the creator of it all, refused him admission. Oscar gave his characteristic shrug and turned away with an aside, 'Oh well, I've seen it before anyway.'

Not all Brazilians approved of moving the capital to the interior, despite the move being long part of the nation's constitution. Rio's whirl and colour appealed too strongly to many people. Being in the roaring streets again after the quiet studio certainly brought forcibly to my mind the old capital's maturity. I could easily see the difficulty of exchanging a city with a past for one with only a future. Rio's carnival really lasted the year round in those downtown streets, which were more sophisticated than Salvador's. The effect of sophistication was marred, of course, when one strayed from the main streets or looked up at the squalor of the shacks on the foot-hills of surrounding mountains, or if one tripped over beggars with diseased stumps of limbs sitting on the pavements. Otherwise, except for the heat, the smart suits, shops and cars gave the Avenida Rio Branco a cosmopolitan air. It was like a London tube station during rush hour and even had its Oxford Street barrow-boys selling fountain pens and cheap bow-ties. There were rather Teddy-boy-looking youths offering watch straps and flint lighters for gas cookers. There were old women selling shirt buttons. There were young women with limbs made grotesque by elephantiasis, or with the flesh eaten away, and who also sat at the side of the pavement begging, with their children around them among heaps of rags.

Brazil is the land of contrast, people gaily said. This was to excuse the horrors of poverty. The phrase insinuated that there was virtue in such contrast. The notion of 'the poor' is by no means dead in Brazil. A beginning has been made to deal with this gargantuan problem. But excessive self-interest and complacency are the bitterest enemies of any progress.

Rio's Fifth Avenue-Champs-Elysées had its crop of contrasts. Not many people stopped to look at an open-air exhibition of fright-ful paintings of thatched cottages, ladies in crinolines, Sacred Hearts and blue Virgins. On the other hand there was always a crowd round the shoeshine man who had no arms. With cleaning-cloth gripped in his toes he did a very good job, sitting on the pavement (the tessellated one), working his legs vigorously up and down. As in Salvador, but out of context here, there were old negresses and their charcoal burners with roasting corncobs and red beans sizzling in oil. Most of the shops along the Avenida had an old-fashioned air, as if they had not been altered since the 'thirties. Their beige-faced models did not bear much resemblance to the beautifully coloured skin of the Brazilians who looked in the windows.

Every few hundred yards there seemed to be a news-stand with illustrated magazines besides comics and cheap thrillers and sex novels. There were postcards and triangular pennants which people buy to show the towns and countries they have travelled in. In Rio, though, you could buy one for each of Brazil's important cities without actually going there. The news-stands advertised the magazines by displaying them open at their most lurid, violent, or morbid photographs. The Latin obsession with corpses and cadavers here found its expression in photographs of car and air-crash victims or just plain, ordinary dead bodies lying in flower-covered coffins. Nothing, except perhaps pictures of footballers, was more calculated to sell the magazines than these macabre *memento mori*.

From gorging yourself at the sight of death you could go to one of the many refreshment bars. Here the choice of fare was more cheerful and much more varied. Sitting on the plastic and tubular steel chairs of a pavement café, you could drink jet-black coffee in polite tiny cups half-filled with sugar. Or, if your fancy was for a cool drink, you could step on to the terrazzo floor of a snack bar and drink juice straight from the sugar-cane. At first I thought these bars were warehouses, because of the tall green cane stacked round the walls. But the customer chose his own cane and had it crushed in the machine which extracted the juice. One bar which I frequented more than any other sold enormous glasses of diluted fruit syrup with ice, for fourpence. I drank gallons. So many other people did also that instead of holding up the proceedings by paying over the counter there was a special pay-box which issued blue discs which were then exchanged for the drink. Another method of quenching the thirst engendered by the Avenida was to go into an office building and up in the lift to a floor which had a cooled drinking fountain. I only did this once, not because I felt guilty of trespassing, but because I sweated so much going down in the crowded lift that I was immediately thirsty again.

I failed to see how the *Cariocas* could stand it. Of course, they were used to such a climate—or were they? People seemed to be sweating in the humid midsummer heat as much as I. What Rio must be like in February, round about carnival time, when, so I read in the newspapers, the temperature went up to 110 degrees, I could not imagine. How had Rio's first white settlers coped with the heat? I was sure they had nothing comparable with the underground ice-houses which eighteenth-century mansions in England possessed. But since the settlers were Portuguese they were used to a certain amount of heat. Nevertheless, the habits in the newcomers' settlements must have astonished the local native Indians, who called the white men's houses *Cariocas*. This name stuck and survived. *Cariocas* today are still those who live in Rio, and the whole city is known as *Carioca*.

But modern life has stresses and strains unknown to Brazil's sixteenth-century colonizers. An unusual sight for South America were the queues at banks and exchanges and for buses. Quite unchanged, however, was the *Carioca*'s appreciation of and appetite for beautiful girls. There was a local song, *Every time I pass a girl I fall in love*. Who would not, passing Rio's women in the Avenida Rio Branco? There was every shade of skin, every kind of noble face formed from European, Indian and negro origins. There was no false modesty by either sex. The men turned to look after the loveliest women as they, with no uncertain flame in their eye, looked at men who took their fancy. Conventions were not entirely lacking in the city. Men were not allowed, for instance, to wear shorts in the downtown streets. Sanctimonious as this rule seemed, there was a rather alarming habit among men, rich and poor alike, of giving themselves outrageous and prolonged scratchings.

Never to have seen a Rio tram was, quite simply, never to have seen a tram. When the sea goes out at low tide it leaves rocks scaly with limpets. That is what Rio trams looked like. They were covered only by a kind of delicate iron verandah, completely open. Along the sides was a step up from the street and on this, clinging for dear life, were dozens of outriders. The first one I saw came charging across the Avenida Rio Branco like a bull. I jumped aside to let it pass with its cheerful load of acrobats in a double layer down the sides. Except at the sharpest bends, and not always then, the hangers-on clung with only one hand. The other was needed for gesturing, the essential part of Brazilian conversation. Each tram had a star acrobat in its conductor. The seats extended across the full width, leaving no gangway, so the conductor was obliged to collect fares from the running-board. When this was loaded he had to work his way up and down the tram by clambering crab-wise over the crowd. But the fare seemed hardly worth collecting. The cruzeiro notes which he folded and held fan-wise between each of his fingers were old, torn and dirty. Many of them consisted more of adhesive tape than original note, whether of one cruzeiro or a thousand. The tram's outriders were called the *turma do descanso*, the resting brigade, because at every stop they got off to rest their strained arms. They also rode on the buffers at front and rear and even on the roof.

The trams running across the Avenida seemed to carry more sailors than anybody else at certain times of the day. Their glistening uniforms looked like white flowers clinging to an old wall. I secretly believed that the *Carioca* loved tram rides as much because they were dangerous as because they were cheap. There was only one fare, and it was twopence. For this you could go for an exciting two-hour journey to the furthest of Rio's outposts at the mountains' feet. I had never seen anything like the *bondes*, the Rio trams, except refugee trains in the East, covered outside by figures in turbans.

It is not by wine or language, or by pavement cafés or by non-stop sunshine that one knows that one is out of England, but by bidets in bathrooms. I had a lovely one in the private bathroom attached to my room on the fourteenth floor of the Grande Hotel São Francisco. It might have been in San Francisco, too, or Chicago, rather than on that corner of Rio's Avenida where the trams crossed. The shipping agent put me in there as soon as I had cleared customs. Like a dog gyrating before settling in its basket I sniffed about the room, noting the view from the window, the springiness of the bed, the capacity of the wardrobe, and the printed advertisement pinned on the inside of the lobby door. It showed at what times a lawyer's office was open for consultations. This set my mind whirring as to

Monument on the plain—twin towers and domes of the national congress

Working palace for the president—marble, glass, and a view of Brasilia's plateau
House for the Indian—straw roof, earth floor, and a view of the alligator river

what complications people in strange hotel rooms could possibly be in which might require the urgent assistance of a lawyer.

My conclusions were so alarming that I went down to street-level. Here I had my first, and last, meal in an air-conditioned restaurant. There were some of the Americans who rode in the hotel lift (oil-prospectors? construction engineers?—anyway, something of the sort, for they wore silvery tin helmets and were red-faced and hard-bitten and spoke to each other by clipped mono-syllables). There were also a number of wealthy business men and their secretaries eating iced melon. Three waiters waited on me and I hated it, so I resolved to find smaller places to eat, where I could find the real *Carioca*. Rua Marechal Floriano ran up beside the hotel off the Avenida. I did not have far to hunt, since Rio teemed with hungry people.

The Rua Mar. Flor., as the town maps call it, became my favourite street—perhaps because the trams went along it, or perhaps because it savoured of an Oriental bazaar. Shops elbowed each other on the pavements and all the way down there was music from radio and gramophone shops. Rhythm beat in the air in a wonderful din. Here there were many little restaurants and bars jammed in between shops which sold shoddy furniture and ill-fitting clothes and shops with shelves full of wax *ex-votos*. And where they stopped at the other end was the pink and white sugar palace of Itamarati. To the street, Itamarati presented a very sparse front, but made up for this by rambling back in a charming, inconsequental way among court-yards and gardens. This housed the Ministry of Foreign Affairs.

Nobody could guess that the low building contained such long, marble halls, staircases, cool *salons* and a large pool flanked by imperial palms. The Foreign Office itself was always referred to as Itamarati, so that it was easy to forget that originally it was a big private house. If there is such a thing as Italian neo-classical architecture, then Palácio Itamarati has it, according to the books. It just struck me as being rather pleasant in a nineteenth-century sort of way. Somebody had entirely ruined its charm during the 1930s by adding a pompous temple colonnade to one end of the large courtyard where swans swam in the pool. A merchant built the palace and lived there until 1889, when presumably there were no more slaves to keep it going. When Brazil became a republic, the provisional government liked the palace so well they moved in among the Aubusson tapestries, Persian carpets and priceless paintings. Although the arcaded loggias, the reflection of Doric columns and palms in the still pools had a certain appeal, I thought altogether too much fuss was made about the palace. Salvador's churches excelled Itamarati and similar showplaces, and Rio itself had new buildings infinitely superior as architecture. But it certainly gave an indication of how the wealthy lived when Brazil still rested on a foundation of slavery. And the living for the masters must have been gracious indeed.

So much, however, could not be said about the shacks on the foothills behind Itamarati. Any street leading off from Rua Marechal Floriano led up to the precariously perched huts on the Morro da Conceicão. These shacks showed the other side of Rio's life. The postcards and glossy volumes of coloured photographs illustrate the Sugar Loaf and Copacabana beach, but they are not the whole Rio de Janeiro. By looking from their windows at the courtyard palms, Itamarati's officials could remind themselves of Brazil's great hinterland and its jungle. The palms, which slyly imitated the Doric columns, were entwined with *monstera deliciosa*, making them like the carved and gilded columns of São Francisco in Salvador. Brazilians called *monstera* Adam's rib, an allusion to the slots in its fleshy leaves. But the visitor to Itamarati could remind himself of the Brazil which is less remote than Amazonian jungles. By walking a few steps from the pink palace he could look up to the steep slopes of Morro da Conceicão, to the huddled groups of shanties, the *favelas*.

Life in the *favelas* flourished with the exuberance of the *monstera deliciosa* on Itamarati's imperial palms. And the shanty towns clung in much the same way, entwining themselves round the main trunk of the city itself. The mountains imprisoned Rio in its golden cage of Guanabara Bay. The city could not expand. Yet wherever it touched the mountains the shanty settlements sprang up, beyond the fringe of everything except life itself. I had never believed that man lives by drains alone, nor by paved and lit streets, nor even by piped water. In Ireland, I had walked countless half-miles from house to spring-well with buckets of water for washing and drinking. And in dry summers I had often to go twice as far to draw from a three-landlords' drain. But the water was fresh, the way cool with shade, the air sweet in the fragrance of meadows. But in Rio's driftwood and oil-can slums the women and children had to clamber over the dry earth in their bare feet. With oil-cans balanced on their heads they picked a way down the steep hill, avoiding the miniature gulches which served as sewers, open in the heat. This done, they reached the first tap at which to fill the oil-cans and so return up the hill amongst the uncleared, stinking garbage.

Of course, people in the *favelas* have before their very doors one of the world's most marvellous spectacles—the splendour of Guanabara Bay. But only the fittest survived to see it, and life was not supported, after all, only by beautiful views. Nobody was responsible for those people. They paid no rates or rents, bore no responsibilities in Rio's civic system and consequently derived no services from it. But there were so many thousands of squatters, living on left-overs from the city's regular life, that no administration could ever clear them without causing serious riots.

In any case, there would be nowhere for the *favela* people to go, and even if there were, they probably would not want to go. Other things being equal, nobody would want to swop the heights of Rio and the view of Guanabara Bay for a concrete skyscraper with nothing but a view of the next concrete skyscraper. Caracas in Venezuela had a similar problem when I lived there. The Government built many tall apartment blocks to be let at nominal, subsidized rents. But the squatters were not interested. They preferred their huts, proximity to the earth and the promiscuity of an almost communal life.

Where it not that Rio's *favelas* result in suffering and deprivation, I would agree that as a method of living it was an excellent one. But I could not help feeling when I looked at the *favelas* that an enormous human potential was being wasted. For those who survive at all thrive with a richness and humour and zest for living which it takes a mixture of negro, Indian and European to achieve. What writers and artists and scientists or teachers and doctors was Brazil missing because this rich vein went untapped? Some idea of what might be can be gleaned from the fact that a number of Brazilian musicians came from *favelas*, including the writers of popular sambas. This situation is not exclusively Brazil's. One need only remember Sicily and Danilo Dolci to realize that. Contrast may have been the Brazilian speciality, but as I saw it, on leaving Itamarati after my first visit, the contrast was really a gulf, fixed and apparently unbridgeable. As though to stress the sinister presence of the *favelas*, black vultures circled slowly above the huddled shacks. They turned on their wings, fluttering against the blue sky like the ashes of burnt paper carried up from a bonfire. They were the urubu, a smaller bird than the bald-headed vulture, and the *favelas'* sole scavengers.

It was unlikely, then, that the *favela* people would ever reach such eminence as to be able to sweep through the doors of the Copacabana Palace Hotel (*the* hotel) or into Rio's French-looking, exclusive Jockey Club along the Avenida Rio Branco. They could, however—and did—go into the Praça da Republica. This was a public garden near Itamarati. It was also opposite the War Ministry, a monstrous building, as big as it was bad. The Praça was a curious place, planted with that odd, stiff formality common to municipal gardens in South America. But the informality of those who used the place more than compensated. There was stiff grass for children to romp on, there were trees to give shade and pools to give the illusion of coolness. Entrance was free to this fresh-air club, anybody could be a member without wearing the ties or jackets which were Rio's symbols of respectability. Naturally, the people came down from the nearest *favelas*, bringing their gaiety with them. The Praça became my club, too. From a fruit-stall outside I would buy a fresh, peeled pineapple and take it into the park for breakfast.

The Praça's cats were not interested in pineapple. For strays, which they were, the scores of cats prowling about the tame jungle were extraordinarily fastidious. This may have been why they were so pitifully thin. Like young lions they sprawled by the dozen on the paths, or chased each other among the carpets of Brazilian prayer-plants. Poor things, their bones showed plainly under their fur. Many *Cariocas* brought food for them. One man brought a saucepan full of fish heads and a bundle of newspapers every day. He carefully put out equal portions of fish in the newspapers and put them on the ground. One day I counted over forty cats feeding around him. But nothing seemed to fatten them.

Much more interesting for me were the *cotias*. These agoutis also abounded in the gardens and amused me much more than the ever-hungry cats. The *cotias* had perfect manners for rodents. They were about as big as a hare, with coarse golden coats. Their fore-paws were small and similar to a squirrel's. And such morsels as they could pick up they nibbled with extreme delicacy, like dining duchesses. As distinct from the disdainful cats, the *cotias* were great ones for bits of pineapple, although their good manners and shyness would not allow them to beg openly. I think they were faintly schizophrenic. Suddenly, they would drop whatever they were doing and dash madly into the undergrowth, and just as suddenly stop again to resume perhaps a punctilious washing with fore-paws. I became a great admirer of the *cotias*, but they were as spoilt as the squirrels in New York's Central Park or Copenhagen's pigeons. They always ignored my overtures, being far too superior to talk to foreigners.

Abundant fish thronged the Praça's two lakes. A mere crumb could be thrown into the water and swarms of black fish would appear from nowhere fighting each other for the morsel. In the middle of these two artificial lakes were little islands where lime trees grew. Small boys left their clothes on the mainland and half-waded, half-swam the twenty yards to fill their pockets with the hard green limes. And not-so-small boys did this, too, for one day I saw three men in nothing but soaking trousers being turned out of the park for a similar theft.

On the whole the Praça was a very free place. Only a few police appeared from time to time, in clean khaki linen uniforms and round tin helmets, looking like American G.I.s. They always pounded the beat in pairs. *Cosme e Damião* the Brazilians call them, after the two inseparable saints. After dark they patrolled on horse-back. By then the Praça had become lovers' lane. At the short twilight, the Brazilian prayer-plants lifted up their leafy hands in supplication. Under the silk-cotton trees a dense shadow developed, ideal for loiterers. Even by day the great silk-cotton trees cast gloom, creating an uncanny atmosphere with their strange ribbed roots like flying buttresses. It was those trees with their grisly foliage which more than anything created the impression that the garden was a stage-set and quite lifeless. There was none of the billowing movement of trees in a breeze, or Wordsworthian dancing daffodils. Neither the luxurious growths of aloes or *euphorbia pulcherrima*, nor the fleshy, red-veined caladium could break the deathlike spell.

Nevertheless, life went on, with greater energy after dark than before. The agoutis started romping in the deserted playgrounds. On the concrete seats old women prepared their bed of newspapers and took a puff or two at their pipes before turning in. Old men, despairing less easily of life's pleasures, filled tins with water from the lake and got their friends to shave them. Then they were ready to catch the eye of the girls who appeared by this time and who were slinking up and down the grand paths hoping to draw the young men. Not all the young men followed the girls, however, and many were their rivals. At times, in the dark, it was quite difficult to tell from the silhouette which was which.

Not all such matters at the park were clandestine and examples of men loving darkness rather than light. One afternoon I found quite a crowd gathered in the Praça. A large negress was champion of the cause. The cause itself, I discovered was the repeal of a recent official decision to ban the homosexual ball, one of Rio's carnival highlights. That it was homosexuals who were to be victimized alarmed nobody particularly except the people concerned. But the idea that *any* official should dare to lay hands on *any* part of the carnival alarmed everyone. Rio would die if its carnival was to be emasculated and at the merciless hands of the pious.

Yet puritanism, contrary in all things to the spirit of carnival, was getting a foothold—even in the Praça da Republica. My Sunday afternoon doze was disturbed by the unlikely but unmistakable strains of Moody and Sankey coming from a loudspeaker by the monument to Benjamin Constant, a one-time Brazilian general.

Curiosity overcoming laziness I got up and went over. A youth handed me a Gospel tract which advised me, in Portuguese, to flee from the wrath to come. I fled. But not far away another militant Protestant sect was giving a children's service. The talk was illustrated by a diagram of toads by a river. I was amused to think what thin ice the Brazilian evangelist was treading, probably all unknowingly, for the toad had played a great part in the sexual magic brought from Africa to Brazil by the slaves.

The negroes resorted to the toad as the Portuguese resorted to the forbearing São Goncalo. In Afro-Brazilian belief nothing was better for consummation of marriage beds than a bit of dabbling with toads. Not among screech-owls, bats, tortoises, snakes and doves was there any creature so magically endowed as the toad. The girl who wanted her lover to remain faithful (always a problem in Brazil) had only to keep a live toad under her bed and milk-feed it. And such things were not entirely heathen, as a modicum of Catholicism was involved.

The woman, for instance, who wanted to deceive her husband had to make certain preparations before running off with her lover. First she must make the sign of the cross on her sleeping husband's face and then sew up the eyes of a toad with green thread. As might have been expected, the rabbit got himself involved in sexual rites, too. Perhaps this accounted for the white rabbit-paw charms which I saw everywhere in Brazil, dangling from key-chains, and from the ignition keys on car dashboards in place of St. Christopher! But I strongly suspected that like jeans, the rabbits' paws were originally imported from the U.S.A., where I had seen them in chain stores years before.

The modern Brazilian did quite-well-thank-you without having recourse to toads—especially the women who haunted the dockside bars. Almost under oath I had promised to go to these bars with some of the *Rubens*'s crew. During my first four nights in Rio the *Rubens* was still berthed, and I went from the hotel to call on my friends at the ship. All the way from Swansea they had regaled me with tales of Recife, Santos, and Rio. Now they had to prove themselves truthful. The sailors never wandered far from the ship. The bars were the beginning and end for Jack ashore. I went to the *Rubens* and we picked our way among the piles of unloaded cargo and arrived at the first bar without mishap. It was not too crowded and we sat at a marble-topped table and began with beer.

There were other sailors in there of a dozen nationalities and the ladies of the bars, ladies of all shapes, sizes, colour, age and character. In spite of being professional many of them gave at least the appearance of enjoying their work. Some remembered the *Rubens* boys from one or two trips back and came over to invite themselves to a drink. Some tiny boys, seeing that a party was about to begin, came to sell twists of peanuts, and some older ones, perhaps eight or nine years old, thought we might like to buy a Rio pennant or shirt-collar stiffeners.

The bar was completely open to the outside and no windows or doors shut it off. There was no feeling of there being any illegal activity. After all, it was the world's oldest drama being played again. Not far away there was a bus station and occasionally priests and young seminarists passed with averted eyes. Each of the girls was a character, from the youngest teenager to the middle-aged *grande dame* who looked like a Kensington hostess and specialized in fat ships' chefs and ageing engineers. All tastes, in fact, could be catered for. As the evening wore on a continual procession of girls came and went, changing as frequently and openly as crowds at a railway station. Occasionally hard words were exchanged with the waiters as the girls migrated from table to table, chatting with their friends as a coquettish way of attracting attention or sitting cheekily with the crews. It was comic and pathetic, but human.

Sailors do not have a wife in every port. They never go as far as that. But they enjoy life. Rio had beautiful things to offer besides the land and seascape of Guanabara Bay. Whether negro or Indian, or any of the shades between, or Japanese, or, like the first one to set her cap at me, dark skinned as night but with refined European features, in those girls there was a fire in the eyes, a suggestion of passion which consumed men from the north. Whether this was true, or was just an illusion created by celibate weeks at sea, or whether it was novelty I had no idea. But what I did know clearly was that it was not those easy come, easy go people, or others like them in any of the Seven Seas' ports, who build up racial barriers and colour bars. By Rio's waterfront the British sailor, and the German and Dutch and Finnish, with the Brazilian girls had an animal pleasure in each other's company. Everyone was well aware that the whole proceedings was business. But so are circuses.

The sailor paid for the girl's drinks as well as his own, of course. But how easily the Brazilian beer went down. From time to time my friends asked anxiously if I was enjoying myself and whether their forecasts had been right about South American bars. About Brazilian beer at least they were right. *Chopp* was the nearest thing to Danish lager I had tasted outside Denmark. Late evening retained the day's heat and the ice-cool beer was so refreshing that we drank copiously. This was also easy to do, for instead of paying separately for each large bottle, the waiter brought a beer mat which had the price on it, and the mats piled up until the moment of reckoning. The girls were adept at slipping their own and friends' mats unobserved among the sailor's. Not that the sailor's powers of observation were too sharp by this time. Payment for services to be rendered was also an important point with the girls. They made it their business to learn enough English, French and German to establish their rights in the bargain to be struck. One girl who could not speak English spilled sugar on the table and wrote her fee in it with a forefinger.

Sugar had been spilled in Brazil centuries before for similar reasons. When the sugar-cane was brought to Brazil from Madeira, some sugar traditions travelled with it. The nuns of Madeira were world famous for their confectionery. It appealed even to the Pope himself. He eagerly awaited the sugar-sculpture from the island to adorn his banqueting-tables, especially creations by the Franciscan sister of Santa Clara in Funchal. Their art went to Brazil with the sugar-plant and with the missionary nuns. And this survived four centuries, though in an altered form, for I found many shops in Rio selling sugar architecture, sugar portraits, and cakes elaborately decorated with sugar in the shape of grand pianos and cars.

Rio's waterfront girls formed a sisterhood with skills of its own. More children had been in the bar selling small orange crabs and a girl gave me one. She had transformed it into an obscene figure which would have done justice to any Franciscan sister of the past. Sisters, indeed, were the little girls who wandered in and out of the bar all night, selling the crabs or peanuts or just simply begging. Their dirty brown legs were without shoes or stockings, and as they padded over the marble floor and their sad, beautiful faces appeared pleadingly at our table, I realized that life held no future for them but to take their older sisters' places.

It was a life, I suppose, not without its attraction—continual excitement, bright lights, a certain standard of living higher than their *favelas* could offer, a room of their own and clothes. Nobody could blame them for choosing dockside glamour rather than hillside poverty. There were few occupational hazards that could not be coped with in one way or another. The police did not seem to be much in evidence except to remove one girl who had made herself a noisy nuisance all night to the other girls and their sailors. But she had obviously been in the police van before. No doubt she would be back the following night, lounging in her chair, chewing bubbly gum and blowing suggestive bubbles at every sailor who came in. Whatever else the ladies of the bar were, they were certainly not ladies.

At the fag-end of my first night in the city I was strolling down the Avenida Rio Branco with the dining-room steward from the *Rubens*. We had left the bar, which began to get tawdry long before the high fluorescent lights went out and the big shutters were pulled down and the unlucky girls went to hunt elsewhere. A bullet whined past my head, and struck a building behind me. Then, apparently from nowhere, three pairs of police appeared and surrounded a negro who held his gun in the air. From under a car a little white man appeared and dusted himself down. Then the city was quiet again. I was to find it so on most nights. Those who had not even so much as a shack up in the *favelas* crept into doorways to sleep. And sleeping on rolls of newspaper and on the steps outside a printing works were boys sprawled in Henry Moore attitudes. Neon signs waited for the dawn and in the gutters rats were busy trying to get titbits before the beggars did. For a little while the chasm between the Avenida's skyscrapers was empty.

4

Hymn to Yemanja

At four in the morning Avenida Rio Branco sounded like a farmyard. Nothing could seem more unlikely during the midday fever. But there it was, the call of at least six roosters in the courtyards below. In spite of scraping skies in my fourteenth-floor bedroom, throughout the night I could hear sounds like the open country. The cicadas sang their high-pitched music, so beloved by film directors to give tropical effects. On Rio's roofs they sounded more like the buzzing of a faulty neon sign. No sooner had the cicadas stopped than there followed the sound of horns in the morning—the first cars tearing along the Avenida. Then there were the trams and from half-finished skyscrapers the first hammers began. Rio was awake and at work by the time the maid brought coffee, rolls and cheese at eight o'clock. The *Carioca* must have snatched the barest hours of sleep between late-night carousals and early-morning work.

Rio's dawn chorus was not exactly like that of birds in a Devon wood. Also unlike a wood was the view from my window into the spaces behind the skyscrapers. At the bottom of the pit was a curious huddle of old houses, backwaters untouched by the stream of commercial progress in spate along the main streets. The nearby Avenida Vargas was always in spate with traffic, too, dangerous traffic, out with intent to kill. I called it, with all due respect to the late President, Suicide Alley. Haussmann would have loved it. Avenida Vargas was a monster of an avenue. Guide-books said it was nearly a hundred yards wide and over a mile long, and 'one of the finest in South America'. They omitted to add 'every inch a killer'. At its intersection with Avenida Rio Branco, the Vargas

sucked traffic into itself like a great vacuum-cleaner. For the Rio
pedestrians, avoiding this whoosh of cars and buses and everything
else on wheels had become a game second only to football. To get
across, those on foot had to contend with eight lanes or so of traffic
moving in all directions.

A big, monumental avenue is obliged to have something big and
monumental at at least one of its ends, like the Paris Avenue de
l'Opéra. Rio had the cathedral of Nossa Senhora da Candelária.
This nineteenth-century domed church was better known as simply
the Candelária. It stood on an island isolated by dangerous swirling
currents of traffic that could easily carry the pedestrian out of his
depth. The *lotacoes* were the worst offenders—small buses as swift
as hornets. With their sixteen passengers they lurched into Avenida
Vargas like something in orbit, belching black fumes. The exhaust
pipes were turned up at the back to the roofs to make the *lotacoes*
look like mobile soup-kitchens. That the inside of the Candelária
should be comparatively still and cloistral was not surprising—even
when full, as it was on my first acquaintance.

An open church door has a fatal attraction for me. I enter with
bated breath, believing I am about to be amazed by the architecture.
But this only happens about once in a hundred churches and
Candelária was not one of the ones. It was depressing to find that
even Brazil, home of wild baroque exoticism, had its equivalent of
Victorian gloom and heaviness and bad taste. Not far away was the
15th November Street and the ferries to Niterói, a town across
Guanabara Bay from Rio, where I had planned to go before Candelária seduced me. Candelária's cupola and the ferries creeping
across the Bay were the only things I noticed about Rio from the
Rubens's rails on Christmas Day. All the buildings had looked like
shoe-boxes standing on end, except for the church's breastlike dome.

Candelária rewarded me for paying respects by laying on a high
society wedding, complete with red carpets and orchestra. Hundreds
of formidable dowagers were arriving in Buckingham-palace-
garden-party hats. Bright pink was a favourite colour, and most
suitable, too, because many seemed to be made of candy-floss. These
expensive hats, suits, shoes, handbags and hair-dos, these expen-

sive women, in fact, were the antithesis of Rio's mountain slums. Their sleek, justly-fed and well-preserved bodies were at the opposite pole from the diseased ones of the beggars outside. The nuptials were to be consecrated and celebrated among banks of red flowers piled all over the high altar and the sanctuary. With almost an hour to go before the bridal pair's arrival, I easily got a pew; a brass-studded leather affair like something out of Maple's mediaeval department. The church *ought* to have been all right, for the basic Portuguese formula was there. But the marble coating looked like old salami and took my appetite away. Candelária started life in 1639 when some shipwrecked sailors made a vow to build a church when a burning light appeared and led them safely ashore. After a series of rebuildings the final church appeared in 1898. It looked better with its architecture hidden by the banks of gladioli, Indian cane and birdy-looking strelitzia.

The brocade dresses were getting tighter and shorter and the hats larger and more outrageous the more we waited for the bride. The nave was beginning to be as crowded as the pens of a cattle-market. Men (dark suits and ties or with uniforms impressively draped by loops of gilt braid like the ropes from Victorian curtains) greeted each other in the same way as the women with a handshake, a hug (big hug for special friends) with heart touching heart. There was also a kind of hand-kissing. Those women who could find a seat eased themselves down, for rapid movement was not only impious but impossible in those tight skirts. Then they fanned themselves with fans painted in execrable taste with bull-fights and serenading lovers, together with other scenes equally unlikely to inspire holiness.

The congregation was not, of course, assembled only for spiritual purposes, but also to make a show and to meet friends—white ones, or at least, the whiter the better. For this parade of Rio's uppercrust society showed me that black was out as that year's colour for skins. There was absolutely no colour bar in Brazil; it was just simply that negroes seldom became top people socially or professionally. Lower down the social scale, say among the Avenida's shoeshine boys, you could be blue-in-the-face and nobody would mind.

Meanwhile, if you were black, or near black or a good bit blacker than top Brazilians (who fancy that with their black hair and black eyes and olive skins they are white) and you want to go into Copacabana's best hotels, then you had to think again. And if you were black you were also most unlikely to receive an invitation to become an ambassador or a general. As I was told on a number of occasions by people who knew, there most definitely was no colour bar in Brazil, but the negroes knew their place.

Their place in the Candelária was not difficult to define. Most of them were servants, cooks and mammas and the like, comfortable negresses who doubtless had nursed and comforted the children of the big houses, and young negress maids. The white people, I could see, were terribly kind and nice to them, but obviously would never marry them.

I grew tired of the whole business long before the bride arrived and left to get the ferry to Niterói. They plied frequently across the Bay and were loaded rather as the trams were. Although no passengers actually hung outside, I wondered what would happen in an emergency, especially to those on the deck below. I heard talk of a bridge to Niterói to take the daily commuters. And it would certainly save another episode like the one when some *Cariocas* were stranded at Niterói. They missed the last ferry one night and so set fire to the terminal building. Nobody had bothered to repair it since. The gaunt skeleton was the first thing to greet the visitor to Niterói. Not unnaturally, Niterói had become little more than a dormitory suburb of Rio. Yet even so, for one with a population of some 245,000 the town had a lazy sleepy-in-the-sun air. There was decay, too, a crumbling, a peeling and a flaking not unlike Salvador's. A gentle charm emanated from the cracked stucco, the rusty iron grilles and balconies. The whole was reminiscent of French things— French Empire style in a Riviera town, a touch of Colette, a little perhaps of Renoir's colouring in the villas hidden in sunlit, old-fashioned gardens with sago palms and traveller's trees. Even the potted silk-flower cactus on the windowsills looked forlorn and dusty. The century-plants looked tired. Poor haggard daughters of Cadmus!

Out of Niterói, farther along the coast, the town's quaintness was left behind for a more typically Brazilian atmosphere. The sun stung, the light dazzled. Now I had the splendid vista of Guanabara Bay from the opposite side. It was undoubtedly more beautiful than from Rio's waterfront. Here, too, bordering the coast road, were bright gardens, especially in the elegant Canto do Rio district. Frangipani fell like homing doves on to trim lawns. One stone wall was topped with queen-of-the-night cactus bearing four dozen blooms or so. But the gathering sun had already struck these fragile, faery things. The cornfield of yellow stamens had wilted inside the white chalice of petals which bloom so extravagantly during a single night. This hedge tempted me back across the Bay from Rio on several evenings afterwards. But I never saw the elusive flowers reclining incongruously on the cactus's harsh spikes, as on a bed of nails.

Those gardens, like so many around Rio, were also rich in bignonias. Trumpets of a dozen hues hung wantonly over walls and terraces. How delighted the Abbé Bignon would have been with the limpid lemon and the blushing pink! Extravagant colours were the fashion at Versailles, where women rivalled the flowers for their beauty. Louis XIV's librarian, the Abbé, may have spared time from his books to study nature, but I do not know whether he gave his name to anything in addition to bignonias. The Abbé Bignon and his bignonias may well have been one of Louis's diversions. But the Roi Soleil had other ways of amusing himself. In 1711 Louis gave his blessing on seventeen French ships whose mission was to raid and plunder Rio de Janeiro. They completely sacked the city and made off with its gold. But then, the French were no strangers to the Portuguese colony. As early as 1555 French Huguenots founded a Protestant town in the neighbourhood, much to Portuguese annoyance. An Indian chief helped to drive the French out of Guanabara Bay, and for this he was made a Knight of the Order of Christ and commander-in-chief of his town. This was the present-day Niterói. I found a bust of him in the main square, Praça Martim Afonso, which is called after the name he took when he became a convert to Catholicism.

But interest centred round another Indian when I was there—

this time a fakir. Unlike the cactus flowers, he did repose on a bed of nails. The posters announced the sensational Zamor. He was going to fast for one hundred and twenty days non-stop. I paid to go into the temporary booth near the ferry terminus, and entered under the watchful eye of armed guards. They were there because the previous fakir was a fake. His cronies had stolen in to feed him at dead of night. But the sensational Zamor was definitely going to do or die. So far, Zamor had only been sealed up in his glass case for two weeks when I saw him. He looked a trifle pale and drawn, but otherwise in splendid condition. And he appeared to be undamaged except for holes in his socks caused by the bed of six-inch nails. In spite of, or perhaps because of the crucifix over his head, Zamor was not in a trance, and studied me as if *I* was in the glass box. For company he had some repulsive snakes, of a kind that could also go long periods without food. Pieces of paper were stuck all round the glass and frame to prove that nothing went in or out. Visitors had written names and dates and good wishes on them. I wrote one. By a series of signs the attendant conveyed to Zamor the fact that I was from Ireland and had come all the way to see him, which I thought an exaggeration, to say the least.

More amazing to me, and decidedly more useful than the fakir's talents, were those of Dr. Daniel de Brito, to whom I was introduced through the Foreign Office. With his company and a car I made a journey of exploration. Ostensibly it was of Rio and its environs. But more importantly it turned out to be a discovery of Rio's intellectual life. Through Daniel I learnt of the city's Gurdjieff and Ouspensky centres and of its distinct Kenneth Walker group. There were also devotees of Wilhelm Reich. And Rio had many music groups. My friend and his wife ran a Brahms and Schumann society not only for listening to records but also for playing the chamber music.

For once, communication presented no problem, as Daniel spoke sixteen different languages fluently—including Near and Far Eastern ones. While we talked, the car whisked us up above Rio into the cool hills of the Tijuca Forest, the *Carioca*'s home-grown jungle on the doorstep. An even closer jungle was the political one

The tattoo smile of the hunting Caraja

Indian sylph

into which the *Carioca* plunges without fear. But the Brazilians' aptitude for making the most out of any situation even made politics enjoyable. The names of candidates were daubed on every available blank wall in Rio, along the canal's stone embankments, and even on the trunks of trees. This was the same exuberance of decoration and elaboration as I saw in Salvador. At that time there had not only been the general election, but there were also seven hundred candidates for the thirty places in the Guanabara Bay Chamber of Deputies. And so there were enough names to cover the whole of Rio with mural designs. Brazilians liked foreigners and reserved any xenophobia for their own Deputies, whom they regarded as the lowest form of existence. I saw a lively demonstration in Rio against the retiring city council. A vast, good-humoured crowd filled the square outside the city hall. It booed. Others carried out a mock funeral complete with lighted candles. The city fathers were marooned in the building. A few of them peeped from the windows of an upper chamber, but withdrew hurriedly at the crowd's cries.

At close quarters the hills of Rio were a trifle dull. From the sea those purple humps and switch-back mountains stood one behind another in the deep perspective of distance. They suggested great valleys and all the splendour and excitement of the interior beyond. But when our car got up to the Tijuca Forest I found it was a dense, lifeless wall of heavy, depressing vegetation. The clouds were low that afternoon, so no sunlight pierced the thick woods. We stopped at a waterfall which looked as though it had been made specially for tourists. It was a high, narrow fall, making quite a reasonable splash over the rocks. But the tourists' knick-knackery had settled round the place. Souvenirs of the type found everywhere in the world were on sale. But in addition there was a Brazilian speciality— butterflies' wings done up into tea-trays and wall-plaques. An extraordinary number of butterfly species flitted about Brazil's forests. That was one thing. Quite another was the use of their great gaudy wings for designs showing the Christ statue above Rio, or night scenes on tropical beaches or maps of Brazil. The splash of the waterfall made an ideal background for an olde-worlde tea-shop with check tablecloths laid ready in the garden.

Undoubtedly the most interesting thing about the Tijuca Forest was its origin. It was not, as I thought, primeval jungle, but the result of reafforestation. When a certain Baron of Bom Retiro started, he was dealing with an almost bald mountain. The first woods had long ago been cleared for coffee plantations which were later neglected and overrun. When I saw it the Tijuca Forest looked centuries old, a deception which well showed how rife and prolific growth could be in Brazil.

Farther along a rising, twisting road we came to Alto da Mesquita and a small chapel made famous because it contained a Portinari triptych. This painter earned fame by the *azulejos* murals he designed for a number of famous modern Brazilian buildings, including, of course, Rio's Ministry of Education. He alone perhaps brought this ancient craft to life again. But Portinari's early panel painting in the Mayrink Veiga Chapel (of a Madonna standing between two monks) was disappointing, though at least he had the courage to do a bright yellow-clad Virgin instead of the usual blue one. The style reminded me rather of Hans Feibusch, who painted so many emotionally moving murals in Europe after 1945, including many in England.

Our summit conference was postponed because of the mist. Daniel wanted to show me the view of Rio from a high terrace. But we could see nothing but the tops of the nearest trees below us and a few birds flying swiftly among the trees or on to the terrace balustrade. The air was damp and scented as though with honeysuckle. Our driver filled the leaky car radiator from a little fountain, carrying the water in one of the hub caps. But from then on the problem of heating up the engine was less acute, because our way ran downhill towards Rio's beaches. Guanabara Bay was held, as it were, between a thumb and a forefinger of land forming an 'O'. On the finger sat Niterói and Rio on the thumb. And the thumb with its mountains and beaches, the *praias*, was the most spectacular part. Those beaches surrounded the knob of land with great scooped out, shallow curving bays, each roughly two miles long. Copacabana stole all the limelight. This was only partly because of its natural magnificence. But perhaps more than this was its association with the scintillating luxury which burst on a black-out-blinded, ration-starved Europe just after 1945. 'Copacabana' is a word which does to modern ears what 'Eldorado' did to seventeenth-century ones. To live, love, laugh and play on the sands in the sun at Copacabana was not at all the same as doing similar things on Bournemouth beach. Yet Copacabana was only one of similar beaches in similar bays, Flamengo, Ipanema, Leblon among them. *Cariocas* had, in fact, begun to push out farther than Copacabana. Too popular to be distinctive any more, Copacabana was no longer the exclusive haunt of the rich.

Thirty years ago those glistening, green, Atlantic breakers broke on the wide white sands. But there was nothing there in those days except the little fishing village of Copacabana surrounded by sand-dunes. Then the Bay's scimitar curve suffered the transformation. Up went the luxury hotels and apartments, down came the fisher-men's shacks, in went the wealthy and out went the poor. Almost in no time Copacabana emerged from obscurity to fame and became the playboy's playground. While the fastest and latest and biggest motor-cars sped along its wide avenue, while the new inhabitants walked in enviable idleness along the tessellated pavements and disported themselves in the soft, fine sand or flung their tanned, beautiful bodies into the green waves, the eyes of the world turned in marvelling unbelief to Copacabana.

Copacabana became a subtle symbol. The sound of its name roused dormant desires. Repressed primitive urges surged to the surface at the mere mention of Copacabana. Who, in the whole wide world, did not want youth, vigour, a beautiful healthy, brown body and another similar body for company and an income before which troubles dispersed! No ad.-man with his battery of psycho-logical guns could ever have invented a symbol as powerful as the image of Copacabana. The facts, of course, had no need to enter into the matter, any more than they need, into, say, Edward German's *Merrie England* or Richard Strauss's Vienna in *Der Rosenkavalier*. That Copacabana beach is too hot, too crowded, often too dangerous to swim from, and that its architecture is vulgar, and that it is en-tirely without incident or accident of nature from one end to the other—none of these things has any connection with Copacabana the myth.

Our car drove slowly along on that Saturday afternoon and I saw for the first time what I returned to again and again afterwards. For, once one dismissed the myth and accepted its faults, Copacabana beach stole one's heart away. In reality it was not the sporting ground of the rich, but for every kind of *Carioca*, especially those living in the slums behind the grand façade of skyscrapers. And more perhaps than for swimming, the sands of Copacabana were used for football. Football in Brazil was not so much a game as a religion, and it obsessed the Brazilians. It occupied a place almost like the games in classical Greece. The players were national heroes; the match results, especially against foreign teams, were looked on as national victories or defeats. Almost from the time they could stand on their own two feet, Brazilian boys used them for kicking a football. They went on playing long after adolescence had past. Building labourers played football near their sites. Under ragged working trousers they wore swim trunks so that during spare moments they could strip for a game. Any bare patch of ground was used for a pitch, in labourers' camps and forest clearings, in city streets and village squares, and always the sandy beaches. The wide curve of Copacabana was perfect.

Along Copacabana's entire two-mile length, pitches were marked by goalposts and teams played in the sand barefoot, as they did everywhere even on the hardest ground. They wore proper coloured football shirts, except for the players who were too hot and ran about in shorts only. I never found out *how* they managed to kick the ball so far without boots. Some said it was done with the toes, others that the ball was kicked by the instep. Whichever was used, the ball went with great force, sometimes sailing high in the air, to rival the kites flying there. From our car the kites really looked like the urubu vultures after which they were modelled. But the kites' reds and yellows against the blue sky were not so sinister as the real birds' black, winnowing wings.

Passing along Copacabana in the car was like watching a travelogue film. Along the glaring sands the goalposts and the sweat-glistening figures enhanced the beach's immensity. Beyond the strip of blinding sand, translucent waves turned over, innocently concealing the treachery of undercurrents. These were the life-guards' enemy. But at last Copacabana ran out and the car brought us to the base of the cable car going up to the Sugar Loaf.

The Sugar Loaf is to Rio what the Eiffel Tower is to Paris or the Empire State Building to New York. Although Daniel himself had been up to the peak of the Sugar Loaf many times he thought it highly improbable that many *Cariocas* had. Riding in the cable car was not a Brazilian sport like the skin-diving or water-skiing, yachting or polo, and even crocodile-hunting, in which the wealthier Brazilian indulged.

The *Carioca* knew his bay-bound city well enough from the ground without going up 1,200 feet to see it. For the stranger, Rio was too complicated to understand at ground level, even with a map. But from the Sugar Loaf the whole city was revealed at once with its incomparable setting of hinterland mountains, swooping bays and wide island-dotted Guanabara Bay, and against all this the Atlantic, glazed in the afternoon sun. This panorama of Rio and the Bay was only the climax to the ride in the cable car itself. We swung over trees below that became green cauliflowers, high above swimmers and motor-boats with a trail of foam who became insects, over footballers on yet another beach who became ants on some mysterious business, and over the water that lapped the Bay like clear soup in a plate.

Sugar Loaf travellers were obliged to change cars half-way on an intermediate rock, the Morro da Urca. I hid as best I could my fear that the cable would snap. But this was an event so rare, apparently, that the last occasion was remembered in detail, including the fact that nobody was hurt, and that the emergency cable had saved the day. All that happened was that the passengers were suspended in mid-air for nine hours or so. They must have been rather bored with the view by the time rescue engineers brought them down. As we sailed over the first void and I suffered the same feeling as I do when a plane takes off, Daniel was talking unconcernedly about the last days of Gurdjieff and asking me about the vodka sessions at the

Rue des Colonels Rénards. As though it would collide with us Morro da Urca rushed towards the car, but missed by inches and we climbed out at the station. Across the second, greater gulf up to the Sugar Loaf itself the cables stretched away into space, sagging at first and then almost disappearing in the distance. A small silver car was hung out there, descending imperceptibly to our own level.

The Sugar Loaf was like an island in the sky. We soaked ourselves in the prospect of Rio. Then we sat on the little restaurant's terrace and drank beer. Inside, the counter displayed butterfly art similar to that at the waterfall. But in addition to these blue, iridescent wings there were some frames containing huge crab-spiders—an unpleasant reminder that Rio was in the tropics and that the jungle was at its door. But even from the Sugar Loaf this was not easy to forget. Though obvious tropical features, like the palm-tree, did not stand silhouetted against the sky, the whole landscape was totally different from the non-tropical. The hills were clad with trees and were far from being scorched dry by the sun like the arid, dusty hills of the Middle East. Yet, in spite of its verdure, this nature was in utter contrast with nature as humanized by the Renaissance. Claude or Poussin could never have created such scenes. Lully could not have written songs about those woods. Guanabara Bay was beautiful, but it was fierce and brooding. And Rio, spread before us along its coastal strip, did not and could never belong to the landscape as did Cuyp's windmills. And certainly, English romantic landscapes could never do to those tropical mountains what Paul Nash or Christopher Wood did to the English scene. Seen against such barbarous magnificence, anything done by man looked precarious and temporary. Perhaps this was basically what I sensed, that men conquered Brazil yet always remained fighters against the land. They never became part of it. Nothing showed this more than the architecture, as I was to see later in Brasilia.

Because the Sugar Loaf trip is made mostly by visitors, I suppose they feel impelled to leave some record of themselves. Hundreds of signatures and initials were scribbled over many years on available walls. But I could only discover one in English and that, obviously, inscribed by sons of Ulster,

LONG LIVE KING BILLY'S BOYS,
REMEMBER 1690. J.H. & L.B.

I tried to explain the subtleties of the Orange cause to Daniel, but he was much more concerned with the cosmic laws of three and seven. We went down to earth again, back to the heat beating off pavements and the happy Saturday afternoon couples. They wandered about arm-in-arm, starry-eyed not so much from love as from the music of the tiny transistor radios they carried. These were switched on permanently. But when the owners actually wanted to listen as distinct from having just a background noise, they walked along with the sets held against their ears. This happened everywhere in Brazil, and people even crossed the most dangerous streets in this trancelike state. The *Carioca* did not feel dressed without his pocket radio.

The afternoon was waning. The heat remained. The light lost its blinding intensity and instead glowed all golden. Shadows fell sharply. I could not bring myself to realize that it was New Years' Eve. Daniel invited me to his apartment in a tall block near the sea, which we had seen from the Sugar Loaf. I could not have a meal that evening because, according to the Brazilian New Year custom, he and his wife were dining with their parents, but separately—he with his own and his wife with hers. However, there was time to see what he termed 'an ordinary middle-class apartment'. But I could not help wondering where else in Rio, or indeed in how many other homes anywhere in the world, such a polyglot library could be found. Besides sections in most European languages there were bookcases devoted to ancient Hindu scriptures, Slavonic classics, shelves of Russian, Arabic, Chinese, and Latin. They were not decoration, but books he used from day to day, often in his teaching. When I mentioned a review in *The Times Literary Supplement*, Daniel opened a cupboard stacked with copies going back many years. He hunted through and found the particular article.

Daniel and his wife followed the old Brazilian habit of speaking French with each other and Portuguese to the servants—yes, servants for, of course, the Brazilian middle class had servants to wash, cook, clean and do all the things which drive the British housewife frantic. Unlike most of Rio's flat-dwellers Daniel had a garden, raised strangely on a huge rock outcrop behind the flats. We crossed a concrete bridge to it. Milky-blue hedges of plumbago lined the path to the swimming-pool. And here I saw my first Brazilian humming-birds: kiss-flowers as they are called. They flitted away at our approach, delicate, nervous and insectlike.

I had never seen anyone have their hair washed in champagne before. This extravagant gesture to the imminent New Year took place in the little restaurant where I ate supper. Four people drank eight bottles in an hour, one of which was poured like a sacrificial libation by a girl over her boy-friend's head. He did not seem to mind, although he was paying the bill. But this would not be enormous, because the champagne was Brazilian at seven shillings a bottle, hardly more expensive than the best shampoo. But there was, after all, something very Brazilian about Carmen Miranda and her famous song *When I love, I love*. When the Brazilians do anything, they *do* it. Like the ticker-tape welcome given to the New Year.

This started the day before New Year's Eve, on the Friday. At first some sheets of paper fluttered from an office window, high above Avenida Rio Branco. They floated down like a flock of doves. I thought an unlucky typist had left a file on a window ledge and that a breeze had caught it. How mad her boss would be, losing a year's correspondence! *Her* New Year would start with getting the sack. But, of course, this was Rio, not London. And the boss *wanted* to get rid of the past year's letters, bills, receipts, invoices, ticket rolls, typewriter ribbons. Soon, from every office window, clouds of paper were showering on to the Avenida. Offices open on the Saturday morning waited until then, but already the Avenida's trees were white with paper snow. Drifts of paper lined the gutters and lay heaped against the buildings. Festoons of lavatory paper sailed across the street like Chinese banners. Some aimed their rolls at near windows, and other rolls were dangled in an attempt to ensnare passers-by in the street. This un-puritanical merriment perhaps was a modern version of the jokes played on their guests by the former nobility.

New Year came in at the fever pitch of excitement. Rio throbbed with life, for down from the *favelas* came the negro musicians, few at first and then many different bands. The drums of Africa rolled and thundered along the main streets with ceaseless pounding and booming. Long before midnight the negro drummers and dancers appeared, a slow-moving nucleus of gyrating, sweating men and women, boys and girls, and babies in arms, moving in samba rhythms. Each group had perhaps a dozen drummers weaving fantastic, insistent rhythm, that ran in the veins like a fever. Crowds grew and swayed to the music of a band and followed it in procession. The air was electric. I found my way to the Praça Marechal Floriano and stood on the Opera House steps. Thousands of people thronged the big square. I looked at the negro faces passing before me—enraptured, shining faces with lips parted, white teeth gleaming, eyes bright. Occasionally I caught a glimpse of muscular shoulders or a bare brown chest as a dancer or drummer who had taken off his shirt passed by, oblivious of everything except the rhythm that pounded like heart-beats in the ears. The insistence of the drums seemed to open some secret way into rhythms that drive the universe. The drums seemed to probe the deepest experiences of the body, exciting it to all movements of which it was capable. The drumming was an intoxication and all the streets of Rio whirled drunkenly.

Then I realized what was happening. The bodies of dancers and drummers were themselves becoming instruments of rhythm. They were no longer *listening* to the drums, but were drums themselves, totally possessed by rhythm. No longer were the negroes playing sambas, but were being played by them, involuntarily. Like a great fire with a red heart the men in the groups' centres were the most affected, the heat of this transformation cooling towards the crowds' fringes until a mere spectator, like myself, was no more than an unconsumed stick, with the sap singing from the fire's proximity. When I stood to watch, my feet tapped to the rhythm; when I walked, my feet carried me along in step with the sambas.

The negro has never lost the sensual capacity of the human body as Europeans have. Perhaps that is why his figure is often more perfect than the European's. It is a living thing, sensitive to every stimulation. Having no cause to fear his body, the negro allows it to carry him away, to transport his mind. So I was witnessing what perhaps would be called mass hypnotism. With the approach of New Year, many of the negroes were in a trance of movement. This was not the motionless trance of the saint's soul, but a trance of the body in motion.

Trances are exhausting. Even saints faint. So I was not surprised to find a prone figure propped against a tree. He was a young negro and at first I thought he was dead. His friends had carried him from where he had collapsed. They opened his thin cotton shirt and massaged his heart, and put their ears to his chest. They slapped his face and forced his eyelids apart. Someone blew in his nostrils, like God with Adam. This young Rio Adam seemed, however, determined to remain clay. His face was that ashen colour which negroes have when they are sick. Then, quite suddenly, life returned. He began to weep, quietly and dreadfully. Tears ran beside his nose and dripped on to his chest. He cried as though all the sorrows of all negroes through all ages were visited on him. And perhaps they were.

By eleven o'clock I was feeling exhausted myself, in spite of the excellent meat-on-the-spit I had eaten earlier. But there were plenty of things to eat on sale in the street. The old negresses were out in force with their Salvadorian specialities, their mountains of pine-apples and horned-moons of water-melons. I worked my way towards the beach. There, at midnight, the serious ceremonies of *Candomble*, or rather *Macumba* as it is known around Rio, would be held in honour of Yemanja. The black Mother of the Waters would receive offerings and prayers which would outshine any made on the Virgin Mary's high days. This pagan worship underlay the whole of Rio's street celebrations, and into the dancers' entranced bodies would enter the deities of *Macumba*. The special New Year celebrations for Yemanja involved the sea itself. Along Rio's many beaches the sea-goddess's devotees would gather. Earlier in the evening I had seen groups of people dressed completely in white, waiting for buses to take them to the remoter beaches. They all carried bunches of white flowers. I wanted to watch the festivities on a beach near the city centre, and so I decided to see only the *Macumbas* by the Avenida Beira Mar. This was on a stretch of reclaimed land where Rio's great Museum of Modern Art was being built. This was not one of the fashionable beaches, and the poorer people used it for swimming during the day.

The beach was protected from the sea by lines of boulders and here I found Yemanja's faithful already waiting. It was uncannily quiet. If people spoke at all it was in whispers. The loudest noise was of the sea lapping among the rocks. Thousands of candles burned on the boulders, some so near the water that unexpected waves came in and doused them. I saw several women who stood facing the sea. Rosaries hung from their fingers and their lips moved. But their prayers were to Yemanja, not the Virgin,

> *Mother Yemanja, look down upon thy children,*
> *Look down upon thy children, Mother Yemanja.*
> *This is a new year full of lights,*
> *I'll light up my candles*
> *So that the Mother of Waters will bless me.*

But the whole theology of *Macumba* and *Candomble* was like a car made entirely of spare parts. So many things were mixed in from other religions that possibly even the devotees had no very clear idea as to exactly what, or to whom, they were praying.

Along the sea for many miles the candles burned low, and when they gutted were replaced. The solemn faces shining in their light were not all negro, unlike the drummers in the streets. Yemanja received prayers from all Brazilian types. I saw one man arrive in a large car. From the boot he took a huge bouquet of white flowers. With this and a small packet he went to find an empty place among the rocks. Midnight was not far off and fireworks had already started to explode with sharp cracks over the city. Many worshippers had already made their principal offering. I could see their white flowers still floating on the sea where they had been tossed. The business man with the outsized wreath lit his candles and laid some cigars in front of them on the rocks with two boxes of matches. He threw the great bouquet into the arms of Yemanja. She sent a wave which carried the flowers away. The cigars, I discovered afterwards, were an offering made to *Macumba's* Evil Spirit, Exú. Cigars were used instead of voodoo's black hen. I was told this was quite a common practice. Additional purposes could be served by cigars. The ghost of an old slave might return and want to blow cigar smoke contemptuously in his white master's face.

Yemanja's New Year ceremonies were certainly attractive. Possibly that was why, again, as a counter-attraction, the Roman Catholic Church also had a big water ceremony, the *Festival do Senhor Bom Jesus dos Navegantes,* carried out in various parts of Brazil, especially around Salvador where *Candombles* are so strong. But perhaps it was only natural in Rio to celebrate New Year by the sea, because the place was actually discovered on 1st January 1502. Goncalo Coelho, the Portuguese navigator, always named newly-discovered places after the saint whose day it happened to be. But 1st January was saintless. Goncalo Coelho thought that Guanabara Bay was the mouth of a great river and called it the River of January —Rio de Janeiro.

That was wrong and that there was, in fact, no great river, no longer matters. The name persisted and survived. Another survival was Brazil's patron, Nossa Senhora do Conceição da Apareçida. She was curiously like Yemanja in that she was black and also connected with water. This statue of the black Virgin Mary first appeared to some fishermen in a river, but they threw it back in the water again. Miraculously, the image was carried upstream instead of downstream. Obviously this was a powerful Virgin and she was fished out again and today is enshrined in her own cathedral. She also appeared, however, all over modern Brazil. The black Virgin smiled from pictures on lorry-drivers' cabins. On medallions and key-rings she was modelled in relief. Fully coped, crowned and coloured she could be bought as a china statuette. And, of course, Mary of the Apparition was a favourite name for Brazilian girls.

The slaves, when they were brought from Africa and forced to become Christians, heard of Nossa Senhora da Aparecida. But they probably also heard about the native Indian river goddess Yara who lured sailors to their death, like the Lorelei or the seal-women of the Faroes. However, Brazil might almost be said to have had a complex about water goddesses. Even Copacabana itself was named after a Virgin. She was Nossa Senhora de Copacabana, a statue which was the sole survivor from a Chilean ship. It went down early in the nineteenth century offshore, opposite the now famous beach. The Virgin floated safely in and was picked up. In those days the beach was known by its Indian name Sacopenopan. But this was promptly changed to Copacabana—the name of the famous shrine on a Chilean lake.

What on earth, or rather in heaven, I wondered, could the poor slaves have made of all this? Their own gods and idols were complicated enough without the added mystery of multi-racial, water-borne Virgins, to say nothing of saints and martyrs. Even less could I unravel all the strands which were tangled in *Macumba's* water worship. But the rosaries that New Year's Eve on Rio waterfront were certainly being said to the glory of Yemanja. But then the whole scene was a strange mixture of familiar things, candles by the sea, flowers floating on waves, rich and poor, black and white alike perched silently like mermaids on the rocks, and all the time, over this ancient magic, the night planes coming low over the sea to land at the Santos Dumont airport. Brazil's contrasts were difficult to digest. Where, I thought, except in Brazil could a native Indian be heard to say on seeing his first car 'Look! Look! An aeroplane without wings!'

Finally, at the stroke of midnight the whole of Rio behind us crackled and sparkled with fireworks and the beach worshippers clasped each other and kissed. They danced. On top of the Sugar Loaf, where Daniel and I had been earlier in the day, the lights winked on and off. I wanted to kick off my shoes and follow an old negress priestess in long robes who went to the sea's edge to get the first wave of the New Year. But I could hum the haunting tune of their hymn to the sea goddess,

> *Yemanja, my mother,*
> *Pity us and help us,*
> *For though the world is great*
> *Your strength is even greater.*

5

Mirage on the Plain

Although I kept a lookout from the plane's window, I was thinking about those five dusty cards in the Rio planning office. They reminded me of the miracle of the five loaves and two small fishes. Those scrawny scribbles of Lucio Costa's had been miraculously multiplied to produce a whole city.

The broad landscape glimpsed beyond the aircraft's silver wing was not the most dramatic I had seen from the air. But it was green all the way to Brasilia. Shortly after leaving Rio and striking inland towards the new capital we passed over folded, indented mountains. Then began endless rolling plains, green but tinged with red like shot silk. Thin paths traversed the plains uncertainly, wavering or changing direction suddenly. Of the desert in which English people had told me Brasilia stood, there was no sign. Nor was there any jungle or wilderness which others had variously described. There were plains, dotted here and there with isolated signs of human occupation, and threaded with heavily-wooded river-banks, but nothing more.

Two hours later, quite suddenly, Brasilia appeared. And there, below, reproduced perfectly on the ground, was the birdlike shape of Costa's city. The likeness to the shapes on the five dusty cards was startling. Shining in the morning sun was the great artificial lake, embracing the city within its two arms. On a promontory stood a gleaming white building—Palácio da Alvorada, Palace of the Dawn, the President of Brazil's residence.

As we touched down and sped along the runway I could see the coarse growth of the *cerrado*. At close quarters the plains were like English downland, though rough with stunted trees and tall grasses.

This surrounded Brasilia, making it like an island in the sea. Yet between the green waves, soil showed through, brilliantly red. Indeed, giant earth-moving machines had excavated so much earth that the city looked as though it floated on blood.

Few of the passengers bothered to look at either landscape or city from the air. They slept or read magazines or looked as though the journey was no more to them than a short bus ride. This was exactly how people, or at least inter-city commuters, used planes in Brazil, particularly between Rio and Brasilia. Those who worked in one or both cities wanted to cover the six hundred miles between them as quickly as possible. Not many people had either the time or the energy to drive along the 750 miles of road, which usually took up two days, compared with only two hours of flying.

Most people in the plane were returning to Brasilia after celebrating in Rio. Some carried Italian *panetone* cakes under their arms like footballs. The man next to me was distinguished by having on one of his hands only two fingers, and this by birth and not accident, as with a maximum of tact I managed to discover. But in Brasilia later I saw children with like deformities, especially those with extra fingers.

Another passenger was an Egyptian Jew now working in Brasilia as a government lawyer. He kindly offered to give me a lift in his jeep. My day had begun at the irritable hour of four o'clock. Brasilia itself was still in the earliest throes of getting down to work when we came out of the airport building. A flock of toucans kicked up a din and flew off amongst the trees. How *could* they fly, those clumsy, colourful birds all beak and no body? Inevitably, I thought of Guinness. When the jeep passed one of the lake's extremities I saw some great white heron, surprising me as always by their gracefulness.

It was unfortunate that the Brazilian's addiction to danger for danger's sake found such an easy outlet in driving cars. The jeep careered along at a speed which made it quite clear that Lucio Costa's design of the roads was beyond criticism. In a series of whorls and arabesques we fled round flyovers and bolted over bridges without let or hindrance. My friend knew his Brasilia. He chose exactly the right roads. Without getting tangled in traffic lights, because the city had no need of them, we rushed along the fourteen-lane highway.

And immediately, Brasilia the plan became Brasilia the reality. I saw how the whole city was conceived around the idea of fast easy and safe traffic circulation. The main highway was like an artery, the roads leading from it were like veins. They fed off on either side at intervals to a chain of residential squares, each about the size of a London square. The squares were arranged two deep each side of the central road, and the complete series was formed into a vast crescent, more than six miles from tip to tip. Across this enormous crescent Lucio Costa placed the city's noble monumental avenue like an arrow in a bow.

Not many of the squares had been completed, but the city pattern was there clearly enough. Although by now we were well within the city our jeep hurtled on as fast as ever, since the central highway had a six-lane express-way in the centre. On each side was a set of four lanes leading by flyovers to the squares and providing local inter-communication. Nevertheless our speed, though exhilarating, filled me with apprehension.

'What is the speed limit here?' I asked meekly above the roar.

My friend indicated that he had not the foggiest idea by lifting both hands from the steering-wheel and driving fifty yards with them in the air. I did not ask him any more questions. Gesticulation was best for pedestrians. But I did ask lots of drivers later on if they knew the speed limit. Not only did they not know, but they did not care either. They ought to have done, because in spite of Lucio Costa's roads the most terrible accidents occurred every day: one just on that morning of my arrival. We saw a crowd and pulled up. A lorry had been knocked backwards over one of the flyover bridges. The car which hit it was crumpled up like a soiled handkerchief. I thought I caught a glimpse of something bloody inside, but I did not look too closely. The breakfast on the plane had not been at all substantial. The lorry's front bumper had a painted motto *Driven by Manoel and guided by God*. Poor Manoel had obviously misinterpreted divine guidance that morning.

Having had our fill, like spectators of a gladiatorial combat, we got back in the jeep. *It can't happen to me* was the only possible motto, I thought, if one was going to venture on Brasilia's roads. On most days afterwards for the whole of my three months in Brasilia I saw such things. Cars which had solo damage, running into lamp-posts and denting wings, or hitting kerbs at 90 m.p.h. and overturning, were littered about Brasilia like wastepaper. But nobody paid any attention to small fry like that. The better kind of crash, involving three or four vehicles and a suitable number of deaths usually got a front-page presentation in the newspapers.

I began to make a collection of lorries' bumper mottoes. The drivers themselves thought them up and painted them on. They were more decorative, with their flowers and black Madonnas, and much more interesting than Christmas cracker mottoes. Above all they helped to give personality to the lorries—*I love only my mother* or *A woman without pride is like a flower without scent* or *Lifts on the way back only.*

When I was a little boy and went to the seaside I could never be bothered with the settling-in at strange houses and the unpacking in which the grown-ups indulged. I always wanted to get straight away down to the sand and the sea. So it was in Brasilia. As soon as I could, I was into one of the supersquares, snooping about among the blocks of flats. I thought they looked like plywood sideboards in a cheap furniture shop. To begin with they all stood on ugly legs. They were all boxy in a sideboard sort of way. Most of them had whole, huge sides without windows or balconies or outside stairs, or even washing hanging out, or any of the things which show that houses *are* houses and that there are *people* in them. In addition, all the sideboards were identical in height and similar in length and were arranged at right-angles to each other in the most unimaginative and boring way possible.

'You exaggerate,' said an English friend some time later when he came up from Rio for the day and I put my views to him. 'I agree it's monotonous. But a provincial borough surveyor at home would do worse.'

I had to agree. And from then on I began to take a more cheerful view of Brasilia's squares. After all, the sun blazed away every day, and the squares were filled with the lively, smiling, carefree, mahogany-skinned Brazilians, which was enough to transform anything. It seemed that when the squares became landscaped and the local schools and shops and churches and cinemas were built in them, the hard edges would be softened. At least the inhabitants would be able to live their daily lives more or less free of dangerous traffic. Their children could go to school without the menace of being murdered by motorists, since fast traffic was kept well away from the squares. This was also why few pedestrians were involved in the fearful motor crashes.

Although the squares were safely separated from the main traffic roads, unfortunately they did not work out as Lucio Costa, the city designer, intended. His idea was for everybody, rich and poor, to live in them. But Brazil was hardly ready for such a social change. Apartment rents were so high, in any case, that they automatically became exclusive. The poor had to make do as best they could, as I was to see. The poor existed in the full Victorian sense of the word. Yet in Brasilia there seemed to be work for most people. Luckiest in this respect were the *candangos*.

Every morning, noon and night the *candangos* made spectacular entrances on the scene. They rode about the city packed on to lorries, standing in the back, forty at a time. The *candango* was essential to Brasilia, for he was the peasant come in from the north to work in thousands on the building sites. A wide straw hat, often tied with string under his chin, was his hallmark. At night, cool breezes blew across the city out of the *cerrado* from the secret places of the plateau. Then the *candango* threw round his shoulders a blanket, like a poncho from the other side of the Andes. When he rode to and from work on the lorry the *candango* looked as though he were riding a wild horse. His straight black hair flew back in the wind, and his high-cheeked Indian face smiled with the pleasure of the wind.

Afterwards, in his wooden encampment he would eat his black beans and rice and stewed meat. Then, exhausted by a day's or a night's twelve-hour shift, he would stretch out in his wooden bunk and abandon himself to dreams. Perhaps he dreamt of girls, for there was a marked shortage of them in Brasilia. Or perhaps he dreamt of the little holding in the north-east where he was born and grew up. Almost certainly, older friends would have told him of the big cities in the south and of São Paulo's coffee plantations. The *candango* would remember the north's bad times in the dry season when not a single raindrop fell. Across the parched landscape every green thing withered. All died and were like skeletons, all except the *juazeiro*-tree. In the days before the construction of Brasilia the men had left to work on the great coffee plantations, until the rains came back and the baked earth of the north was green again.

The building of Brasilia was a lucky break for the *candango*. It provided him with work all the year round and did not take him so far away from home. The new roads to the interior and the north which led to Brasilia were opening up vast new tracts of Brazil. No longer was the *candango* so remote from the *Carioca*. Indeed, in Brasilia they met and worked side by side in rushing the new capital towards completion. With infinite patience, limitless energy, the *candango* worked also on Brasilia's landscaping. I saw many hundreds of them crawling crabwise across the vermilion soil. putting in individual grass plants by hand. This was as urgent a work as building, for the soil was migratory. In the rainy season, sudden torrents of rain swept the soil away and poured it over the roads like rivers of thick red oxide paint. But in the dry season, in the utterly rainless months, the wind turned the soil to powder, caught it and carried it along the roads as dust-devils. Swirling bits of paper and rubbish were caught in them as though rushing across the hot plains of India.

The umbrellas reminded me of India, too. Many men carried them for both rain and sun, especially the *candango*. They strode about Brasilia looking absurdly incongruous with this symbol of elegance. Although more often than not the *candango* was handsome, he was never elegant. But the black, rolled umbrella was a necessary defence against the sudden downpours. Raincoats were too hot and could not be used as sunshades after the rain. The *candango* working on building sites could always take cover from a deluge, but not those engaged on landscaping. So their umbrellas sat upright beside them, points stuck in the ground, like watchful vultures.

When Haussmann cleared Paris and drove his great avenues through the city he had to carve his way through dense and crowded quarters. Much of the old vital Paris went for ever. The Boulevard des Crimes, reproduced so excitingly in the film *Les Enfants du Paradis*, went in a cloud of dust. All its roaring life was silenced. No sacrifices were demanded for the construction of Brasilia's wide avenues. The city's great monumental axis was laid where only the sharp-bladed glass and stiff stumpy trees had been. And only a few pampas-ostriches were dispossessed and driven to hunt their snakes on the outskirts.

Mankind discovered the formula for monumentality very early in his cultural history, and no other method has ever been invented. All monumental avenues and squares, from the sphinxes to St. Mark's Square, Venice, from the Champs-Elysées to Brasilia, are all essentially composed in the same way. Their secret lies not solely in great size but in the use of a significant form. This form has to be quite unassociated with the trammels of ordinary, everyday life. The monumental form has to be outside life. And it is nearly always larger than life. There is nothing suburban about the Doge's Palace, and nothing domestic about the Arc de Triomphe. Nor is there anything bourgeois or provincial about Brasilia's monumental avenue.

No committee ever produced a work of art. No panel of experts ever produced a work to astound by its beauty. Such things have always been the work of the individual genius. The committee of distinguished architects which met at New York to design the United Nations buildings produced nothing. They disagreed violently until Niemeyer produced his sketch idea to which they all assented. And the influence of genius is why Brasilia takes its place along with others of the world's beautiful cities, in spite of its drawbacks. Brazil was fortunate in possessing its own genius, just at the highest point of his ability, just at the moment when the decision to build Brasilia was taken. It would have been built anyway, whether a genius was to hand or not. In fact, Brazil had been *talking* about moving the capital to the interior since 1789, when it was suggested by the Minas Conspiracy, an early group who sought independence from Portugal. While he was British Ambassador in Lisbon, William Pitt gave his views in 1809 on the subject, and thought the move should be made; 1808 in London saw the publication of *Correio Brasiliense*, a Brazilian newspaper, and this also urged the move. But only after 1955, when Kubitschek's government took office, was the immense scheme finally launched. And the genius was ready.

This was Oscar Niemeyer.

Lucio Costa's general conception of the city was already established when Niemeyer began work on Brasilia. But the creative act had still to be done. The clay body was there, as it were, but the breath of life had yet to be breathed into its nostrils. And this was what Niemeyer did by his architecture. He had to invent the significant form which would turn Brasilia into a capital with a worthy monumentality. He shunned, however, any suggestion of imitation. What he produced was unique and a work of art. It astonished me every time I looked at it, or passed it, while I lived in the city.

Lucio Costa laid out his monumental avenue at right-angles to the six-mile residential crescent. This ensured that the parliament buildings which terminated it, as the Arc de Triomphe terminates the Champs-Elysées, could be seen from everywhere in the city. To dominate this composition he indicated a tower and a great square. And this was Niemeyer's starting-point. With Niemeyer rested the responsibility of making Costa's great conception as noble as the city deserved.

As its terminal point, the main monumental avenue had the Congress building. Slender twin skyscrapers reared against Brasilia's spectacular cloudscapes. And below, catching and reflecting the light with the subtlety of a Greek temple, were the two gleaming white domes, reposing gracefully on the ground. Inside the domes were the two chambers of the Brazilian parliament. The dome of the lower chamber was inverted to form a bowl. Framing all this in a classical perspective of recession were the ministries on either side of the avenue. Farther away from the Congress and terminal point stood the theatre on one side and the cathedral on the other. Both were unfinished when I was there, though for different reasons.

The theatre came rather late in the building programme and was taken only as far as the huge shell of the building. The end of the Kubitschek presidency did not see the theatre's completion. Not unreasonably, people were asking what would be played in the theatre's two auditoria. It would probably be many years before Brasilia had its own opera and drama company, and the city was too remote to bring companies frequently from Rio or abroad. But in nothing was Brasilia timid, and it had its gigantic theatre, with stages and seating far below ground. Only the stage towers were above ground, and Oscar Niemeyer put these under a gigantic concrete tent, as impressive as an Aztec pyramid.

The cathedral was left in a similar condition also—raw concrete, and an indefinite future. It, too, was designed to be partly sunken. Nothing but its high, beautiful lantern was visible from the avenue. The decision to finish it rested with the Roman Catholic authorities. There were rumours that the Archbishop of Brasilia preferred to found a seminary. But with an unfinished cathedral the city's monumental avenue could never reach perfection. There were those in the city who remembered the fate that befell another of Niemeyer's churches. That was the chapel of Pampulha, near Belo Horizonte. For fifteen years after completion it awaited dedication. Its forms were considered unusual at that time and so were deemed unliturgical by the hierarchy. When I met Niemeyer I talked to him about Brasilia's cathedral. In spite of being a Communist, he was sorry that his kinsman, the Archbishop, was postponing the completion. I thought of the gimcrack horror which was soon to be erected in Liverpool and wished that the hierarchy *there* would halt proceedings indefinitely. After all, Liverpool already has one beautiful cathedral, while poor Brasilia has none—not even a major church of any kind.

Perhaps one of the hardest things to grasp about architecture, and consequently about cities, is that empty space is about the most important thing of all. Once understood this is the most rewarding. Brasilia's monumental avenue ends in empty space—though, of course, the way this is imprisoned is the secret of its magic. There is no other great public square in the world like the Praça dos Tres Poderes—Three Powers Square. Venice's St. Mark's Square, Italy's example of the art of the empty, is similar. It ends abruptly in water. Brasilia's Praça ends equally abruptly, but in landscape. Perhaps not since the Greeks built their marvels on rocks, such as the Athenian Acropolis, or Louis XIV put up Versailles in the middle of nowhere, has architecture and nature been seen in such abrupt proximity. But even then nature at Versailles was very much trimmed to shape by Le Nôtre. At Athens or Sunium and at Brasilia, nothing was trimmed, neither architecture nor nature. Niemeyer is an artist of drama in space. There can be few nobler sights in the world than the Three Powers Square when it is crammed with people, brave with flags, blazoned with military colour. The dove-white marbles of Niemeyer's forms are as clear and subtle as a Doric colonnade. They are no less monumental. The perfection of swanlike shapes is enhanced by the rolling hills against which they curve from ground to sky.

The term 'rolling hills' sounds perhaps like a stage contrivance which rolls hills into position for the next scene. And Brasilia certainly was not without its theatrical element. Yet the country which surrounded the city and touched it so closely at the Three Powers Square was typical of the whole Central Plateau. It was like an overgrown orchard in a forgotten garden. The grass and undergrowth ran wild among twisted, stunted trees whose leaves were thick but concealed no fruit. For the first months after I arrived in Brasilia I walked every day through this country to go into the city from my lodgings to eat and post letters. I got to know it well and to recognize which paths might be dangerous because of poisonous snakes.

Although I had been assured that the greater numer of ophidians were non-poisonous, it always seemed to be the dangerous ones I met. They were recognized by their thick, short tails and vertical pupils—not that I stopped until I saw the whites of them. My first acquaintance was with a coral snake, with tiny eyes and a skin of the most handsome colours. He was killed a few yards from my bedroom. The biggest snake I ever saw, however, was very much alive, a black, oily thing coiled round a young blood's wrist. He often drove through the town with his grotesque, terrifying pet draped round the left arm while he drove his sports car with the right.

Most of the trees wore a dried red mud bustle built by termites, though these bulges were not so large as the enormous red anthills which the ants seemed to abandon as soon as they were completed. Huge prettily coloured butterflies drifted inconsequentially about, and from the blue clouds of wild lupins monstrous, droning bees appeared, black and weighted with pollen. Grasshoppers and cicadas sang with their unmusical noise of high-powered drills. Then, as though a factory hooter sounded, they all would stop together suddenly. A flock of green parakeets might take advantage of the silence then to swoop screeching under the twisted branches.

On the hottest days and the wettest days I hitch-hiked into the town from my lodgings by the lake. The road was circuitous but had the advantage of passing the Alvorada palace—Brasilia's most beautiful building—and the most beautiful in modern Brazil. It ought not to be, for it breaks all the cherished rules of both academic and twentieth-century architecture. But it is not less wonderful than Gabriel's Petit Trianon at Versailles, which for me is one of Europe's most beautiful buildings. In a way that horrifies the modernist, Niemeyer spurns functionalism, but equally shocks the Academician by refusing to make bogus duplication of the Classical —though nothing could be more classical than the Dawn Palace. Its forms are quite new, yet they have captured popular imagination—which architecture always used to do until the Academies made it a cult for the few instead of an art for the many. The graceful curves of the Alvorada's marble façade have become Brasilia's theme. People should not be blamed for using their curved diamond-shape in the same way as the Eiffel Tower is used, on girls' headscarves, on supermarket paper bags, on ash-trays and key-rings and postage stamps, in fact on anything where a device could be printed.

By good judgement, NOVACAP had forbidden the shape to be used in actual building anywhere in the city, so preserving the purity of the original. The name NOVACAP sounds rather like a firm making funny paper hats for Rio's carnival. In fact, it was the public company formed to produce and run the new capital. I lived at a NOVACAP hostel, an affair of fifteen single-storey wooden blocks by Brasilia's lake. The place was called Do Re Mi, reputedly because there used to be radio music all day and all night there. While I lived there, the hostel was filled with the humbler contributers to the new city. Do Re Mi catered for carpenters, foreign architectural students, bus drivers and mechanics and any passing waifs and strays who fell on governmental mercy. Nobody so high in NOVACAP's hierarchy as Dr. Israel Pinheiro would stay there. He was the company's president during the first years of Brasilia's life. Then he became the first mayor. NOVACAP's new president was a man called the Holy Ghost, and the mayor who succeeded Pinheiro later was called Paul of Tarsus! We were all in a flutter when the newspapers announced that Paul of Tarsus was coming to look into the 'Irregularities' of Do Re Mi.

Saul, Saul, why persecutest thou me? might well have been asked of the mayor if he had been in office when the Vila Amauri was removed. This was the lakeside shanty town removed because of the rising waters. The people simply took their few sticks and moved a mile or so away. Most of the remains and wooden ruins were submerged under the rising lake when I was there. Stumps and posts stuck out of the water. At its edge, wooden flotsam and jetsam floated, as though the innocent lake was full of drowned ships. The shore ought to have been beautiful. On days of brilliant sun, the water had a surface of lapis lazuli. Yet the Vila Amauri people had left behind so much of their squalor that it littered long stretches of the shores. In vain did the tomato and marrow plants of the slum gardens run wild in an attempt to cover the filth and rubbish. And like ghosts come to haunt the former shanties, boys stood motionless in the lake, fishing. With luck they could get up to a hundred perchlike fish in a morning.

Do Re Mi was intended only as a dormitory. Perhaps that was why its windows were too high to see the lovely view of the lake, and why such elaborate precautions were taken by the watchmen, who wandered about during darkness, blowing whistles. I was always out and about in the city, looking at new buildings or drinking sweet black coffee in a low wooden hut near the Congress towers. Brasilia was created in that hut and Oscar Niemeyer worked there. He often sat on the bench outside chatting with the office boys, the porter or the drivers. The ambassadors or film stars or the millionaires who came to do him homage bored or embarrassed him or both. He hated being made a centre of attention. Cameras and tape-recorders terrified him. He hid for several days from some Americans who wanted to add his recorded voice to that of Le Corbusier and Mies van der Rohe. Niemeyer was much too preoccupied with his art and with improving the lot of the poor in Brazil to bother with flattery.

In Rio, Niemeyer had told me he would see me in Brasilia on 'the five of January'. He was truly Brazilian and truly artistic by not appearing until a week later. But we quickly found common ground and he simply became my friend Oscar. I stole his time on many successive days. Two or three hours would slip by while the coffee-cups were replaced and the pile of sketches grew. Oscar talked with his pencil and sketch-pad—one afternoon I counted nearly forty drawings made to illustrate his points.

We would perhaps only break off when a city guide brought distinguished visitors to meet Oscar. One afternoon a small, pale American came in who, within five minutes, had told us of his forty-five-roomed Manhattan mansion (dining-room and seven other rooms transported floorboard by floorboard from an English castle) and his vast collection of Picassos, Arps, Henry Moores, and Brancusis, his plans to establish a nine-acre garden of sculpture, laid out by the Japanese Isamu Noguchi, in Jerusalem for Israel's National Museum, and his intention to attend the Eichmann trial which was then current news. He was now in Brasilia to meet 'the great Oscar', whose work he knew from New York. I had never met anybody before who just picked up stuff as he went along—Rodins, Bourselles, Maillols, Daumiers. Not only did he possess all these, but also the original of Epstein's *Visitation*, of which, he maintained, the Tate Gallery had a mere copy.

He paused and, being in ignorance, I inquired what his name might be. 'You'll remember it,' he said. 'Billy Rose.' I would certainly never forget it. His visit was rather like a Press interview, and indeed a few days later Brazil's newspapers did bear reports of his visit to the city and of his nineteen Henry Moores, the Grinling Gibbons fireplace and the forty-five rooms. The papers also added that Mr. 'Showman' Rose had been two days in the company of Oscar Niemeyer. It was a quick two days, even for show business.

Such were the visitations which often descended on the wooden shed. They left Niemeyer unmoved. Knowing the tremendous poverty behind the developed coastal strip and the ignorance in which almost all the Brazilian population lived, Niemeyer was a Communist. He was not to be distracted from his country's problems by rich and famous visitors. Nevertheless he held a few in great esteem. Jean Paul Sartre's and Simone de Beauvoir's visit left a deep impression on him. So did that of André Malraux. When people left we would return to the wooden bench outside the office to sit with Silvio, the coloured office porter, who was a wise, clever clown.

Oscar's head was always in the clouds. But perhaps it was this high vantage-point which gave him such a clear grasp of real life. This superb creator of illusions in space had no illusions whatsoever about life around him. He lived in one of the three-bedroomed houses of the W.3 district, built by the Low Cost Housing Foundation, destined originally for working people. Brazil being Brazil, however, the working people did not get into the houses, just as rich and poor did not live as neighbours in the supersquares. The houses were occupied by people whose work was not manual. Niemeyer's assistants lived in them, for example, as Niemeyer's own neighbours, and nearby his cousin the archbishop. The houses could sometimes be rented furnished at fifty thousand cruzeiros a month from people who were buying them on the instalment plan. The workmen for whom the houses were designed did not earn ten thousand in all per month (610 to the pound at the time of writing) and consequently had to go elsewhere.

But in no way was this a street of snobbery and certainly not one with a colour bar. I often ate with Gladson da Rocha, one of Nie-meyer's architects. From their windows which slid open to the garden I could see the whole street. Here all the children ran bare-foot, chased dogs, quarrelled or rode each other's tricycles. When heavy tropical rain fell one day, all the children trooped through the archbishop's sliding windows to shelter in his study. Whether the four and five-year-olds with their muddy feet and grubby hands fascinated the archbishop, or whether he held them spellbound, nobody knew. Perhaps the attraction was mutual. At any rate, when lunch-time came he simply asked them to stay and join him. Every time I went to Gladson's I saw the archbishop in his tiny garden plot talking to the children.

Thinking that Gladson's name was curious, I asked him if it was Brazilian. He was born on a farm and a letter was written to aunts who, by virtue of living in a town, were thought to be authorities on children's names. When the letter arrived from the country asking for suggestions, one aunt was reading a romantic novel whose hero was called Gladson. But then, his brothers had unusual first names also—Rubens and Murillo, and they all had an Uncle Beethoven. Many English surnames being used as first names in Brazil probably came from similar sources.

Gladson was fortunate to have a house for his beautiful Mexican wife and four children. In Brasilia's early days, and still while I was there, the housing shortage was acute. People flooded to the city faster than it could be built. From sharing one room with another family (plus their maid) Gladson solved a desperate situation by taking illegal possession of an empty house nearby, belonging to, but not used by, one of the armed forces. It was a demonstration which quickly got him the house I knew in the W.3 district.

Not all were so lucky. The thousands of poor with their bundles who streamed into Brasilia from all over the country had to make huts in which to live. At one time Brasilia was said to have had thousands of homeless, familyless boys roaming its streets. At night the police rounded them up, for there was nowhere for them to go. I knew one of them, a shoeshine boy, bright, cheeky, intelligent, and ten years old. He simply left home for the promised land of Brasilia.

His poverty-stricken family had more urgent things to concern them than worry about him. After all, he was ten. An acquaintance, Countess Helena Tarnowska, one of Brasilia's most intriguing pioneers, was hoping to establish a home for these boys to sleep in at night, so that they should not mix with criminals at the police station. But in many cases the boys were just as likely to corrupt the criminals as be themselves corrupted. Some of the mudlarks stole enough material to build themselves a house. Being worldly wise, they invited the chairman of the juvenile court as their first guest. Unfortunately, the boys soon discovered that besides food stolen to feed themselves, other appropriated articles could be hidden in the house. It was possible, at one time, to go there and buy almost anything. But their antics were soon discovered and the place disbanded.

Around the brand-new city was another and sorry aspect of the truth. Discreetly separated by a compulsorily maintained green belt were Brasilia's slums, the same huts, open sewers, lack of water, the same disease-prone, insanitary slums which overshadowed the beauty of Rio de Janeiro's showplaces. And at this point, when I talked with friends, a discussion always began as to whether Brasilia should have been built at all. It seemed that in part, all it had done was not to solve existing social problems but to create new ones. Euphemistically referred to as satellite towns, Brasilia's outlying shanty settlements were integrally involved in the city's life. To ignore or forget these slums, to excuse or laugh at them, did not alter the fact that Brasilia consisted of those places no less than its shining white palaces.

Brazilia's pioneers, of course, had to camp somewhere, and this was in the Free City, the Cidade Livre, a timber town six miles beyond the city proper. But from housing the pioneers and providing them with amenities it grew until I saw it as a highly developed wild west town, straight from a Hollywood film. Amongst the wooden shacks and oil-can shanties, doctors and dentists, airlines and lawyers had set up their notice-boards. The large all-male population of the construction camps queued at week-ends outside the cheaper brothels. With the Congress's elegant towers shining in the distance, women of the Free City picked their way through filthy tracks and open sewers to wash and do laundry in a drain.

Not all the slums were kept at this respectable distance from the city, however, and some even flourished within ten minutes' walk of the Three Powers Square. It was always a pious, theoretical hope that the Government would somehow do something. But while I was there, this never got farther than enforced removal of some shacks, like the Vila Amauri, to the back of beyond. Poor people who came with high hope to the dream city had their wooden huts pulled down, piled on to lorries and taken out to such settlements as Gama, Taguatinga, or Sobradinho. There, if lucky, they might get a new chicken-house (six feet by eight) in which to live temporarily while they built yet another shack. But alas, one family I saw at Gama, and this was typical, had been there three months and had no plans for leaving their windowless box. I shall never forget Gama, but for another reason.

It was a Saturday afternoon. A little before I arrived a young man had ridden into Gama on his horse to buy milk and bread and eggs for his wife and eight children. Having made his purchases from the shack shop, he stowed the food in his canvas saddle-bags and mounted his horse. Then he fell from the saddle and was dead. When I saw him he was prone on the ground. A wooden box with lighted candles fluttering gently had been set at his head, and round him stood a silent crowd, just looking. Nearby, his horse unconcernedly cropped grass. A loaf of bread was sticking out of the saddle-bag. It had been a hot afternoon and the sun was now penetrating, showing up the stiff concavities of his face. He might have been sleeping, except that the flies were walking, bold and undisturbed, in and out of his mouth. An hour later he was still there. More children had been brought to see the Saturday-afternoon wonder. Mothers suckled their babies as they looked on. In the background Gama's life went on as usual. Some men carried planks for a new shack. Others fiddled in a car's bonnet. The dead man would have to wait until his young wife arrived.

Gladson da Rocha took me to Sobradinho, where his design for the Church of the Nazarene was under construction. Like many other

Nonconformist churches and missions in Brazil, this was led by a pastor from the U.S.A. At Sobradinho there were already Presbyterians, Baptists, Assemblies of God, Church of God, Christian Church, Adventists, as well as the Nazarenes. The Roman Catholics had only one small church. But its priests were not unaware of the rivals which challenged them in every new town throughout the country. The Roman Church could see the Gospel caravans parked along W.3 in Brasilia, selling gaudy booklets and sickly records to entice the country folk into the evangelical net. On my first morning at Do Re Mi hostel I had been awakened by *Onward, Christian Soldiers,* on somebody's radio. But there was a counter-reformation, for the same night, while I was with Gladson's family, a procession of young girls moved along the darkened street carrying a statue of Our Lady of Fatima and lighted candles. They called at every house and asked for the Madonna to be set up and the family to join in a quick decade of the rosary—which was led by a young clerk from the British bank. One could sympathize with the archbishop's wish to train priests before finishing the cathedral.

Brasilia had a night life of sorts, but without appeal for me. I preferred to wander along the lonely roads and perhaps stop at a *candangos'* camp. By the lake and near Do Re Mi there were a number of them, but they might have been concentration camps. All were alike, with severe rows of cheerless wooden huts, some allowing no more than ten square feet per man, barbed wire fences, and guards at the gates, and lights blaring down. Yet the *candangos,* I knew, were happy enough. They tried to make the barracks more homely. Caged singing-birds hung outside many huts, and the men would take them for walks like dogs. The birds' music sounded a long way. The most carrying voice was the big white, blue-cheeked anvil-bird's. His call was metallic and without invention—unlike the red cardinals' more graceful melody—or the *candangos'* own music.

The men often invited me to sit outside on a wooden seat or inside on a bunk while they played haunting music on pipe, guitar and tambourine. Though in the same room, the music seemed to come from far away, in the *candango* country to the north, blown

111

by some wind across the plateau and the lake and the distant, sparkling lights of Brasilia itself. But even during my own months in
Brasilia, many of those clever native musicians forsook their instruments for pocket radios. The flutes would never sound again. And
at Gama and Sobradinho, too, civilization would march. There would
be television sets and washing machines—even if the women had to
walk a mile for water.

When the moon was up, or on clear, starry nights, I walked home
to Do Re Mi along the lake. In such half-obscurity it was transformed. The moon rose from behind the hills across the lake. At
first it was a waxen moon, round and red as a Dutch cheese. But
climbing higher, it scattered silver on the lake. By day, if one thought
of poetry at all by the lake it was probably about hollow men and
waste lands. The decamped squatters were still too much in evidence. But by night a more ancient poetry floated on the air, perhaps the Chinese mysteries of Li Po. Brasilia's night-lake, indeed,
conjured dreams about boats of sandalwood and oars of magnolia,
flutes of jade and pipes of gold. The moon really did seem to burn
the blue water—even if the peach blossom was no more than the
potato flowers forsaken in the backyards of the Vila Amauri.

6

The Hunting Caraja

I did not expect to find worse floods in Brazil than I left behind in a wintry England. But most of Bananal was inundated. After the exceptionally heavy downpours of an unusually rainy rainy-season, almost the whole island lay under sheets of water which looked like glass from the air. Because my visit was privately arranged, I was able to stand in the pilot's cockpit as we flew out from Brasilia for the journey of three hundred miles to the north. Bananal was claimed in Brazil as the world's largest (there they go again!) fluvial island, formed by a 250-mile stretch of the Araguaia river on one side and a tributary on the other. This departed from the main river, leaving a sixty-mile-wide strip of land in the middle, and then joined the main river again.

The pilot took the plane down low when we reached the island, and we flew at about thirty feet over the tree-tops. There was no danger of colliding with towers or pylons or cables, because Bananal did not have such things, but only animals and Indians and a few people from the Fundação Central do Brasil—the Government department responsible for opening up Brazil's interior. The island was itself dotted with islands. These were made by areas of higher ground that had escaped the floods which spead over all the land from the Araguaia river. The wild animals crowded on to these dry areas. From the plane I could see herds of wild horses, deer, and stranded cattle. White herons, gloriously independent, sailed low over the flood-waters and perched superciliously on trees.

But even from my moving eyrie I could see that somehow I was touching for the first time the real heart of Brazil. I knew I would find here the loneliness, the emptiness, the vastness, the richness of wild life which was legendary about Brazil, but whose existence I had begun to doubt in the sophistication of the cities. It had been almost in desperation that I accepted the invitation to go in a Fundação plane which carried daily freight to Bananal. In his great programme of opening Brazil's interior Kubitschek planned for the Fundação to expand the work it began years previously. The practical exemplar was to be the tractor and modern methods of land development and of fishing. One such station was established on Bananal at the little settlement of Santa Izabel, right on the banks of the Rio Araguaia.

Here also Kubitschek built himself a country house—called the Little Alvorada. A tourist hotel was also being built, because the island was immensely rich for hunters. But more than these Bananal was famous for its Indian tribe living at Santa Izabel more or less in their ancient way. I was in no way trying to play the amateur Colonel Fawcett, or to give myself airs as an explorer. But I was genuinely trying to find at least a trace of the Brazil which everybody thinks of as Brazil, even though for most Brazilians it was untypical. Farther up the Araguaia, I was told, there were really primitive Indians, tribes which had only just seen the light of civilization. Some of them came to Santa Izabel during my own visit, in their long boats cut out of solid tree-trunks. One had the biggest smile I saw in the whole of Brazil, which looked particularly effective under an ex-Brazilian army tin hat.

Bananal enjoyed the dubious advantage of being entirely an affair of the elements, at least of air and water. No roads ran to it and so the island could only be approached by plane or boat. This put Bananal in the peculiarly Brazilian situation of belonging simultaneously to the remote past and the hopeful future, but not exactly to the present. I certainly thought the island divorced from the present at the unearthly hour when I had to present myself at the airport. I hate early mornings. Gone are the days when I could get up to watch the dawn flood the summer landscape, gilding the already golden cornfields. I prefer to take my dawns comfortably. But travellers pay for the privilege of travelling by being required from time to time to make movements at impossible hours of day and night. So, well before five in the morning, I was creeping stealthily about my room at Do Re Mi trying to make sense out of my clothes and trying to be cheerful with the Air Force Officers who called for me in their jeep. As they took a plane to Bananal and back on most days of the week, early mornings were no strain for them—at any rate, not apparently.

We drove along Brasilia's lakeside, passing the long row of sites labelled with the names of almost every country in the world, which one day will have fully-fledged embassies. During my own months in Brasilia the great stretch of land had only the temporary embassies of America and France and the British. The latter was a monstrous building like a Nonconformist chapel. Rather tactlessly, the site noticeboard announced '*Inglaterra*', which could not have pleased Scots visitors.

At the military part of the airport used by the Fundação we had to wait an hour for mist to clear. The day's cargo was plaster—presumably to help with finishing the tourist hotel which had already been inaugurated. I wondered what the Indians had made of progress and civilized living. Nothing, probably. After all, the older generation in Britain remembers its childhood, going to bed by oil-lamps or candlelight, the first motor-cars and aeroplanes. Indeed, I once had a farm at Sheldon in the Blackdown hills of Devon. And this hamlet, even in 1956, had no electricity nor did any bus or public transport pass near it. I thought myself fortunate in having a pump in the house for water.

Civilization's encroachment on Indian territory was not novel to the Carajas, the tribe living at Santa Izabel, for they had been contacted some fifteen years earlier. Quite a number came to the air-strip to see our plane land. And as soon as I saw their faces I knew I was going to lose my heart to Bananal. There was gracefulness in those tanned, oval faces. In the black, slightly almond-shaped eyes there flashed a naive, lovely liveliness. The first smile I got on the tarmac landing-strip itself more than repaid my reluctant early rise. Quite satisfied, I could have got straight back into the plane and flown back to Brasilia with the others.

This, however, would have been to miss a hundred other smiles,

115

joyous and mysterious. As soon as we had taxied to a standstill at the runway's end and the propellers stopped and the crew and I climbed to the ground, a naked boy ran from the group of Indians. He crouched on his heels in the shadow under the tailplane, his big eyes missing nothing. Black hair fell to his bare brown shoulders and his body was painted with red and black stripes. Just below the calf of each leg was wound a tight wide band of red thread, ending at the front in a tassel which hung to his feet. Neither he nor anybody else seemed to find his tribal paint and patterns at all incongruous with the plane.

Arriving in the middle of nowhere, as it were, by plane, was like a fairy-story come true—something to do with magic carpets, seven-league boots or flying trunks. At Santa Izabel's air-strip all the usual airport paraphernalia was missing. The radio station was some distance away and there were no buildings at all. That was why the welcoming Indians were themselves so welcome. It would have been most disconcerting to have got out of the plane and found nobody there. The boy who squatted under the tail looked as if he always did that. His older brothers of the tribe helped to unload the plaster, though most of the work was done by Fundação labourers from the cities. A few of the Indian men had been modernized by short haircuts, T-shirts, swimming shorts and an absence of painted decoration. The rest were a compromise between the ancient and modern. Their hair fell like the boy's to shoulder length, they had some paint, and wore a motley of second-hand clothes. Some had discarded Air Force jackets or old, ill-fitting shorts, and these oddments produced a marked effect of poverty and squalor which belied the vigour of their bodies.

The Indian women who came, maintained a respectful distance from their men, and perched on some empty oil-drums to watch the proceedings. I did not see them closely until later, but could just make out similarly handsome faces and shoulder-length hair. They, too, wore odd clothes, including dresses and shawls that looked as though they had come from a jumble sale. One consolation was that the oil-drums had not been made into shanties. I had hopes of finding at Santa Izabel something less degrading than the new capital's shanty towns. But whatever influence Western ways had made so far on the Carajas they had kept their tribal characteristics intact. Their physical beauty was unimpaired. They all had the deeply tattooed circles under the eyes, circles as big as halfpennies which distinguish this particular tribe from others in the region—a region which was bordering, if not actually in, genuine Fawcett country. Though most becoming, the tattoos were made cruelly in early childhood by burning each cheek with the heated end of a pipe, the colour being rubbed in afterwards.

Hours seemed to have passed since my bleary-eyed arrival at Brasilia's airport, but in Bananal it was still only late breakfast-time. Leaving the plane to be unloaded, the pilot took me in yet another jeep for coffee and rolls in the village itself. And here was something else to steal a part of me for ever. From the moment I saw Santa Izabel loosely strung among big mango trees along the river, I knew I loved it, for here was the Brazil I sought.

I am never sure whether to like or to loathe William Morris for his inability to come to terms with the machine. Was it he who began the preservation-at-all-costs craze which has been a British obsession ever since? Or was he himself only caught up in a general panic to keep the beautiful things which the nineteenth-century machine was destroying? Whether he was to blame or not, preservation is certainly a British obsession, but there are so few people who can do it properly. John Betjeman can make people feel guilty if they hate Victorian architecture. Benjamin Britten successfully convinces the musical that there never *were* such melodies as English folk-songs. Old motor-cars have more spent on them in one year than children in orphanages. Women feel positive paupers unless their jewel boxes contain something which grandmama wore. The spirit of preservation was probably what a Brazilian friend noticed about London. Making it his last stop in a literally flying tour of Europe, he said: 'I liked London because it was the only capital where I felt it wasn't the 1960s.' The spirit of preservation, however, is prone to the phoney, and it was with trepidation that I heard about Brazil's Service for Protection of Indians. But protection for the Indians against what and whom? And was an air-strip in their village the best way to do this? Could there be something folk-arty, hand-crafty, back-to-Mother-Naturish about the Service?

But I need not have worried. If anything, the Indians were influ-encing the people who were there to protect them. But there was nothing inevitable or automatic about this confluence of Indian and civilized ways of life. The entire achievement was that of three dynamic Brazilian brothers, Orlando, Leonardo, and Claudio Villas Boas. They were implicitly trusted by the various Indian tribes. They also enjoyed a legendary fame throughout the rest of Brazil, equal to that of Colonel Fawcett in England. For many years the Villas Boas brothers had devoted their lives entirely to the Indians, living amongst them in the wildest and remotest country, quite close to where Fawcett disappeared. It was these brothers who found the body which Fawcett's son denied was his father's. But most people I met in Brazil, including the three amazing brothers, who have seriously concerned themselves with the prob-lem, believe the remains to be undoubtedly Fawcett's.

The house where we went for breakfast was the village head-quarters of the Fundação. It was at once town hall, police station and social club to everybody. In spite of the Indians' totally different way of life the house was theirs if they cared to use it. There was nothing of that unbearable oppressive atmosphere of colonial life with its sharp, unnatural division of those 'native' and those not. The place swarmed with children. Its long porch which shaded three sides of the house was a playground for young Indians, painted like the boy under the plane and for the children of the Fundação employees. The children loved the house and played there with their toys or climbed into the hammocks slung between the porch posts. The Indian children had made their own toys—a stick with the top of a tin nailed at the bottom to make a wheel. No doubt they were Bananal's future tractor and outboard motor mechanics.

Fortunately for me the tourist hotel was not ready for guests otherwise I might have had to stay there, away from the village. But I was invited to stay at the house by Enso Pisano, the island's head of Fundação. Everybody called him Paulista, since he came from São Paulo. With the children's laughter sounding through the open doors and windows Paulista talked about his work at Bananal. But I was more absorbed by the complete happiness of the children. Even some of the non-Indian children had their bodies painted exactly like their Indian friends. The fruit juice used for the skin painting only lasted a fortnight, but I knew they would replace it by other jazzy decorations. President Getulio Vargas, who founded the Protection Service, would probably have been pleased with these results of his journeys up to Bananal. He had become interested in safeguarding the Indian tribes long before Brasilia became a practical matter. But because of the new city, Bananal was now less remote from civilization.

My room in the house faced the river and was a kind of dormitory. The windows had no glass but only blue shutters which were left open during the day. The Indian children with the tattooed circles under their eyes stood solemnly watching any move of the stranger. But I did not stay long in the house. I felt as though the whole Rio Araguaia and its banks were waiting. Unfortunately a lot of things I might have seen were disturbed by the floods. The crocodiles, I was assured, had taken advantage of the unusual flooding and had gone from their usual haunts, farther afield. Nobody knew exactly where to look for them, except in one or two distant lakes which had not yet overflowed.

But there was enough in Santa Izabel to interest me. So far as domestic matters were concerned the Indians kept to themselves, and lived much as they had always done in the palm-leaf-thatched huts, immensely practical for that climate. In telling myself how fresh and cool it was at Bananal on getting out of the plane, I had forgotten that it was still early morning. After breakfast at the house, when I walked across to the Carajas' houses, the sun already felt like a weight. People had warned me that Bananal was hot.

The Indians coped with this climate problem by not making any pretence about work, though they were far from idle. Labourers had to be flown in from Brasilia and São Paulo to work on the tourist hotel a mile or so up river. The Indians occupied themselves in and about their own houses. Most of their time passed in an aristocratic indifference to money or trade. I was told that their own language contained no numbers. Lucky children with no multiplication tables to learn! The grown-ups spent themselves as they saw fit. The men went hunting (Bananal's *raison d'être*) for wild animals or caught fish in the river by bow and arrow. Or they hunted Bananal's beautiful birds to get the brilliant feathers for fantastic headdresses which would be worn at the next tribal feast. I saw one young man taking his pet eagle for a walk on a piece of string. There was nobility about the young Caraja and his eagle, like a Renaissance portrait of a lord with a falcon at his wrist.

Bananal was full of animals. I may not have seen full-sized crocodiles, but I did see a baby one kept in a tank at the radio station. Because it nearly took my finger off with its nasty teeth, when I scratched its back, my interest in crocodiles dropped abruptly. The radio station was quite a zoo, for the operator and his wife could not resist any creature they found. I spent many odd hours there. Always first to greet me was the ant-eater, a friendly soul with a stiff coat, who shared his bed with two dogs. To be lovingly embraced by an ant-eater was an extraordinary experience. He took a particular fancy to my shoe-laces and was generally otherwise inquisitive with his long snout and spaghetti-like tongue. Their young seagulls were jealous over the ant-eater. They could not bear him to take any attention and screamed and flapped their wings and pretended to attack my legs with their extraordinary bills. At first I thought they were a pair of baby toucans, for they seemed to be weighed down by beak. Their black stiletto bills had brilliant orange bases, but both mandibles were solid, except for a tiny part forming the mouth. The gulls were entirely free to fly off and join their friends by the river, but they preferred to stay at home with the hens and the ant-eater— as long as he behaved himself.

The Indian houses had pets, too, though there the variety was even more astonishing. Having seen Brasilia's slums, Bananal's Indian houses seemed to be comparatively clean, as was the whole of Santa Izabel. Even the animals in the palm-leaf huts looked clean, except perhaps for the dogs. This cleanliness was all the more surprising because all the members of each Caraja family lived together in the one room of the house. Both sexes of all ages ate and slept in the smoky atmosphere. All their belongings were kept in the room also in higgledy-piggledy order. Between the Indian and the elements there were only the thin inflammable walls of palm-leaf, yet in most houses a fire burnt on an open hearth. The smoke escaped as best it could through the thatch or through an eighteen-inch gap under the eaves. Some huts were rather grand, with an extension at the back used as a kitchen. No less than the buildings themselves, the welcome I had in each of the thirty-odd houses reminded me of Irish cottages.

All the Indian houses faced the river, a fast-flowing expanse of water a mile and a half wide. The land was so flat and the sky so immense that Santa Izabel made a perfect setting for the titanic electric clouds of heavy yellows and dense greys which mounted the air. It was still the middle of the rainy season, with ceaseless lightning at night, with thunder, and always with anvil-headed cumulus piling up like God the Father in baroque murals. Under these great thunderclouds the water reflected their colour, but added even richer hues. Currents caused the river to swirl and made the surface like old canvases with varnished oil paint put on centuries before.

Kingfishers darted everywhere along the river. They sped under overhanging undergrowth or plunged into the water for fish. Myriads of huge dragonflies hovered uncertainly, like toy helicopters, their iridescent wings catching the sun, their brilliant red bodies like red-lacquered Chinese cabinets. They skittered about like jewels on wings, some orange or yellow, or green as emeralds, although the praying-mantis was the greenest of all, like a fresh lettuce, though it, too, had bejewelled, embroidered wings.

At the village itself the banks were alive with young Carajas diving and swimming or standing poised, slender and naked, to catch fish with their bows and arrows. The boys were as sharp-eyed and as quick and much more ambitious than the pygmy cormorants in their pursuit of the great fish which abounded in the Rio Araguaia. They belonged perfectly to the river and were quite unafraid of the dangerous flood-waters that were sweeping forest debris along. But it was a Caraja belief that they came, like Russalka, from water.

But that year the floods had been so vast and had damaged so much that the tribal chiefs had forbidden many of the usual tribal celebrations. Their long wooden boats were the only means of commuting between tribes and the chiefs thought such travel too dangerous.

Nevertheless certain occasions were so important that even floods could not prevent them. Every palm house that I went into was busy with preparations for one such big party farther up the river. None of the houses pretended to any furniture. There were hammocks and the floor. Both could be used for sitting or sleeping. The floors were partially covered by hand-woven mats. I think it was the mats which gave off the odour peculiar to the Indians' houses. The mats were steeped in oil from human bodies as well as the none-too-savoury remains of food left lying about for the animals. In the first house I visited three vivid macaws clawed their way down the walls and began squabbling over rice left in a pot. They looked revoltingly mangy in parts. But I suspected that this was not disease or moulting, but robbery of their feathers for use in the new headdresses under construction. An agouti and an armadillo likewise foraged amongst a pile of corn-cobs and sweet potatoes that formed part of the family larder, and which separated two sleepers' mats.

The old woman who bade me enter was grinding corn in the hollow of a tree-stump. A watchful parrot pecked fussily at her spillings. Quite the largest owl I had ever seen was sitting tethered to the roof. Although several people were in the hut nobody showed the slightest sign of interest or curiosity in me and this made me feel as though I was a familiar figure about the place and therefore welcome. Whatever people were doing, they went on doing it, and I presumed that this was the Carajas' way of making a guest feel at home. One old man, however, a bag of bones in an Air Force jacket, displayed the greatest, bright-eyed interest in me. He sat on a freshly woven straw mat—an honour given to the old. He had no idea of his age and neither had a boy who came in with his bow and arrows which he carefully stowed away in the roof thatch. He threw his catch of half a dozen fish on the earth floor and lay on his stomach on the nearest mat, propping his chin in his hands. The woman, his mother perhaps, stopped grinding the corn and roasted the fish whole, just as it was, on the fire. At least the smoke drowned the other smells and drove out the mosquitoes, even if it was not the sweetest of incense. The boy looked as if he might be about fourteen years old. But he had not the slightest interest in ages.

The only person in the whole tribe whose age was in any way identifiable was that of an elder, said to be a centenarian. But the Fundação people said he had looked the same for decades. People remembered him from the time when Vargas went to Bananal, and he had certainly not changed since then. His fair fell full and straight to his shoulders as thick, oily, and blue-black as any of the most vigorous young men. He was making material for a woman's dress in the traditional way. The old man peeled a whole tree branch of its bark without either split or cut except down one side. He did this by tapping the bark all over and then finally slitting it free with a sharp knife.

Few of the Indians were idle, particularly the women. A hundred domestic things filled their day. I found one woman crocheting the tight thread band round her young son's leg, similar to the boy's who sat under the plane. This red-dyed garter would possibly stay on for years. Some tribes deformed their legs to a baluster shape by such bands and considered it beautiful. In another house a woman was spinning cotton, pulling the white lumps from an earthenware bowl, rubbing it on her leg before threading it through her fingers on to the spinning yarn. Other women were making the beautiful feathered headdresses, including some feathered caps which would be the envy of any London West End milliner. Hardly to be found in Bond Street, however, was the women's lack of dress sense with regard to bosoms. Mostly these were bare. At first when I went into the house they quickly covered their breasts, having learnt that much at least from civilization. Later, they were not alarmed by my approach and did not bother to be modest.

Mats were being made, too, with special designs, for the tribal gathering. Many of the Indians still had down sticking to their bodies from the last be-feathered display. They had been in full regalia and paint to liven up the inauguration of the tourist hotel. Most curiously, many of their headdresses had lozenge-shaped crests worked into them, like radio aerials. And similar forms were traditionally used in Ireland for St. Briget's crosses. But then, similar shapes were also made by the Huichol Indians of Mexico as 'God-eyes', to protect children and bring them long life. Again, such squares could be found from Sweden to Polynesia, from Australia to Africa. But I could not find out whether the Carajas of Bananal used the crests as charms and magic symbols. Perhaps the form had survived, but an older meaning had long ago been forgotten. And this was just as well, maybe, because some cheap souvenir shops in Brasilia had acquired Caraja headdresses, bows and arrows and had them for sale.

Visitors like to have mementoes of the Indians. I found that the Indian women wanted something from me, too—tobacco. I was smoking my pipe when I went to the houses and was besieged by young girls and old women alike for a fill. A contented expression passed over their faces as they tamped my tobacco down into their stemless pipes. I thought that perhaps tobacco was scarce in Brazil, and I remembered the unofficial traders coming aboard the *Rubens* who wanted British cigarettes. But Brazil was one of the biggest tobacco producers. In the markets and street stalls of country towns scattered around the Central Plateau, I was to find coils of plug tobacco wound like rope round four-foot poles. The smell before smoking was the most delicious I had ever found from tobacco, and in my pipe it had a rich plug tang. The Caraja women also insisted that I try their tobacco, which they had not the patience to cure properly.

But theirs was probably the older method of treating the leaf, because long before the Americas were discovered the Indians were smoking and taking snuff. The Spaniards took tobacco back to Europe before Raleigh did, though smoking's popularity probably can be laid at Jean Nicot's door. He was French Ambassador at Lisbon and he sent a box of snuff to cure Catherine de Médici's headache. Snuff-taking became all the rage, despite a special papal bull issued by Urban VII ordering the confiscation of all snuff-boxes brought into churches. The Czar of Russia went further and ordered the noses of all female snuffers to be slit open.

THE HUNTING CARAJA

In one of the palm houses, quite indistinguishable from its neighbours, except for the number of dogs about it, lived the Caraja chief. His face was familiar all over Brazil, because he had been featured many times by the Press and magazine photographers during his visits to the outside world, especially to Brasilia. He never sacrificed his dignity by wearing a suit, but always kept his own native feathers. For the first mass on the site of the new capital the chief and his warriors were invited to attend in their full panoply of paint and feathers, and thereafter to a number of festivities. The photographs of such events were put up in Brasilia's smarter restaurants and office waiting-rooms, because the Indians' feather costumes were thought to be wonderful decoration, and as essential to big occasions as was the presence of at least one cardinal.

But at home the chief was a different figure. I was as welcome in his house as in the others. The first time we met he was lying on the floor, surrounded by children and grandchildren. The tiniest of these was a girl only a few months old, and quite naked except for enormous earrings made of bright macaw feathers. She looked at me coyly. The chief was without his own feathered finery and wore instead his informal and no doubt more comfortable dress of a singlet patterned by a design from the U.S.A. and a pair of shorts. His eyes were full of humour and when I talked he laughed and rolled on his mat with pleasure. A cardboard suitcase was then opened and a pile of photographs taken out for me to look at. This was the record of the chief's high days in high places with high people. The chief lay gazing for some minutes without any expression at all at one of himself with President Kubitschek at the Alvorada Palace. This must have been his most glorious hour.

Of all the city honours only the photographs remained now, and such delights as bottles of hair oil, tubes of toothpaste, and hand mirrors. The chief's family peeped into the mirrors for a long time, again completely without expression. He was greatly amused by my curiosity over a tiny hole pierced in his lower lip. I learnt from the photographs that this was used for hanging a kind of false beard about two feet long. I thought this might have been made of wood or from a feather, but it was a giant turtle bone. No less aristocratic than the rest of his tribe, I think the chief was fond of a gay life, because preparations were going on for his next magnificent costume, and I presumed that he had a new one for every dazzling occasion. A girl was plucking a beautiful white heron. Its black legs contrasted vividly with the snowy whiteness of its plumage.

The trouble with aristocratic life is that it cannot be so for everybody, and the Caraja chief was more than helped by his huge family who waited on him. This was true of all the men. Although they actually went out to procure food and were very much the hunters, in the house they were served by the women, who appeared to exist for this and for other domestic purposes and to bear children. There was no question of equal rights. Time was subject to them and not the Indians to it. The young bloods seemed to spend a great deal of their time lording it in hammocks. They only got out of them to fetch fruit from the plantation behind the houses, or to fish in the river and at sundown to swim. But I discovered that this was not laziness or overriding male superiority. It was a legacy of the tribe's former life. At one time the young Caraja had to be tuned as taut as the string of his own bow. His physical strength and fitness was the tribe's only means of survival against enemies. To be vigilant against other tribes' attacks, to keep himself strong, to hunt, to make his weapons, fully occupied the warrior. All domestic affairs including harvesting were left to women. The men also used their energies in tribal dancing. But enmity between tribes was reduced to an almost harmless rivalry. The worst they did was to steal children occasionally to ward off the dangers of inbreeding.

So the men's life was without its old purpose and with few exceptions no new one had replaced it. Although normally the tribal dancing went on as in the old days, during my stay in Brazil it had been abandoned. The reason was kept a dark secret. None of the Fundação people could discover from the Carajas why there would be no dancing that year. There might have been a simple reason, or something complicated and mysterious, perhaps connected with the stars, for the Indians knew the stars and gave them names in their own language. The prohibition on dancing was to extend, in fact, not for a year as such, but for a period measured more poetically. The Caraja went by moons, by rains, by the season of turtle-laying or by the ripening of mangoes.

A further custom which showed that the young men were far from being lords and masters was that their marriages were fixed up by their mothers! The Caraja married in his early teens, so a boy's best friend had to be his mother. Those boys who disagreed with mother over such an important matter ran away from home. Some went to other villages along the river. One such escapee went to Brasilia and stayed with my friend Jesco von Puttkamer, who was a clever photographer. Jesco was being drawn more and more to love the Indians and spent much time with them along the Araguaia and the Xingu rivers, always with his cameras. Jesco was a close friend of the Villas Boas brothers, and was himself learning some of the tribal languages. But insofar as modern life had touched the Carajas, except for some of the youngsters, they seemed indifferent to it. The old customs still persisted along the ancient patterns. The Carajas never kissed. This had been taboo for so long that they would probably not know how to. Husband and wife never slept together, neither in a hammock, nor on the floor, where they lay close together but wrapped in separate blankets. The time and place for making love was out among the trees, a beautiful idea, broached when the women went to collect sticks for the fire.

In one house I found a boy of about fifteen lying on the floor. After a while I had got used to walking in and out of the houses at any time of day, and I noticed this boy lying very still. His brown complexion was the colour of wood ash. His father sat near him, his hand under the blanket which covered the boy. I discovered a great tumour on the boy's groin. His father was rubbing it until the swelling was raw. The pain must have been excruciating. But his son lay silently, his beautiful face tranquil, his eyes bright as though with fever. The Carajas were frightened of doctors. I thought, however, that the boy would die, probably from blood poisoning, and so I went to get Wolfgang Gunther of the Fundação. In spite of his name, he only spoke a little German, but more English, which he had learnt from the New Tribes Mission station across the river. He went to look at the sick boy and promised to arrange for Santa

Izabel's two nurses to go and lance the tumour. Feathers and war paint might have been rather jolly, but ignorance and disease were not. And from that moment I began to understand what the Villas Boas brothers were working towards.

Another boy I found was being laughed at by the others, for during a fit of hunger he had roasted his pet monkey whole and had eaten it. And not all the ounce cubs and toucans, the armadillos (even better eating) or ant-eaters could console his remorse, although he still had a fine toad secured by a string to its hind leg.

Beyond the Indians' thatched houses were the buildings belonging to the Fundação workers. These were not thatched, but made of tree branches roughly held together, some of them roofed with tin sheets. The Fundação employees lived and worked here. They kept no animals except hunting dogs and a very cross-looking wild pig which was boxed up for fattening. They also kept poisonous snakes alive in boxes until they could be sent to São Paulo's famous Butantan Institute, where anti-snake bite serums were produced. In return for their snakes the men received free serums. This was a necessary item when they went hunting the larger wild cats whose skins greatly supplemented their wages.

Among the Fundação farm-workers and river-boys I made my real Bananal friends. The Carajas were hospitable, but nevertheless I remained a stranger. Our worlds were too far apart. But with the others I was at home and spent most of my time with them. One morning I was stopped and asked if I had any insect repellent, for these men from many different places in Brazil were being bitten and stung as badly as I was. Bananal's insects were one torment which Dante forgot to include in the *Inferno*. The worst I encountered was a tiny tick which lodged itself under the skin and made a nodule of inflammation which still itched unbearably weeks afterwards. To be stung by a mosquito was almost light relief compared with the ticks.

I discovered my new friends in an earth-floored canteen. They had just finished their midday meal and were resting in the hut. They brought out their treasures. Most of the boys came from cities and found Bananal's wild life fascinating. They had panned in the

This young Caraja cuts his hair—but still paints his body

Her beads and the dug-out canoe are made like her ancient Indian forebears'

The Caraja's river abounds in fish—which can be dried in the sun
Indian boys will be boys—besides squirting, the hole in his chin is
used for fixing tribal decorations

river for some sparkling mineral crystals which were without much value except for their intrinsic beauty. The boys also had little bags full of terrifying crocodile teeth and cougar molars. Such precious things had no doubt taken a long time and much patience to collect, but nevertheless I had to accept a selection of their finds as a gift.

Osvaldo gave me many of his as presents. He became my firmest friend. He was a muscular negro from São Paulo city, and he considered the exchange of crowded streets and noisy traffic for the quiet of the Rio Araguaia a good bargain. He never wanted the rush and tear of cities again. Osvaldo and I spent a lot of time together, laughing more than talking, for he had a mischievous humour. There was no liane forest too dense for his tough bare feet to find a track if I wished to wander away from the village. No island of water-lilies was too far from the bank, or river currents too powerful for him, if I wished to swim out, and no hour of the frog-loud night was too late for us to go on a pleasure hunt.

Fundação put a fast river boat at my disposal. I suppose they must have seen that I could hardly wait to get on to the Araguaia. One of the boys came as crew to look after the outboard motor. We sped among the lily lagoons up-river which so strongly brought Li Po to mind again,

> *On Mirror Lake for three hundred li,*
> *Gaily, gaily the lilies are blossoming.*

The boatman had distinct ideas of what I should see, and, leaving a great V-shaped wake on the still waters (I could never understand why the river could be so placid and yet flow so fast at the same time), we went towards the Little Alvorada, the President's house at Bananal. All the way green forest came down to the water's edge, and this made the hunting lodge seem all the whiter.

We landed on the bank and I went hurriedly through the Little Alvorada, for I thought it had no great merits. The main floor was raised above the ground to give a wide view of the river and its forest bank beyond. Hanging under the house was an orchid garden. The place was also used as a guest house for official visitors to Bananal. When I got back to Brasilia people asked if I had slept in the President's bed. But it was perhaps just as well I didn't, for on that very day of my visit to the Little Dawn, President Kubitschek found a man sleeping in his bed at the Big Dawn. My boatman thought so many tiled bathrooms and kitchens in one house a wonderful thing, and he would not leave until we went to the hotel also, still far from complete in spite of being inaugurated. The workmen were burning sheets of cardboard to make a smoke-screen against mosquitoes.

The river banks teemed with birds. It thrilled me to see a curassow perched in a tree like an overdressed turkey. The brilliant red comb was a sitting target for an Indian's arrow. I saw one quite small boy proudly carrying home three of these fabulous birds which he had bagged with his bow. To dine off such exotic flesh might be expected in fairy-tales, though it was quite common Indian fare. Even finer eating, for those who like greasy food, was a very big black and white wild duck.

But the whole scene was like a fairy-tale full of unexpected and improbable beauty. For this reason, too, I liked crossing the river by going some miles upstream to São Felix, a small village built along the opposite bank. The river was so wide and its currents so powerful that I could not believe how the dry season narrowed it, leaving empty blazing sands along the banks, sands which were finer and whiter than even Copacabana. It was there the Indian boys played football, and where the turtles came out of the water to lay their eggs and bury them in the sand.

No Indians lived across the river at São Felix and perhaps this was the basis of strong feelings between São Felix and Santa Izabel. I discovered that Izabel looked down her nose at Felix. This may have been on account of Felix being comparatively new or because it had bars and shops—which for me was its main attraction, for Izabel had nothing with which to console her guests' dry throats. Further, São Felix enjoyed the reputation of being a smuggling village—right on the Araguaia, remote from official eyes, who could blame it? But with a thirst to deal with after a day's humid heat, I was not disposed to moralize about what Felix had to offer his visitors. Izabel did have one up on its rival by having the hospital on its side of the river. We gave a lift in our boat to a man coming from a friend in the hospital who had been terribly mauled by an ounce.

Perhaps the Izabelians were afraid that their Indians would get into bad company and bad habits by crossing the river. Or perhaps they feared that the Indians would not return, for São Felix was in some ways more attractive than Santa Izabel. Its single main street of single-storey houses was colourful, for the mud bricks had been plastered and gaily painted. From the river street, others ran back at right-angles. They were all paved with grass which was easy on the hooves of the horses and mules which the Felixites used. I saw no wheeled vehicle except some bicycles and a solid wooden-wheeled ox cart pulled by yoked zebus. Most of the horses wandered happily between the houses, munching the pavement, ignoring with lordly dignity the hens who also fussed about in the grass until bedtime, when they went to roost among the banana trees in the backyards.

You would find no xenophobia in São Felix. Among the river-bank houses was a chapel for the Assemblies of God—distinguished by a religious-looking stepped gable. The stranger you were the more they liked it, for then you could tell them about the big world beyond the Rio Araguaia and the horizon's rim of forest. 'Is Brasilia marvellous?' they asked me. I hadn't the heart to say that I preferred their own village. But I did prefer the whitewashed, thatched cottages with half-doors which again reminded me of Ireland, and the liveliness of young bloods riding in from the forest on their snorting stallions for a night's drinking, gambling and love-making. Children were playing in the grassy streets, the youngest ones looking pregnant with their bloated bellies, and all looking beautiful because of their eyes and skins like polished hardwoods. I always walked the same way to get my long, cool drink, first passing the women slapping their washing on the river stones, and then by the village shops—especially my favourite one with two pressure lamps and a dozen pairs of pink brassieres hanging from the ceiling like well-cooked hams.

But, of course, São Felix was not paradise and must have had its own problems, otherwise why should the bar-cum-general stores have sold revolvers over the counter? Among the sad rolls of cloth, sad green crêpe paper in boxes, American sailor hats, cans of Singer sewing-machine oil, and the ubiquitous but nevertheless startling Fockink gin, there was a heap of revolvers. Customers could go in and buy a pair of hand-made boots, a comb, a packet of airmail envelopes, and that revolver there, thank you. Then he could pocket his purchases and drink a cold beer at a table. Who shot who about what I never found out, fortunately. Probably when the men from the backlands came into São Felix, besides pacific topics like the sale of a cow or the birth of a daughter they discussed more belligerent subjects which only pistols would satisfy. But I never heard of, nor saw any shooting, nor any disturbance loud enough to frighten the horses with beautifully tooled, high-pommelled saddles, which they hitched to the rails outside. It was surprising that nobody shot the bar proprietor for charging more for beer that they did even in Brasilia's bars, which in turn were much more expensive than Rio's.

Like children everywhere, Santa Izabel's Indian children hated going to bed. After a send-off from São Felix with lots of hand-waving from the women and children, and after our boat passed the deserted cemetery and the flooded forests, the lights of Santa Izabel swung into view. And the Indian children would be playing until the last possible minute by the electric lights of the Fundação house. The tribal chief might also have walked over, honouring the occasion with some old Western-type clothes which did little to hide the paint on his arms and neck. I was usually ravenous by this time and went in to demolish a mountain of rice and black beans without a care as to whether the drinking water was boiled or filtered, and without a thought about such niceties as shaving. Afterwards I sat with the chief on the verandah, or lay in one of the hammocks there—if the beautiful servant girl would let me. Her great sport was to rock the hammock until I almost fell out, and laugh when I was annoyed.

Osvaldo and the river-boys would be waiting, and rather than stay to watch the Indian children playing whist, I went to join them on some evening jaunt. As I walked by the Indian houses I saw their mats placed on the ground outside and silent figures rolled in a blanket, already asleep. Continuous, but thunderless lightning showed up the scene uncannily. Perhaps from the open-air sleeping the Carajas developed both their interest in the stars and the poetry of celestial names. I wondered for how much longer the Caraja would name his own stars. Every year, indeed every month, modern life was attacking them like the hostile tribes used to. Not at Bananal but farther in the interior around the Xingu river I heard that the Indians' ground was being bought and sold from under their very feet by racketeering real-estate firms operating internationally. The Villas Boas brothers, the Protection Service and the Fundação were all fighting against such evils and the tragedy which would follow. At Bananal the opening of the tourist hotel would reduce the Carajas to the role of familiars about the place, awaiting the summons to appear in paint and feathers before important visitors.

Perhaps somewhere a middle way would be found whereby the Indians could retain their physical beauty and nobility of character, yet also take part in Brazil's expansion without being exterminated and at best degraded, as many people feared would happen. To secure at least territory for them, plans were afoot for forming vast reserves, kept entirely free from industry or real-estate sharks. It would be idle to suppose that the Indians could live in a vacuum hermetically sealed against the effects of modern life. Even the deep forest tribes which were still undiscovered and whose existence was only suspected must have seen planes flying over their jungles. The men and women working with the Indians were well aware of the dangers of confronting the people they loved. Some openly declare that in ten years the tribes will have vanished, defeated and corrupted by civilization.

On going back to Brasilia, I met two or three Caraja tribesmen who were living in the city. Their long hair was cut, their feathers exchanged for jeans and shirts. One of them worked at the military airport because aeroplanes fascinated him. Yet by their broad smiles they were obviously completely happy. I took hope that change for the Caraja and the other tribes would not mean destruction. Perhaps they would remain as undisguised in character as they were physically undisguised in Brasilia by the indelible rings under their eyes.

At night in Bananal from several of the huts came an awful wailing. It rose and fell on two notes only. Wolfgang Gunther told me that women were wailing for the dead, and that this moaning and rocking to and fro were not to the Christian God, but to the elements—the sky, the lightning which lit it, and the fast-flowing river, their godhead. By night the Indian houses were different than by day. The wailing went on for hours. I could not understand how the people in the house could bear it, to say nothing of the neighbours. But then neither could I understand official propaganda which showed the Indians in feathers and paint attending the first mass of Brasilia and also pointed out that the Indians' forebears helped to carry the great cross which Pedro Cabral erected on first coming to Brazil in 1500. But perhaps the Indians managed to combine both, for even Irish Catholic women used to wail the *caione* and smoke clay pipes at funerals not so long ago.

Being careful not to tread on sleeping dogs or other Indian pets, I eventually found Osvaldo. Our meeting almost invariably coincided with the evening downpour and thunder. I never believed such waterfalls could empty themselves out of the sky. In a moment the ground was swamped and new rivers went rushing down to join the Araguaia. Osvaldo would sensibly be wearing only his swimming shorts, the muscles of his dark torso glistening in the pale purple flashes of the lightning as we went through the forest or stood under the wide thatch eaves of the Fundação's tractor shed. When the rain came I simply took off all my clothes and put them in a plastic bag. Once I was caught without my bag and arrived back at the Fundação house as a sorry, soggy mess, dyed like an Indian by red mud. Ironically the water supply was cut off at the house and so I stood naked under the flowing eaves and took a shower bath.

The rooms were open to the rafters and the pantiles. A few inconvenient gaps in the tiles let the rain through—especially, I thought, where I had to sleep. Enso Pisano played musical beds and shifted them round to avoid the worst drips, but I continued moving at intervals during the night because the rain seemed to follow me round. The river creatures provided the music, a noise that seemed quite impossible when I looked at the innocent river banks the next morning. A whole aquatic world woke after dark and took possession of Santa Izabel. Frogs were barking, croaking, squealing, rasping, piping, warbling. Could they be as big as elephants I thought, lying awake, although I knew that the loudest voiced were as small as thimbles. When they stopped, all at once for a few seconds, I could hear the cicadas. And between thunderclaps which shook the house, the old women's wailing went on, endlessly. But somehow, I managed to sleep. And then hardly had the bull-frogs stopped than the Indian children were back, too bright, too early, wanting to open my wooden shutters on another glorious day of sun on the Rio Araguaia, on new hunting, new cloudscapes, and new stories to hear in the cool pools of shadow under the mango trees.

Osvaldo had some new finds from the river for me to keep, new fangs from the forest for me to have as talismans. And one of these was very lucky indeed—a tooth of the ounce which had attacked the man now lying in hospital. But whether it was just for luck or to act as a defensive amulet I could not find out. I knew, however, that the tooth was not a gift which cost the giver nothing, for all those objects had commercial value. City jewellers mounted animals' teeth and claws in gold and sold them along with *figas*. But as a boy I had taken my fill of charms—literally, for I often ate written charms or washed the words from a written page and drank the inky water.

The technically-minded modern world laughs at the magic of crooked sixpences and four-leaf shamrocks. But such things still played a part in Brazil, where the Church so prized its relics of the saints, and often housed them in special chapels. And this seemed no different from the Basuto boy who would wear a kite's foot to make his own feet swift, or the East Indian who would keep elephant's hair to make himself strong, or the Japanese youth taking the hair of the girl he wants, and knotting it into his own. These and ounce teeth and the priest with saints' pickled hearts or martyrs' toenails are the same. The power, after all, is in the mind.

7

Landscape with Sharks

Like Louis XIV, President Kubitschek of Brazil will be remembered for his outburst of building. Just as the French king built a new capital (this is almost what Versailles amounted to) so Kubitschek determined to put Brasilia on the map. Another coincidence is that Louis began (though rarely completed) immense water undertakings to supply his various palaces. And so did President Kubitschek. The difference, of course, is that Louis, egged on by the wily Colbert, was after self-aggrandisement, whereas Kubitschek's sole purpose was to open the lost world of Brazil's interior. Of these intentions Brasilia stood as the primary symbol. More technical, but none the less romantic for that, was the immense dam at Tres Marias.

During my first weeks in Brazil there was a spate of inaugurations of new developments—roads, industries, major civil engineering works. The President seemed to open something, somewhere, every day. Although not all the works were finished, Kubitschek wanted to baptize them, because his five-year term of office was all but expended. For Brazil, these projects meant the release of a tremendous potential, contemplation of which even amazed the Brazilians themselves. Brazil of the future will be quite another thing from Brazil of the past. People's image of Brazil must change, and radically.

I was excited to be invited to the opening of the Tres Marias dam. It blocked the vast São Francisco river, making one of the world's largest hydro-electric stations. The river's destructive floods were now controlled, and the terrible drought that used to follow the floods was averted. The opening ceremony was a national occasion, for not only would power lines thread throughout an enormous area, but the whole river valley itself would become fertile, right down to its starting-point well north of Salvador. And because of the dam the Rio São Francisco, the most important Brazilian river, was made navigable for a thousand miles through the whole year, so joining north and south of the country. And further, the vast reaches of parched land will blossom because of the network of irrigation canals. Brazil's rice-fields will treble their harvest. Not unpoetically, in this promised land, the garlic of Egypt will be forsaken—in 1958 Brazil bought garlic from the Nile's banks to the tune of many millions of cruzeiros!

As requested, I was at Brasilia's military airport early but not bright (as usual) for the plane, to be precise, at 5.30 a.m. We left four hours later—long after I had recovered from alarm-clock shock. Sixteen reporters from all over Brazil were in the plane, and for two hours during the flight they were like a Sunday school outing with the curate standing ice-creams all round. The hilarity stopped when instead of green valleys below we saw the gleam of water, the scoured red earth and the great wall of Tres Marias itself, and beyond the cocoa-coloured streams which fed the great river, the sad forests being drowned for ever, and the plains newly planted with thornless cactus—cattle feed through many a long drought. The plane circled, cameras clicked and whirred. Then we went down, squeezed a landing-place on the tiny, overcrowded airport, and were given linen lapel badges and an envelope with scripts of the dam-openers' speeches. My heart sank. There were pages and pages. Then a way was cloven through the crowd. We poured into a bus—a bus beautified by red and yellow wax roses and a crucifix and long lengths of yellow fringes. Perhaps as a warning to impious pressmen there was also a sign assuring us that,

> GOD IS PRESENT IN ALL THINGS,
> IN HEAVEN, IN THIS BUS,
> IN THE EARTH AND IN THE SEA.

Figuratively speaking, there were roses all along the way to the dam, and little knots of people waiting to see Kubitschek pass by. At the site itself there was a real crowd, plus a traffic jam and parking shortage. Even most trees were occupied by tied mules and horses for out-of-town members. The sky's glare was intense and the heat radiation from high cloud was more uncomfortable than if the sun had actually been shining. Hundreds of umbrellas were up—though, equally, they might have been protection against the vultures circling overhead. Vultures, after all, resemble pigeons in some respects. Although the President's plane was also circling overhead by now, publicity cars were still darting about like scalded cats, bill-sticking walls and tree trunks with posters. They showed Kubitschek standing between the famous scalloped screen of the Alvorada Palace. He was certainly Brazil's most photogenic president ever. JK, as he was called, was also one of Brazil's most popular ones, for when his car approached the dam the crowd crushed in on him. And when he got out it was just like a member of the family coming home. Every little girl wanted to kiss his hand and present him with flowers, every grown-up wanted to give him a good Brazilian bear-hug, and every housewife wanted JK to look at *her* poster of himself. President Kubitschek untied a ribbon and walked across the high top of the dam. The crowd surged. The pressmen preceded him, walking backwards, using up reels of film.

A shiny band struck up music on the dam's further side. But orderly progress was rather difficult and we all got separated from the President. I was wedged in behind a dear little archbishop who was beetling along magnificently and using his umbrella as a sort of crowbar. Brazilians were so accustomed to seeing bishops and archbishops walking the streets in dusty soutanes, queueing for stamps at the post office, or waiting to use the public telephone, that no notice is taken of them at all. This was perhaps only to be expected, since in Brazil the Roman Catholic Church was disestablished when the country was declared a republic in 1889. And also, there were so many archbishops. Scarlet-hats, of course, were better off, for being Princes of the Church they had international status—quite a different kettle of fish. And in my time in Brazil the Church's fathers were very different, too, from those around Salvador in Le Gentil de la Barbinais' time. Apart from one or two priests always found in smart restaurants, most of the clergy seemed to be poor and hardworking.

LANDSCAPE WITH SHARKS

At last, archbishop and all, we got to the dais. It was already
loaded with generals and admirals, senators and mayors and all
sorts of things. It must have been a bit of a squash getting that lot
in behind the President and the bottles of mineral water. The
bottles almost caused a battle among the women who wished to
minister to the presidential thirst.

The speeches started. Now the chairman of the waterworks was
in full spate with a flow of words that would have done credit to a
revivalist preacher. A look of boredom possessed the President and
he kept crossing his legs. No doubt he had already heard such
flowery words every day that week. His eye roved among the pressmen for familiar faces. He told a guard to turn the muzzle of his
machine-gun aside so that a little girl could give him a toffee.
Another bishop, dangerously near the dais's edge, took off his shaggy
soup-plate hat because of the heat. Underneath, his bright magenta
episcopal skull-cap was an island in a sea of sweat. The speech was
still only on page six. Bishops were not sufficiently high up on the
V.I.P. list to have seats on the dais among the municipal fathers.
To hug his friends he jumped up and down, showing a lovely length
of episcopal sock to match the skull-cap. Nobody kissed his enormous ring, although he gladly accepted cigarettes, especially filter-
tipped.

A senator spoke next on behalf of the upper house. He was well
trained, and exploded apoplectically in alternate sentences. His chin
was well up over a stiff collar and both arms went round the micro-
phones. The pressmen counted the pages of the typescript to see
how much more he had to do. The exalted ones behind him began
reading yesterday's speeches in today's newspapers, as they would
read today's speeches in tomorrow's. Then a congressman gave his
speech. He spoke in a more restrained manner, gesticulating at the
President, who was wilting and mopping his brow, and at his wife,
whose make-up was starting to run in the heat. The old men in the
back row put the newspapers over their heads and slept. Somnolence
threatened everybody until the congressman's hairy arm emerged
from a cuff and he waved a fist and shouted. This woke everybody
up. They gave him a lukewarm clap. Bible-thumping was really the

139

favourite. All the speakers had a hug and a handshake from the President for the honeyed words. Within the following days many of them would have gone out of power like JK himself. The opening of Tres Marias dam was their last occasion for performing in front of an audience.

A luncheon was thrown in after the ceremonials and the pressmen rushed to get further shots of JK arriving for his meal. The bus drove us at breakneck speed to the huge contractor's shed set out with hundreds of beautifully laid and flower-and-fruit-decorated tables. But the President had given everyone the slip and was off to the airport for a well-deserved weekend in Rio de Janeiro. So our gang dashed off once more, careering along the narrow, rutted country lanes to the airport, and was rewarded by the sight of the President's plane taking off. Only one thing was left to do now— eat. We rushed back to the huge shed again and were the last of the thousand guests to sit down. The army of specially-flown-in waiters in white had an excellent five-course luncheon served to the thousand in no time. But time was our enemy. At one end of the shed the São Francisco valley industries exhibited free samples of their wares—goods that were already proof of the dam's efficiency. Women, who I thought had gone to the lavatory, were now returning in their fine clothes, laden with wooden boxes of sweetmeats, garlands of garlic around their pearls, coconuts bursting from their string bags. They had come prepared.

The Press forgot about the luncheon's last course and went to get the exhibition's leavings. Being a foreigner, I came away modestly with only a chain of some fifty garlics, ten pounds of sweetmeats and four pounds of scrubbing soap. The sole person out of the whole thousand who seemed not to be helping himself was the dear little archbishop. He was gallantly reading the posters about the various products, though the stalls and shelves had been cleared of the actual articles. The archbishop laughed when I pointed out my garlic rosary.

Tres Marias was already settling back to normality by the time our bus took us to the airport. Farmers were riding their horses and mules home along the lanes. And instead of squeaky loudspeakers, macaws squawked, and sambas vibrated like swarms of flies round every shack-café. The bus stopped briefly at a village bar-cum-shop so that the pressmen could buy cigarettes. Outside, a sow found a mate. On the still-crowded airfield the pilots and crews woke from sleep under the shade of the planes' wings. Cattle-birds flew back to de-tick the humps of the zebus. At the edge of the airfield some children emerged from the trees carrying enormous bundles of firewood on their heads. Three Marys was forgotten as the plane roared us towards Brasilia again, and everybody was wondering when the plane would leave the military airport for the next inauguration.

Five courses with Three Marys was more than enough for me. I never entered the Press Sunday school races again. But I did go many times out of Brasilia, to see as much as I could of the thousands of square miles of the Central Plateau. Quite a number of these trips were due to my friend Herbert Konen, manager of the Bank of London and South America. He was of German extraction from São Paulo and was one of Brasilia's pioneers. Herbert knew the city when it was nothing but heaps of red dust. His family and the young bank assistants piled into jeeps at the weekends and we went twenty miles south of the city to some waterfalls and natural pools for swimming. This place had the marvellous name of Saia Velha—the Old Skirt!

We went bumping over country where pampas-ostriches lived (nandu or rhea, and *strauss* in German. Can *Tales from the Vienna Woods* ever be the same now that I know it was written by a man called John Ostrich?) The building of Brasilia and new roads had not driven the ostriches completely away. The giant bird was un-disputed king of the plateau. To see it fleeing along a track in front of a car and changing direction with violent, sudden swerves, I could easily believe that no other animal in the world could tack so rapidly when pursued. Once I saw a whole family: a cock and his six wives. Mr. Nandu was a very faithful husband and attacked any uninvited flighty Miss Ostrich who strayed into his harem area. The nuptial dance was quite a performance with the cock roaring in two distinct notes at regular intervals, like an animal. His neck shot bolt upright like a poker and his breast swelled up like the peacock curtains of the pantomime theatre in Copenhagen's Tivoli Gardens. There must have been many of the ostriches still remaining, for rich and poor alike (they were not often alike in Brazil) had the birds' feathers as dusters about the house. In some parts of the country ostriches were kept as pets, because their favourite food was snakes—though other people kept snakes as pets because snakes ate mice. But ostriches were not seen so frequently as the long-legged, stately bustards. I often saw these dainty, disdainful birds in the wild stretch between the Three Powers Square and the President's palace.

The Old Skirt waterfalls and pools were not high so much as beautiful, not spectacular so much as good for swimming. We had to leave the jeeps and walk through woods and waist-high grass, and cross boulder-strewn streams to climb up to the pools. Only one was wide enough for swimming and deep enough for diving. It also offered the most dangerous sport. This was to climb on a ledge of rock close behind the roaring cataract and work across, with the pounding water almost touching one's nose. I only made this perilous journey once, cutting my bottom to ribbons in the process (at least it *felt* like ribbons afterwards). One slip from the shelf would have been fatal. Not even the boldest dared to plunge in at the foot of the waterfall. But we always seemed to be in the mood for tempting providence. After the first swim we would climb above the waterfall and explore the river's upper reaches. When the rapids became too fierce, we resorted to the densely overgrown banks. Since we only wore swimming shorts and were without shoes we had no defence against snakes and scorpions—though I only found poisonous spiders and wild bees' nests. And those bees *were* wild!

The Konens also took me farther afield from Brasilia—one day to Goiania, a town not thirty years old and capital of Goias State. The way lay through Anapolis, by means of the new Brasilia-Anapolis highway, another important development for the interior. Beyond Anapolis this fantastic road joined up with one of the finest of all Brazil's achievements, the 1,418-mile road up to Belem in the Amazon's mouth. Not long ago people said that such a road could never be built. But Kubitschek set his heart on it. By incredible endurance and skill Bernado Sayão, the engineer, constructed it in an extraordinarily short time.

The road was cut through thick forest which nobody had ever penetrated. Three new Indian tribes were discovered as the road slashed farther across unknown land. On it went, mile after mile, the whole way strewn with giant trees, some 230 feet high. Bridge building feats were performed as a matter of course. It was a vital link for Brasilia with Brazil's far north and the Amazon valley. In Brasilia I saw people from the north lay the foundation stone of a group of apartment blocks which would bear the names of northern states, so in this small way making a contribution to the new capital's representative character. I was ill afterwards, for at the luncheon (shades of Three Marys!) I ate Amazon turtles straight out of the shell. The turtle was called 'the ox of the Amazon', since it sells by the kilo in Belem shops. I certainly thought that an ox was trampling in my stomach.

The new roads opened the interior more than anything else. They were, quite simply, the constructions which meant that the rest of the world must change its way of thinking about Brazil. Already the roads were doing more than carrying goods and people. This was almost a secondary function. More importantly, along the roads, in the hitherto hidden valleys, people were settling and beginning to farm the rich, virgin soil. Blackened stumps of burnt trees stuck up along the Anapolis road for miles where the jungle had been pushed back. But the ground was already lush with pasture, patterned and ribbed by hillsides of maize and rice-fields and cane-crushing mills, fat flocks, trim farmhouses, coffee plantations, cotton-fields, banana and orange groves. As we sped past these things, Herbert saw many signs of change since his first journey two years previously.

I began to see how Brasilia's site differed from most of the surrounding country, although all of it belonged, in spite of considerable variation, to the great Central Plateau. The landscape was totally covered by verdure. In one area there were many abrupt hills thrust conically out of the plain, but ancient geological movement had truncated them. The greenness flowed up from the plain and covered their sides and tops. There were no bare rocks any-where. In other places, the landscape repented of abruptness and rolled in smooth, gigantic waves, like the Sussex Downs.

All new buildings were horrid, and belonged to the worst type of sugar-icing villa. But the older mud-brick houses with thatched roofs belonged to the land, as indigenous buildings always seem to. Modern civilization had forced open the land which had lain closed through the centuries. Yet already its own peculiar emblems were planted in the greenery—enormous advertisement hoardings for Goodyear and Firestone and Dunlop tyres. The simple, white wooden crosses marking roadside graves, or the many vultures hovering or cleaning up the remains of dead horses seemed to belong to the age before the silent interior was invaded. But then our own jeep, and the loaded lorries and the express buses and the fast cars were so different from the farmers on their horses, bare-footed in their stirrups and draped with long capes against the rainy season's downpours.

And so we came to Anapolis. We left behind the farm labourers cycling along the roads, one hand on the handlebars, the other holding an umbrella. I began to look for things other than eagles, buzzards, and vultures in the sky. The most interesting so far had been the variety of hawks. They had the ostrich's partiality for snakes. After cruising and hovering they dropped like stones, rising up again almost at once with their prey. Not to have pity was barbarous, but I could not feel sorry for the wriggling snakes whose poisonous fangs were for once helpless, caught as they were in the hawk's talons.

Anapolis was comparatively an old town where the old ways still lingered. In the outskirts the houses had long gardens walled by deep red mud-blocks. Horse taxis went at a sprightly speed along the road. Those gaily painted spring-carts were India for me, with its jingling *tongas*. There was a country-town richness in the air, and the smell of animals going up the cobbled streets to market. We passed a hunter bringing in tiny deer no bigger than roe to be sold as live meat in the market. Women, hurrying in the same direction, flapped over the stones in their home-made slippers of rice straw.

The soapstone prophet Joel declaims to a vanished eighteenth century world of gold-mining

The prophet Isaiah is another of the twelve by the crippled genius O Aleijadinho

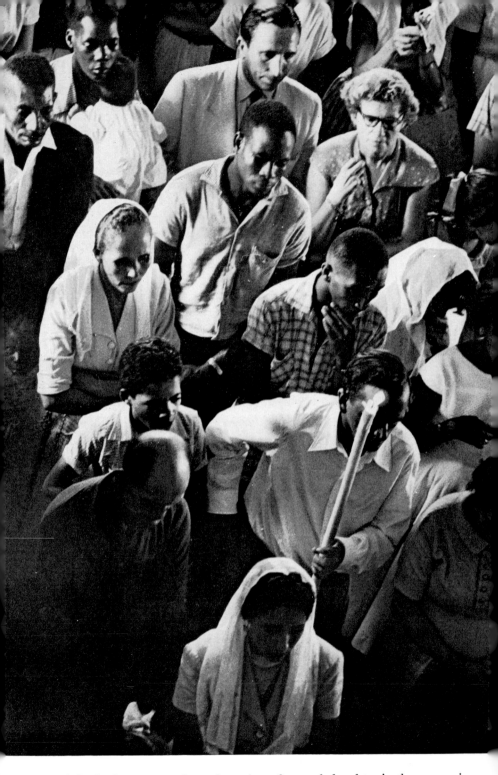

A hushed moment, solemn faces, but afterwards laughter in the sun again

Overfull gardens spilled their plants across the pavements—Michaelmas daisies, hibiscus, blue and white agapanthus lilies, dahlias, roses, and the most brilliant blues of morning glory draped the red walls. But in Brazil the morning glory was outshone by another ipomoea of the same genus of the convolvulus family, the *ipomoea cairica*. This white flower bore the faintest blush of pink, and deep in its trumpet was the bright stain of crimson.

I saw also araucaria pines. These trees were not used to gratify a gardener's fancy but as a major Brazilian export. Luckily for Brazil, millions of acres were covered by araucaria. The *Rubens* often carried cargoes of it back to England. But we did not linger in the town, for Goiania was our main objective—including a *churrascaria* to whose meat-on-the-spit my thoughts were already turning. Just outside Anapolis we passed a band of ragged gypsies with tents pitched and horses tethered. And afterwards the landscape changed again and all the thriving greenery grew to greater height. The stunted trees which dotted the plains around Brasilia, and the low bushland we saw on the way to Anapolis, now became real Brazilian forest. But burning and clearing was going on there also. Forty-foot-high trunks stood scorched and dead, spaced in the maize-fields. The herds were bigger. Creamery lorries passed us more frequently.

On most farms the palm-trees, of course, had been saved in the clearing process. Humboldt referred to the carnauba palm as the 'Tree of Life'. This was true, but real credit should have been given to the ingenuity of the Brazilians who used it. They put this palm to a hundred uses, and built houses and bridges with it. The trunks could be used for making telegraph poles. The leaves and tough fibres also had endless purposes, from mats to fishing nets. Poor people used its seeds instead of coffee (in Brazil!) and the ashes of its roots as salt. In the north-east *candango* country the carnauba was called the 'Tree of Providence.' English ships' captains would have agreed, for a cargo of the wax which seeped out of the palm's leaves meant big money. They would rather carry a tiny cargo of the wax than a large one of pine timber or coffee.

Goiania's saving grace was its beautiful avenues of trees which both shaded the streets and helped to hide its nondescript buildings. Gardens and flowering things were everywhere. Palms lined some of the streets and in others there was the flaming splash of flamboyant still in bloom. Creepers mercifully concealed much of the offending architecture. Goiania had enough atmosphere to keep casual visitors happy without realizing the town was only in its third decade. My visit with the Konens was during carnival, but except for negroes dancing in an unfinished building and children walking about with grease paint and paper hats there was nothing to be seen. There was nothing approaching Rio's carnival extravagances. In the letting down of hair, Rapunzel of the fairy-tale had nothing compared with Rio's four mad days and the *Cariocas'* release of a year's pent-up inhibitions. This return to the wild excesses of Brazil's early colonial days was not without its cost. Nearly seven thousand people were treated in Rio's hospital for carnival wounds and bruises, while police did their best to cope with thirteen murders, three suicides, nearly ninety assaults and almost five hundred fights. Not bad going and, from the *Cariocas'* point of view, perfectly plausible in the face of forty dull Lenten days to follow.

In Goiania it might have been Lent rather than carnival. But we made our own celebration, for young Carlos Konen bought a cylinder of ether and perfume—the carnival weapon. It cost ten shillings and was soon replaced by another—an expensive though sure way of attracting girls' attentions. The ether and perfume were packed under pressure in the canister. A plastic button released a thin, numbing jet. By the time we left quite a few shapely calves, brown arms and round young necks had felt the sting of Carlos' aim.

Like the palms, this carnival liquid could be used in many ways. Formerly it was packed in glass bottles, which often exploded. President Janio Quadros, Kubitschek's successor, got his eye trouble from the liquid fiend. For years it was banned, but nevertheless sales soared. Some people drank it, and even in quiet Goiania we saw some youths inhaling from handkerchiefs and doping themselves to induce the carnival mood. Doctors have used it in emergency as a local anaesthetic. But in spite of such goads, Goiania plodded on undisturbed by carnival. It was hot and we wandered through the market and into the town's surprising number of bookshops, where favourite biographies seemed to be of Oscar Wilde, Disraeli, and Madame Curie. We left in the late afternoon, using up the rest of the ether spray long before we saw Brasilia's towers shining on the plain again.

More exciting fare than the wholesome capital of Goias was a small settlement on the Rio Araguaia several hundred miles south of Bananal. An hour and a half's flying from Goiania brought me to Aragarças—a flight which finally convinced me that I could never be a hero. I went with Dr. Raul de Oliveira. He was secretary-general of the Fundação Brasil Central. The previous day a party had left to fly up to the Xingu, deep in the Indians' country. The three Villas Boas brothers had arranged for orange trees to be taken from my friend Jesco von Puttkamer's farm. The brothers were hoping in this way to start improvement in the Indians' diet and so help to secure the tribes' survival. Numbers had declined drastically. From a once flourishing tribe only one male remained, and was the only man left in the world speaking his own language. It was in the Xingu region where the brothers found what they claimed as Colonel Fawcett's skeleton.

Unfortunately I could not travel with the group going to show the Xingu Indians how to plant and cultivate the trees. But I went next day to catch the party on their return journey at Aragarças. Raul invited me to share his little plane. I felt nervous as soon as I saw the toy thing parked at the side of the airport runway. The inside was smaller than a small car. The Brazilians called the craft a *bonança*. Raul said that the Fundação had owned one previously, but that it crashed, killing those on board. Fortunately the plane could only hold the pilot and two or three passengers. We left Brasilia, making a detour to Goiania to pick up some rabies vaccine. Somebody at Aragarças had been bitten by a mad dog.

Fortunately our pilot had many hundreds of flying hours in the difficult interior region. This and newspapers helped to keep me composed for the first part of the flight. We stopped to eat at

Goiania's tiny airport and during the meal I discovered more about Raul. I already knew that he was one of Brazil's heroes in the Second World War. But Brasilia was always full of rumours and romances and Raul was always too busy to talk about himself. And because he was so quiet and retiring, I thought possibly my informant had exaggerated. But while we were lunching, Raul accidentally knocked his side and it made a most alarming sound. He laughed and said that his body was encased in metal plates because of his war wounds. The rest of him was also fairly well shot. In fact, he had been blown up in one way or another three times in the Libyan desert. By coincidence, an English ambulance man who once came to collect the pieces of Raul which remained, did so a second time. Raul still remembers his four-lettered language of surprise. 'Why', he asked me in Goiania, 'do English soldiers use this word?' It was difficult to explain. Then Raul told me that he had not waited for Brazil to enter the war, but had joined the French Foreign Legion as a teenager. He stayed with the Legion for four years before being discharged as a physical wreck. In fact, he went off to the war so quietly that even his family knew nothing until a B.B.C. telegram arrived, asking them to listen in to a message from Raul at the front. But I found him the same about his position as head of the vast organization which was responsible for opening up the interior and preserving the Indians' identity as a people. Nobody would suspect his character from his appearance, any more than they would suspect the genius from the appearance of his friend, Oscar Niemeyer.

During the first hour of the journey to Aragarças I tried to snatch a siesta. But the words of an Australian flying-doctor I met in Brasilia kept recurring—never fly in a single-engine monoplane. He had said the doctors in the bush were advised not to do so. And there we were, thousands of feet above uninhabited Brazilian forest. Whether this was better than the tree-hopping I did around Bananal I could not tell. But then I saw with relief the gleam of water ahead and Raul pointed out the Araguaia river. Then we were flying low over the little town of Aragarças. Raul showed me the diamentiferous beds where we could see a few black figures panning hopefully in the mounds of stones by the river. Unlike African diamonds,

Brazilian brilliants were not mined from rocks. They usually occurred inside river-bed pebbles, or on mountain-sides. Some finds had even caused world attention, like the Star of the South, and the fabulous green *Diamante de Dresde*. The Getulio Vargas diamond found in 1938 took third place in the world heavyweight championship with 745.5 carats. There were diamonds at Aragarças just for the asking. At the hotel in the evening a man came up with two quite big yellow stones in his pocket.

More remarkable, and to me at least, more beautiful, was a small spherical boulder given to Raul. It was perfectly rounded by being rolled over and over in the river bed. Its yellow, marble-like stone was smooth and seemed to hold sunlight like a ball poised on a gatepost in an Italian garden.

Unexpectedly, Aragarças' surroundings were quite Arcadian, an effect produced mostly by slender, delicately foliated eucalyptus trees. The hotel had a cloister-like arrangement with a central arcaded courtyard. It temporarily housed the local museum's collection of stuffed animals and birds, until the new museum building should be completed. I lighted on these with a gleam in my eye, for they promised to tell me the names of many birds I had seen. But alas, the man who carried them thence from the museum was illiterate and he had hopelessly mixed up the identification cards. There was no solution to the puzzle. I hoped more than ever that, besides building roads and dams and opening the interior, Brazil would also grapple with its problem of an illiterate population.

Raul had Fundação affairs to attend to. He arranged for a jeep to take me across the Araguaia over its new bridge and, of all things, to some hot springs. Brazil, apparently, had no end to its surprises. Little Aragarças itself had attained minor fame. Besides diamonds, it was noted for its connection with an Air Force insurrection during the Kubitschek government. When we got out of the tiny plane at the air-strip, I had noticed some jagged wreckage at the side—the revolution's sole remains. At that time, Captain Galvão and the *Santa Maria* were still headline news, not without a certain wicked delight for me, as I was once on board the *Santa Maria* and involved in a fight between Portuguese and Italian immigrants. But the

Brazilian airborne revolution came to nothing at the hands of a few paratroopers.

The sulphurous radioactive hot springs were not in Goias State, but across the border into Mato Grosso. This state was *grosso* indeed, being very much larger than the whole Iberian peninsula but with a population of only half a million. The way to the springs lay along quite a pretty lane. At places it deceived me into thinking it was Irish, and especially as we passed a boy wheeling a barrow of the same size and shape as the turf-barrows of County Meath. But such strange similarities occurred throughout the whole of South America. Another was the *faja*, a woven belt worn by bachelor Otavalo Indians in Equador, a belt with the same design and colours as the *criss* of the Aran Islands.

In Ireland, however, one would be unlikely to be joined by a farmer carrying the spotted skin of a *jaguatirica*, a sort of jaguar. He had shot it three days before near Aragarças. We halted the jeep to give him a ride and he told me that wild life abounded in the district. His interest was only in the skin trade provided by the big cats and panthers, otters and deer. There was even a big, sandy wolf which did much damage to the flocks and herds, though it did not run in a pack and was a notorious coward.

The farmer also carried a very high haunch of tapir, a meat which I ate and enjoyed on two occasions in Brazil. This curious-looking creature was known in the Americas as the king of the animals on account of his size and great strength. A Brazilian legend tells of the tapir and the ant-eater. Once in the year King Tapir gave a feast to all his animal vassals. Everyone went and were on the best of terms, eagles chatting merrily to the weakest of lambs, ounces purring into the ears of deer. The party had an early start, for King Tapir was an early riser and expected all his guests to greet him as soon as the sun came up. But it was already midday before the ant-eater appeared. In his shaggy coat he carried a vast swarm of ants. He looked apprehensively at King Tapir, for those were the days of yore in South America where lateness was the unforgivable sin—indeed, latecomers were never pardoned.

But the poor ant-eater begged leave to present his case. Going along the road in excellent time he had met the ants all done up in their finery and also making an early start for the party. They asked the ant-eater to give them a ride and he, being a considerate animal, agreed. But it had taken many hours for the stately ant procession to get aboard his beautiful, droopy, umbrella tail and on to his back. Hearing this, all the forest beasts fell silent and waited with bated breath for King Tapir's judgement. Looking at the contrite ant-eater, the tapir noticed his fine teeth, the best teeth, in fact, of any animal present. King Tapir mitigated the usual harsh sentence for lateness, and decreed that the ant-eater should lose his teeth and have instead a long thin tongue. Ever afterwards this would enable him to destroy the ants which had caused his disgrace, so that to this day the ant-eater's tongue can worm its way into any anthill.

Our farmer got out of the jeep to talk with a man on a horse. The man's left leg was much shorter than his right and had no foot so that the stirrups were accordingly adjusted. We passed through the grassy streets of the old Aragarças village, which much reminded me of São Felix. And then we got on to a rough track running at the foot of forest-covered mountain. There was nobody at the hot springs. I walked down a bank to a swift brown stream and saw the pool beside it. A faint steam curled up from its surface. But it was crystal clear and crystal coloured and had a smooth sand bottom. I lay in it, floating without effort because of its strange buoyancy. There was no noise except the stream's babbling and the forest's sounds. Insects kept plopping into the pool from the overhanging trees.

I relaxed and floated in the slightly vaporising water without a care. This was more than I had done in the Araguaia river at Bananal. It had been wonderful to splash in the shallows with the Indian children. And when Osvaldo took the boat and we went among half-submerged forests and lily lagoons, I thought the river was the most beautiful thing in Brazil. Yet treachery was concealed there, not because of the flood-season's currents, but because of *piranhas*. These deadly fish swarmed in millions throughout the vast length of the Araguaia river. They were meat-eaters, devourers of living flesh, and were equipped with teeth as sharp as razor-blades for cutting their unfortunate victims to pieces. A single drop of blood in the water would attract dozens of them within seconds.

Indian fears about their boats being overturned on the river during bad weather were not so much concerned with alligators and water snakes as with *piranhas*. There was no escape for man or beast when they attacked. Waving red rags at bulls was no doubt just an idle belief, but throwing a red rag to the *piranhas* was said to be a practical way of decoying these insatiable bloodthirsty fish. When *piranhas* have surrounded small boats on the Araguaia a red cloth thrown out has supposedly drawn them off for a while. It deceived them into thinking a patch of blood floated behind. Fortunately, I did not have to try this myself—although when I was a small boy I courted danger by waving my cousin's Salvation Army jersey at a whole series of bulls without rousing a trace of spleen.

On the bank above the hot springs, a lorry arrived with a rowdy crowd of thirty boys, besides men with their young children. It was bath day. The women and girls went off to an even hotter spring while the boys jumped into mine, whipping and churning the water as excitedly as any school of *piranhas*. The older men sat shaving at the pool's edge, allowing the rotund babies to paddle. The youths took deep breaths and submerged themselves to see which of them could remain longest under water. Because none of them owned a watch, I did the timing.

Even though it was the coolest spring, the heat of the water affected the adolescents in a most uninhibited fashion. But no one, not even fathers or older brothers, took the slightest notice of what to some British eyes, say on Brighton beach, would have been an outrage. Once or twice older youths got out of the water to cool off. They took revolvers from their high boots and fired a whole maga-zine into the air, out of sheer joy and to hear the animals' fright and the birds' flutter. Though darkness now seeped through the forest, they all continued to lie in the pool like obstinate water-buffaloes refusing to budge from mud-holes.

The others of our party were back from the Xingu where the orange trees had been planted that morning. We sat down together in the hotel dining-room, whose roof was held up by lopped tree-trunks, and set about a delicious, hefty farmhouse meal. The party was curiously and accidentally mixed and so made conversation as good as the food. There was the president of the high court of Goias, Fundação heads of departments and two women writers. Both of the latter had once been pioneer farmers out in the Central Plateau long before Brasilia appeared on the scene, and could make their own clothes from home-grown, home-spun cotton. There was also a university lecturer, and a shambling Vaughan Williams-looking sort of man, hiding shyly behind dark glasses. He knew more about Brazilian Indians than anyone else had ever done—Claudio Villas Boas.

I had wanted very much to talk with Claudio, but both Raul and Jesco warned me how difficult it was to get to know him, although both of them had worked with him over the Indians for many years. I had already spoken to his two brothers, but at my first meeting with him Claudio had only smiled. However, I could not restrain the urgent feeling that I had to talk with him.

At about that time Jesco had been living up in the Xingu area and, as usual, taking hundreds of his wonderful photographs of the Indians. Among them was one of a little girl holding up what looked like a stone, scored with lines. In fact, it was one among thousands of ceramic fragments lying buried under forest undergrowth. These pieces of ceramic pots were of three distinct kinds and were obviously the remains of some civilization quite different from that of the Indians. More exciting still was the remains of a great ditch which Jesco and Claudio discovered. Running for over a mile, it protected the landward side of a promontory at the confluence of the Xingu and a lesser river called the Suiá-missú. The burning question was, had there been a highly developed settlement within the confines of the moat and the rivers? And was it the lost city Colonel Fawcett sought on his last and fatal journey to the mysterious 'Z'?

Ironically, Claudio actually lived on this site. In that region, some miles away, the brothers had found the controversial skeleton. At this point one had to tread warily with Claudio Villas Boas. All those present at the hotel knew the story of Fawcett's surviving son, Brian, and how the group with Brian in Brazil had opened up the grave, and how they disagreed so fundamentally with the brothers about the skeleton's identity. Claudio rarely discussed the matter. Being certain and adamant in his views, beyond that he had no further concern, certainly not from a publicity point of view. But rushing in where angels would have feared, I inveigled the shy Claudio into my room.

We had some difficulty over language, but I managed to convey to him my interest in the 'book'. Ah yes! Claudio beamed, was this the book about the Xingu by Adrian from Oxford, who had lived with Claudio in his Indian hut for eight months, some years back now? No? I showed him some photographs I had taken of birds and Indians to keep Claudio's interest up. Then elliptically, I veered back to the topic of English writers who had come to pry into the secrets of the Xingu. Claudio's face brightened again and he grinned like a great boy. Ah yes! Aldous Huxley. Claudio had got on fine with him. A splendid man who wanted no truck with newspapers or Indian bows and arrows to sell in souvenir shops.

Equivocation was getting me nowhere—so I asked outright about the grave of the Englishman, *the* grave. Claudio withdrew at once and sat clenching and unclenching his hands. Then he affirmed quite simply that he was without any doubts whatsoever that the human remains he had discovered were those of Colonel Fawcett. Claudio had his good reasons for being certain. But he was not prepared to give a 'story' about it. He wanted no limelight himself nor unwelcome, disruptive and perhaps mischievous attention focused on his Indian friends. A knock at my door saved him. He jumped up to open it and escaped. At our meetings afterwards, including a long journey together, Claudio never mentioned the subject again.

Raul told me of Claudio's pre-eminence in all Indian matters for many years. He, perhaps more than his brothers, had risked his life in ending hostilities between warring Indian tribes. That was a claim of significance, for Claudio was not alone among the brothers in this. A recent article in *Time* told how Orlando turned down President Janio Quadros's request for him to be head of the Indian Protection Service. The magazine then gave some amazing accounts of Orlando's escapes over the years from flying hostile arrows. It was to Orlando's credit that he turned down this offer of high office to return to the Indians' country to live 'native', even to the extent of eating locusts and wild honey when there was nothing else for the tribesmen. But the elusive Claudio kept even more away from any limelight. There were no photographs of him in *Time* magazine. Nor was there even mention of him in *Exploration Fawcett*. There Brian Fawcett referred to Orlando as the 'Great *sertanista*', that is a man who lives in Brazil's back of beyond. But the savage tribes Brian's father encountered have called Claudio their 'great white father' for years.

The Xingu was known as 'the Scientists' Grave'. One of Colonel Fawcett's last letters told how they encountered the first of the still-wild Indians, 'naked savages from the Xingu'—much to the delight of Jack, his eldest son, who was on the expedition, too. Many learned men went into the forests, but not all departed alive, and Claudio was not going to betray any tribal secret concerning Fawcett's death. Such a secret certainly existed among the Indians, so I was told, and if anyone knew it Claudio Villas Boas did. He had no objection to people planting orange trees or helping to fight disease among his Indians. But Claudio definitely had no story for pressmen and no fanatical interest in one dead man's bones. He had only the care and nurture of his people at heart, those whom he wished to protect from corruptions of civilization and the real-estate sharks—the *grileiros*.

Perhaps the Villas Boas brothers were reluctant to go on about the Fawcett affair because there had been so much pointless discussion and theorizing by outsiders ever since the party's disappearance in 1925. Besides, the brothers had the protection of the whole region around the Xingu and Araguaia rivers almost entirely on their own shoulders. It was both tragic and intriguing about the three Englishmen. But staring the brothers in the face was a far worse destruction of human life. More pressing than concern about three dead Englishmen, more alarming by far was the imminent, threatened extermination of whole Indian tribes, of noble savages, if savages they must be in Fawcett language.

The *grileiros,* the real-estate gangsters, brought all the latest equipment to bear on their inhuman activities. Complete and detailed aerial surveys had been made of the Xingu area, so that the land could be parcelled out in lots for selling. The real-estate companies evaded the Government restriction on the amount of land which any one person or company can purchase by having hundreds of owners whose ownership was nominal only, for a suitable fee. The whole area had now been bought up by this means from the state of Mato Grosso. It was the most fertile land of the whole region, the only land where the Indians could, in fact, survive. Many tribes had migrated to the Xingu basin because of its fertility. Yet the real-estate sharks had no care as to what sort of land it was in which they dealt. Barren or fertile, necessary or not to human life, it represented to them only so much satisfaction of their vile greed.

The aerial survey made for these companies has been called an 'infernal instrument' by a well-known Brazilian engaged in the fight against the murderous speculation. The Brazilian Indian in his natural state was noble indeed. Now that the Villas Boas had pacified many of the tribes, their way of life had dignity. Physically the Indians were strong and handsome, morally they were uncorrupt. Yet because modern Western ways had not touched them, it invariably destroyed them when it did. There was no gradual adaptation.

But perhaps an even more direct form of extermination was threatened. In Rio de Janeiro I heard rumours, which were from clergy and said to be true, that the Xingu land was being sold guaranteed free from Indians. No less than eighty Indians were said to have disappeared at once from one area. This news came from a missionary down in Rio from Mato Grosso. Yet what could be done? The real-estate transactions were just on the right side of the law, in fact they had support from high political officials who had long harboured animosity against the Villas Boas brothers. To police an area of the interior which was as big as Europe was impossible. Whole tribes could be murdered and nobody would ever know. Even before his 1961 assumption of office Brazil's new President, Janio Quadros, had interested himself in the Villas Boas' work, and had made it clear where his sympathies lay. He had been to live with the brothers in the Xingu on three occasions, and he alone had sufficient power and authority to stop the rot of corruption, or at the very least let his Government make 28,000 square miles of the Xingu an Indian reserve. Janio, as he was known popularly, came to power with a broom as his symbol. While he was Governor of São Paulo State he cleared out much of the corruption. His maiden presidential speech reaffirmed that he had brought 'the big broom' to the whole country. But Janio was soon in exile. Perhaps his successors will continue his opposition to the *grileiros* before the fate of North America's Red Indians in the last century overtakes the Brazilian Indian of this century.

It would be tragedy indeed if so high a price had to be paid for Brazil's bold advance from the coast to the interior.

8

Gold Rush

Brasilia always seemed to be more sky than land. Also, the sunsets were spectacular, whether there was an aerial lake of flamingo, or gilded towers piled in the clear darkening blue. Some such towers reared in the sky when I left the Do Re Mi hostel for the last time. A tall column of cloud stood up from the horizon, like a painted wooden cloud in a baroque niche. The cloud-tower's sides were coloured white and yellow and pink. Its edges were touched with gilding. Spread fanwise behind, rays shot out, one of light and the next of shadow, as rays come from the Holy Ghost dove in religious carvings.

Nothing could have been more appropriate. I was going to Ouro Preto, a little town of carved masterpieces which hid itself in the mountains near Belo Horizonte. I had decided to travel from Brasilia to Belo Horizonte not only by bus, but also overnight. This meant that although I would lose all sleep during the fourteen hours' journey, I would at least see dawn taking the beautiful landscapes of Minas Gerais unawares. And dawn, after all, ought to follow sunset.

Brasilia's sunset sky was so exaggerated in its beauty as to be almost in bad taste. Yet while leaning out of Herbert Konen's jeep to watch it, the sun went lower and all the colour faded, leaving the cloud as nothing but a grey lump in the sky. Herbert was taking me to pick up the Belo Horizonte bus after a last beer together. This last beer included, of course, my friend Bob Tanner, whose cheery talk and yarns about his long life in the army had livened up many hours for me in Brasilia.

Whenever we met, we 'split' a beer, as he called it. Bob was in Brasilia as security guard of the British Embassy, and I first visited him when he was isolated in the Ministry of Works' nasty new building. He was its sole occupant until a skeleton staff moved up from Rio de Janeiro. Because so much of the city had still to be built around the embassy, it might have been a desert island, but Bob did not remain completely alone. One day a ginger kitten attached itself to him when we were having lunch in the W.3 district. The kitten went home in Bob's shirt. When the time came for me to 'split' a last beer, the kitten had already grown into a cat of character. But Bob was no fonder of his stray kitten than he was of the homeless urchins who came begging along the W.3 road. They always knew that his wallet would be opened with some feigned gruffness, some expression in the strange Cockney-like tongue which they did not understand. In official records, Bob was only a security guard. Yet he was known and liked by Brazilians and was more likely to achieve friendly relations by his ever-ready smile under a shock of white hair than ever would the dark suits and dead-pan expressions of *socialité* diplomats.

So Bob and Herbert both came to pick me up at Do Re Mi. Had she seen my things being loaded into the jeep, Creepy would have come to the bus station, too. She had been another star of my Brasilia stay; literally, for she was really called Estrelita—Little Star. 'Creepy' was my nickname for her, because as she went round cleaning my block at Do Re Mi every day her thoughts drifted away into dreams. She would stand by a window, her black Indian-looking eyes bright, and then at my approach glide away with a mysterious smile. I had always found it hard to believe that Creepy the dreamer was practical enough to build herself a wooden hut near the hostel, put plants in pots by its door and turn it, as far as huts can be, into a home. We had to pass the hut on the way, and so I could shout '*Bo' noite*, Creepy!' as I had done on scores of nights when going home late to Do Re Mi. Creepy and Bob were also on excellent terms. On her side their acquaintance was tinged with awe. Bob's portly figure, florid face, white hair and his impressive manner made her believe that he was the British Ambassador himself. And Creepy refuted any suggestion to the contrary.

The jeep hurried past the hut, where a square of window and

cracks in its wooden sides glowed with oil-lamp light. But the city was already a brilliant beacon in the wide darkness of the plateau, as I had seen it every evening at sundown. Now the clouds were lead instead of gold. The sky's majestic black, in which all the firmament would be hung, was still dreamy with the pasty wash of the last sun. This lingering light was cold and blue. And when it fell on the Congress towers and domes it changed them into the frailest, most delicate of Wedgwood china, ivory against the muted blue of the eastern sky. And in this exquisite form, Brasilia's centre appeared to me for the last time. It was how I had always imagined visions ought to be, ethereal, insubstantial.

To leave Brasilia for Ouro Preto was merely to exchange one vision for another. Unfortunately, to attain the second vision I would have to pass through Belo Horizonte, a town against which I was admittedly prejudiced. At best I expected to find Belo Horizonte surrounded by ugly suburbs, crammed full with monstrosities of modern architecture in the centre, besides being difficult to get in and out again. This idea of mine was pieced together like an old *azulejos* mural, from other people's experiences. But it proved, in the event, to be fairly accurate. With Ouro Preto only a further two hours' bus ride away up in the mountains I could not resist the temptation to pretend that Belo Horizonte did not exist. So I made my farewells to Bob and Herbert and prepared to face the all-night rush through Minas Gerais State.

I found it hard to believe that after so many years of wanting to I was actually on the way to the tiny mountain town. Its hills, I knew, were each crowned by an exquisite rococo church. And there were carved saints and prophets, angels and martyrs, altarpieces and ceilings, and a flood of other rich carving which revealed the eighteenth-century vision of heaven. But, though beautiful, the paradise revealed by Ouro Preto's architecture and sculpture was decidedly a paradise promised. For most of its inhabitants, Ouro Preto's heyday had been hell. It was especially so for the slaves who sweated and suffered in its goldmines. And perhaps for more than anyone else it was hell for the man who saw heaven and fashioned it from the stones of the earth.

GOLD RUSH

Antonio Francisco Lisboa, given world recognition since as a sculptor and architect of genius, was called *O Aleijadinho*, The Little Cripple. In spite of his physical agonies he, more than anyone, brought heaven to Ouro Preto. And because of his own pains he may have brought hope into the desperation of captivity he saw around him. O Aleijadinho well understood what slavery was, for his own mother Isabel was an African slave. He was a dark mulatto himself. And to be so, even by a quarter part, in the Ouro Preto of those days was to be socially outcast, even though Antonio was himself born free. Undoubtedly from his mother he caught the fever of spirit, the emotional intensity, and the feeling for plastic form which made his sculptured heaven so human. If tears and suffering and the love of God made Man have ever been expressed in art, then The Little Cripple did so. Black blood lent him passion, and his negro spirituals were of stone and wood.

From his mother the passion, but from his father the skill of eye and hand to give the passion its outlet. O Aleijadinho's father, Manuel Francisco Lisboa, was a Portuguese master builder, and undoubtedly skilled in his craft. He built churches, often making the designs himself. The designs were patterned on the Portuguese twin-towered type of church as adopted in Brazil, in a plain fashion by the Jesuits and more ornately by the Franciscans. Manuel would remember the churches of his homeland, for he was an immigrant from Portugal, and was not born in Brazil. He was probably drawn like hundreds of others to the mountain town, attracted by the gold rush.

Unlike most other gold rushes, the one in the late seventeenth-century Minas Gerais left a permanent architectural mark of great beauty. There was nothing similar to the Australian ghost town or the Klondike straggle of shacks. No doubt the Brazilian adventurers thought the source of gold inexhaustible, for among the mountains of mist and sun permanent towns quickly appeared—Mariana, São João d'El Rey, Sabará, Congonhas do Campo. And, of course, there was the chief among them, Ouro Preto—Black Gold.

Originally, the place had a more plebeian name—Villa Rica, Rich Town. From the beginning it thrived more than the other towns and was more ambitious. The goldmine owners were ruthless and more brutal to slaves than were even the sugar-planters of north-east Brazil. Masters and slaves alike lived wildly, prodigally. Emotion and lust went unbridled. There was neither prevention nor cure for gold fever.

It was to be the role of the nineteenth and twentieth centuries to express the possession of wealth by debased art and the destruction of landscape. Perhaps this fitted the worship of mammon. In eighteenth-century Ouro Preto, the Trinity, the Virgin and the Saints were worshipped. This may well have been a strictly practical affair, ensuring for the masters wealth here and life eternal here-after, and for the slaves comfort, and a hope for the easing of their pains after death. For whatever reason, God was worshipped. And for this purpose His churches were set on hills.

The aim of the church builders was not only to provide a place where masses could be said and relics housed but also to make visible the invisible. If the air around them was full of angels and spirits and if God looked down, as in Ouro Preto they thought was the case, then such things could be made plain for all to see. As the priest turned bread and wine into the divine flesh and blood on the altar, so the sculptor and the painter turned stone, wood, canvas and paint into no less real presences. Where The Little Cripple excelled was in the unique intensity of his vision and his unique skill in bringing dead material to life. He also possessed a strong sense of narrative, so that his carvings telling again the story of the Passion could add an emotional content no doubt present at the event, but absent in the sparse Gospel accounts. But more than this, he told the story of Ouro Preto's febrile life, and most of all the story of his own burning, yet poignant experience.

Isabel, the negress slave of Manuel Lisboa, the master builder, bore him this illegitimate son at Ouro Preto in 1730. The gold rush was already in its fourth decade, and a pattern of existence had emerged, a pattern of violence. The possibilities of rebellions by the numerically superior slaves were never out of mind. There were outlaws, too, who terrified and robbed the quieter citizens. And there were always rumblings of revolution amongst the miners against the Government, which took a fifth of their findings as tax. Once a year the Portuguese shipped their treasure from Brazil to Portugal. In 1753 the argosies carried bullion valued even in those days at three million pounds. This gold was used partly to pay English manufacturers and merchants who had sole rights to sell in the Portuguese empire. Ouro Preto was therefore important to Portugal, and governors who ruled the town were velvet gloved and iron fisted. Miners' insurrections were put down by a force and cruelty equal to that which the miners used on their own slaves. Ouro Preto's life from the beginning was fierce and hot-blooded and only the sudden exhaustion of gold in the Minas Gerais hills and rivers brought an end to the pattern.

No doubt the little coloured boy, Antonio, grew up happily enough, living at first with his own mother, and afterwards with his stepmother when his father married. But it may have been during these formative years that he began the neurotic tendencies which developed more fully under the stress of his later mutilations. Antonio was healthy, and nobody could have guessed that a terrible disease would strike him in early middle age. He was also sensitive and receptive. With Ouro Preto still growing, the boy had plenty of activities to interest him. The nearest to hand would have been his father's building sites and work-shops. Artists and decorators from other parts of Brazil worked in the town, and although none was of great note, at least young Antonio had a new world opened to him.

Like most boys, Antonio probably tried his hand at making things in wood. He was almost certainly apprenticed in his father's work-shop while still a boy, and later was hired by master craftsmen who were working on church decoration. It is not known that he was ever trained by an artist. Nor is it known whether there was anybody wise or knowledgeable enough to observe that the boy was exceptionally talented. When he was twenty-eight years old Antonio Francisco Lisboa was recorded as being a self-employed craftsman.

But Antonio was an artist by temperament and, after a little while, by achievement also. This and the tempo of Ouro Preto's life, it may be supposed, led the young Antonio to spend himself completely. Descriptions exist which show him as a lusty, energetic young man, as aware of his body and others' as he was of his soul. Yet other suggestions have been made since that the aggressive moroseness which coloured his later years would have been there anyway, disease or no, because of repressions in Antonio's youth. This is possibly partly true, for being a mulatto he could not join his fellows in everything, nor yet was he a slave. To be neither one nor the other in a society which was exclusively on a master and slave footing would certainly have meant being a misfit.

The shadow was already round the man Antonio which was to darken his later life. Nobody knows exactly what the disease was. Nor do they know whether he inherited it or contracted it himself. What is known, is the bitterness of his losing struggle. Antonio led a normal life until he was forty, though church accounts exist showing expenses for having him carried to it. This might mean that his disease began even earlier. Whenever it was, the malady consumed him, eating away his flesh and bones, not even sparing his skilful fingers.

The pain was a fire which burned not only Antonio's fingers and feet but his whole body. And the fire was never extinguished until the sculptor's ravaged body was dead. But the fire was slow. The man who now became O Aleijadinho, the Little Cripple, worked on the churches of Ouro Preto and the region round about for another forty years. During those years his finest work was done.

The Little Cripple was equally adept at carving the rococo façades of the churches or at decorating their interiors. He could work on their bold masonry modelling, or on the elaborate and fantastical altarpieces and groups of figures. The various religious orders who were building the churches all wanted his services, and he was never short of commissions. Sometimes, perhaps because of the pressure of work, he made designs which others executed. At Congonhas do Campo, a town near Ouro Preto, he used other craftsmen to do the heavy roughing-out on his statues of the twelve prophets, but by then he was an old man weakened by long years of disease. These were noble, declamatory prophets standing about the steps up to the church of the Good Jesus. The Little Cripple gave them vigorous forms, and made their gestures and faces full of forceful utterance. The mining community was as wayward a people as the children of Israel, and well might the Old Testament prophets address them. This emotional work, together with six life-size Passion scenes full of pathos and suffering was, and still is, considered O Aleijadinho's masterpiece. But he *was* a cripple and in his eighties before the figures were finished. The disease had been devouring him for decades. By this time Antonio could no longer walk. Instead, leather pads were fixed to his knees and he crawled along the scaffolding of the churches. His hands were likewise destroyed, but Antonio's fierce determination drove him to the stone walls or the sculptor's yard. The tools were strapped to the stumps which were all that remained of his hands. For the Little Cripple, life was not a struggle for survival, but a struggle for the creation of sculpture.

O Aleijadinho's chisels rang against the Minas Gerais stones and each blow of the mallet must have given him pain. And this was the relentless artist in him driving him on. But there were other, no less compelling forces. They were ghostly.

O Aleijadinho was caught up in mystical existence. The heaven which he and other artists were carving and chiselling was not merely a way of demonstrating what the priests were talking about. The beautiful figures of flying angels, of saints in glory, or of the Virgin amid moon and stars, were fragmentary glimpses of the heaven which they thought existed all around them. The priests could reveal it to human eyes only in the host, but the artists could display its actual glory. In a sense, as much as any mystic or modern worshipper of *Macumba's* gods, O Aleijadinho was possessed by these spirits. For how could he, The Little Cripple, have belief any longer in the power of flesh?

So he, whose flesh was fallen away, subdued it to his will. The pads and straps and cold chisels were fixed every day to his stumps and crumbled bones by his faithful slaves.

And here again there was a curious paradox. A century and a half later it seems impossible to believe that such an extraordinarily powerful atmosphere of religion could have surrounded and inspired

such a commercial undertaking as the gold workings of Minas Gerais
—the General Mines. Still more extraordinary for British eyes
accustomed to the even glare of state welfare, are the violent contrasts of social shadow and highlight which the spiritual authorities
not only condoned but actively promoted. Ouro Preto's life flourished
only because the slaves suffered. The Church saw no wrong in this
and was itself deeply involved in the slave business. Three centuries
had passed since the Pope had ordered Saracens and the like to be
reduced to slavery. What was originally a matter of faith had now
become a matter of commerce.

Wealth and slavery, mysticism and art existed side by side. Even
O Aleijadinho, son of a slave women, owned three slaves himself.
They were hands and feet to him. Doubtless he treated them kindly
enough compared with the brutalities of most masters. Maria
Graham would have found little cause for complaint. She was an
English lady who travelled in Brazil early in the nineteenth century.
Many of the things she saw in the way slaves were treated displeased
her, though at home she would probably have turned not a hair at
chimney-sweep boys or sweated labour in England's new factories.
However, Maria Graham *was* shocked by cruelty in Brazil. She
noted in her journal that she saw 'a white woman, or rather fiend
beating a young negress and twisting her arms cruelly while the
poor creature screamed in agony until some of our gentlemen inter-
ferred'. Noncommittally she reported that the youngest child she
saw offered on the slave market was only two years old.

Maurício, Januário, and Agostinho served their master well. But
the relationship was not without piquancy. Januário, for instance,
was bought more or less fresh from Africa. And on finding himself
owned by such a horribly disfigured master, he tried to commit
suicide with a razor. But luckily, all was not lost and he was snatched
from such an untoward death. In time he became devoted and
faithful to The Little Cripple, and led the mule which carried his
master when he had to go long distances. Maurício, on the other
hand, was singled out for special favour. Although he was a slave,
O Aleijadinho regarded him as an equal. Maurício received a half
share in whatever profits were going from the work in which

Maurício himself took part. The profits, however, were by no means certain, for though the churches wanted his master's work, they did not always pay up. In 1808 O Aleijadinho was complaining of the Carmo church that for his work on two altars there he was paid in 'fake gold'. But, and this Maria Graham would *not* have approved, The Little Cripple was so ill and possessed of such a fractious temper at times that he often beat poor Maurício soundly with the very hammer which the slave had just strapped to his stumps. Maurício was undoubtedly the hero of the hour. At any rate, he stayed inseparable from O Aleijadinho, and Maurício's death must have been one of the most tragic moments in a life of tragedy.

As the disease gradually took possession, defiling and distorting his body, O Aleijadinho withdrew from ordinary human society. His sensitive artistic spirit suffered because people were revolted by the sight of him. The comparatively carefree young man became the embittered middle-aged one. He had nothing to live for except his art. The three slaves transported him from site to site, managed the contraption of straps and pads for his limbs, erected the screens behind which he hid himself, and generally made his existence feasible. He almost certainly taught them his technique of carving. But Maurício always remained the favourite. Perhaps he was the sole human being with whom O Aleijadinho had any communion during those terrible years.

When he got the commission for his figures at Congonhas do Campo, O Aleijadinho went with Maurício. And there, while work on the masterpiece was in progress, Maurício died. Besides pain, desolation was now added to The Little Cripple's burden. Without Maurício he was utterly lost, for nobody knew his needs and whims so well, and certainly nobody could bother to learn them now. But O Aleijadinho worked on. When the sanctuary of the Good Jesus was finished, he returned to Ouro Preto. There was always something to be done to the rich embellishments of São Francisco, a church he had worked on during most of his career.

Somehow, the wreckage of the man drifted into old age. He was poor, and had to work alongside one of his disciples, Justino Ferreira de Andrade. They both lived in a house belonging to a religious order. But the arrangement did not work. Besides being a helpless octogenarian, O Aleijadinho was blind by now. Yet Justino went off for a holiday, leaving the old master quite unable to fend for himself. Earlier in life The Little Cripple had produced a son, and in desperation he crawled along the street to his daughter-in-law's house. The loathsome creature, all that remained of greatness, was taken in. O Aleijadinho lay on some bare boards, longing for death to release him, longing to enter a blissful, ghostly heaven he had spent his life depicting. He knew it so well. But he had to wait two further years on those bare boards before he reached his real heaven. And that was in 1814, on 18th November.

The dream survived the dreamer. Untouched, except by such changes as time could make, O Aleijadinho's marvellous work outlived the gold of Ouro Preto. It came to have a value that the precious metal never had, for what he wrought was priceless. Reckless life ebbed away from Ouro Preto. Its hill-top churches were stranded like hulks blown on to rocks by a storm. The tides of life swirled elsewhere and after the gold was exhausted, never touched the town again. Ouro Preto's population of 100,000 dwindled in a century and a half to 10,000—not even enough to fill all its churches on a feast day. The tides receded down the valleys, away from all the once-rich mountain towns. Heavy green undergrowth healed and covered the old scars of mine workings, and mists came down to move mysteriously as though the gold fever had never been.

Only the wondrous churches remained to speak of the past. São Francisco de Assis at Ouro Preto was among them, and the one I most wanted to see when, if ever, my bus journey ended. Strangely enough, another São Francisco de Assis church also clamoured for attention, and this was the one at Pampulha, near Belo Horizonte. Yet I obstinately refused to budge from Belo Horizonte's bus station, not even to go and see the once-controversial chapel by Niemeyer and Portinari, not even to go and see Niemeyer's latest work, a new yacht club for the city. Being, after all, only in transit between two visions, Brasilia and Ouro Preto, I was in no mood to be reminded of the here-and-now of which Belo Horizonte's suburbs were a most unpleasant reminder. This was not entirely a

rarefied aesthetic reaction or a *fin de siecle* sensitivity to the rudeness
of the modern world. It was simply that Belo's suburbs were sordid
to a degree. They consisted of terrible icing-sugar villas all pink and
consumptive green, filling stations, and waste sites quite unglorified
despite their waterfalls of tumbling morning glory, and a general air
of *nature morte,* very *morte* indeed.

Perhaps I was in an arch mood after travelling in the all-night
bus. But quite definitely, Belo Horizonte could go to the devil so
far as I was concerned, and judging by the number of priests and
nuns at the city's bus station, it must have been considered by the
hierarchy to be already well on the way. While waiting for the
Ouro Preto bus, I sat on my suitcase next to a postulant nun who
had a rucksack on her back and a fat breviary in her tiny hands. A
regular stampede of clergy was in progress. They darted hither,
thither, and back to hither again in a positively gaga manner. They
were not at all helped by their clinging soutanes which were in all
sorts of chic colours besides being faded, soup-stainy and exuding
bus-crowdy smells and, of course, the odour of sweat. Next to the
postulant nun a woman sat all on her own. I could see a brown
breast as she suckled a young boy who was not her last born. Calm
in the centre of the storm.

Having come in at one side of Belo Horizonte, I went out of the
other, rising up at once into the mountains to an accompaniment of
huge advertisement hoardings. These had the dubious honour of
screening from view some of the suburbs on distant hills. Fortunately, civilization stopped very shortly and one of the most beautiful landscapes I had seen anywhere took its place. First we rushed
between long swells of green downland, great rounded folds of hill
shoulder, reaching from climax to climax in smooth leaps. The air
was clear, the light bright, and the sky a limpid, watery blue.

The hills' profile against the sky was sharp, and as I followed
those swooping, graceful curves I wondered where I had seen them
before. The way that the flanks and valleys folded into one another,
the way that their ridges flowed and joined in a pattern of shadowed
surface, was familiar, too. And they were familiar not because of other
landscapes, but from some other shapes which I could not identify.

But when my thoughts strayed again to O Aleijadinho, I knew immediately, for, of course, the rococo curve of pediment and window-head, of dome and scroll, the folds of drapery on those heavenly bodies, were all in the landscape, too.

I found this antiphonal response between Minas Gerais's highly-contrived, voluptuous rococo and the untrammelled run of hills, most exciting. For I believe that nature is made in imitation of art and not the other way round. The English landscape looks like Constable, because we look at it through Constable's eyes, or Cotman's or Bonington's. Nature looks exactly as we want it to look, and if it does not, then we do not look at it. So the Minas Gerais hills, with their gaps allowing glimpses of a vast, serrated blue beyond, looked as though the eighteenth-century Minas Gerais artists had carved them, as though The Little Cripple had been a giant cripple with giant chisels.

The journey up to Ouro Preto delighted me. The shapes of the hills were a preview of the gorgeous carvings I had wanted to see for so many years. So exact was the reproduction in this landscape of the sculptor's typical shapes, the sinuous curve, the fold of drapery, that I was tempted to revert to the idea that artists borrow from nature. *Had* The Little Cripple and the other carvers taken their ideas from the landscape? But no, this was impossible, for everybody knew perfectly well that the style they worked in was the Portuguese edition of the Churrigueresque manner. Their art also came by a rather long and roundabout way from the effervescent style of the Franciscans and from the Jesuits, who got it from the mother country, which got it also in a long and roundabout way from Mannerist Italy with a bit of Vignola's Gesu church thrown in for good luck.

Yet, the Brazilian churches flourished with unique exuberance. The spicy, racy lacing of African culture in Salvador must have influenced architecture there. So in Minas Gerais the potent presence of the hills with their strong sculptural forms probably influenced the native artists, even if only subconsciously.

It was Palm Sunday. By hairs'-breadths only, our bus missed groups of children who were walking home with green palm fronds from the country churches. Palm Sunday was more easily managed in Brazil than in England, where a dried-up strip of palm leaf is all that can be offered to the congregation. But those Minas Gerais children carried great leaves such as only a bishop would have in Ireland. I saw one farmer riding home on his ass from church and he was using his palm branch to beat the poor beast. I wondered what G. K. Chesterton would have thought of that.

It was Lent and the colour of Lent was everywhere. From flanks of the steep green hills, and from pretty, sylvan coppices by the road, clouds of purple blossom shone radiantly. Trees tossed masses of purple flowers on every bough and twig. Down in the valleys and up on the hillsides acres of land were draped for Passiontide. I put my head out of the bus window to see the brilliance of these trees in blossom. The flowers were saturated with colour, a royal purple that sang in the sun. I stared as we sped along by those drifts of gleaming colour, as though by opening my eyes wider I could take more of it in. This was the way I stared at fifteenth-century Flemish altarpiece panels, which glowed with the glory of the artists' transparent paint. But the purple trees of Minas Gerais outshone the Flemings' colours.

In Brasilia I had grown accustomed to the green and olive-green monotone of the stunted plateau bushland, to the hoary-leafed *lixeira* and the milk-juicy *mangabeira*. It was possible to forget what real trees were like. The hills around Ouro Preto seemed so rich compared with the poor growth on the upper plateau. Yet the purple trees were not exquisite solely because of contrast with the scraggy uplands. No daffodil, however gently blown by spring winds under English trees, could ever convey Calvary with such majesty. Deservedly, the purple tree was named after purple Lent— *quaresma*. And the English daffodil, however its trumpet might catch a fitful April sun, could not blaze for Easter with the yellow of yet another blossoming tree in Minas Gerais—the *ipe fedegoso*. The golden drifts of this rivalled the purple and both were ignited by the sun.

The bus climbed up into the mountains and the air grew clearer. The hills were steeper now and gorges yawned beside the road.

And I had a sense of elation, perhaps because of the air, as we dropped a passenger off at a little town called Nova Lima and then ran along the last escarpment to Ouro Preto. And then I saw it, straight ahead. First one church on a hill, white with two towers, then another, and a third, and yet more until the whole town came into view. It lay below us, for the road in was at high level on a shelf half-way up the mountain's flank. I looked down at this exquisite town of mottled pantile roofs and white walls, of steep streets, and crowning churches, each a jewel of architecture. There was profuse vegetation among the little buildings and beyond and above the ring of closing hills.

The apparition vanished in a cloud of dust and the bus dropped like a thunderbolt down to Ouro Preto's square. For some unaccountable reason I kept thinking of Lewes in Sussex. Perhaps it was the streets' steepness, or the pressing presence of the hills. Or perhaps the quiet neatness of the Georgian houses in Lewes was similar to the plain harmony of Ouro Preto's colonial houses. Or I might have thought of Lewes because its peaceful streets had once, like Ouro Preto's, been the scene of martyrdom, and there had been the burning of Protestants at the stake where now the buses start for Brighton.

So, too, in Ouro Preto's square, where I climbed out of the bus from Belo Horizonte, there had once been martyrdom. Violence beyond the normal violence of Ouro Preto's life was done there to the man who roused the greatest passions about Brazil's freedom and independence from Portugal. He was Tiradentes—the Tooth-Puller. My arrival from Brasilia had links with those far-away events. Ouro Preto's bells boomed and echoed round the square for Passion Sunday. The bells had always been renowned for their sonority. At Brasilia's inauguration as the new capital of Brazil, the bells of St. Peter's Rome rang in rejoicing, together with those of Lisbon and of Vienna. Yet Ouro Preto's bells meant more to Brazilians than did all the European carillon. For in Brasilia itself there was one bell from the little mountain town, sent there for the inauguration by order of the Archbishop of Belo Horizonte. This bell was a symbol, for in 1792 it rang to tell the people of Ouro

Preto that the Tooth-Puller was dead, a martyr on the gallows in Rio de Janeiro.

In those days, the goldmine town was still called Villa Rica. It was not only rich, but reluctant to part with its riches in the form of taxes to Portugal. Mad Maria I had forbidden any kind of industry in Brazil except the manufacture of rough cotton cloth for slaves. Yet in spite of this Brazil was wealthy. The Minas Gerais people in particular had ignored her order. This was one reason why they plotted against Portuguese domination. Ouro Preto, still Villa Rica, was the main centre in this matter as in others, and the leaders had their headquarters there.

Most outspoken among them was Joaquim José da Silva Xavier, nicknamed Tiradentes. A revolt was planned. He went down to Rio de Janeiro to rouse support there, and while he was away one of his companions betrayed him. Twelve of the conspirators (the Inconfidentes as they are known in Brazilian history) were condemned to death. But eventually only the Tooth-Puller himself climbed the scaffold on 21st April 1792 in Rio de Janeiro. His body was quartered. Then it was salted. And afterwards the bits and pieces were sent to be exposed along the road to Ouro Preto. The pickled head was reserved for display in Ouro Preto itself, as a salutary warning to other would-be revolutionaries.

This grisly exhibition had taken place in the square where the bus set me down and which was appropriately named after Tiradentes. A Victorian-looking memorial to the Tooth-Puller occupied the square's centre. But as he was a martyr of independence and therefore in a sense a founder of free Brazil, he could be excused any traffic jams, or rather donkey jams, he caused by his memorial. Tiradentes was still a popular hero, for amongst his other achievements was the first idea of moving the capital city inland. So he might also be called the father of Brasilia.

Partly because he was the patron saint of the emerging Brazilian nationalism, his beautiful home town has been carefully guarded against vandalism. No new buildings were allowed to be put up in Ouro Preto and no old ones could be pulled down. This may be considered a highly doubtful manner in which to display a town's

173

character, an unjust triumph for the antiquary. I was to meet young people in Ouro Preto who thought so. But Belo Horizonte, thriving city of the mid-twentieth century, was the proper place for philistines.

Ouro Preto was as famed, and probably more so, for the Tooth-Puller as for O Aleijadinho, his contemporary. But the town was anything but a museum-piece quietly decaying, with cats sunning and smiling to themselves on doorsteps, its cobbled streets the haunt of old ladies trying to remember the old days. Ouro Preto was none of that, but a lively cheeky place, no doubt because of its students. There were also old ladies—one in particular. She met the bus. I thought she had dressed up for some of the weird folklore ceremonies which I knew took place in some Brazilian towns and villages. Her face had once been handsome, but now the flesh on the fine bones was cracked like stucco on a Venetian water palace. Indeed, the too-liberal mask of rouge was like a coat of colour flaking from an old wall. Somehow, the rouge had got entangled with her grey hair and with the flowers on top. A bunch of flowers was also tied to the top of her over-sized shepherd's crook. Round the old lady's neck hung jewellery most effectively improvised out of two or three rosaries, all doing duty as a necklace. But she obviously felt greatest pride in her Passiontide robe of *quaresma* purple.

Ouro Preto was neither too hot nor too cold, yet the lady of the apparition wore an ancient golden fox fur about her shoulders. When I asked her name she said something which sounded like Igreja Olimpia Angelica Ameba Secca Copa. She then insisted that I wrote it down. As I was a special friend I was to call her Apassionada. An onlooker was impressed then to take a photograph of us standing together, Apassionada making sure that her purple robe was well in evidence. Then we parted—temporarily—and I was free to go. I bought postcards later on and found one of the old lady, whose proper name, it appeared, was Dona Olimpia. After religion, her veneration was for tourists' cigarettes.

But already I could see that Dona Olimpia was by no means Ouro Preto's only outstanding figure. A number of young men lounging about the square or sitting over a beer in the tiny bars opening off it were similarly conspicuous. They belonged to the town's celebrated School of Mines. Unable to hide my curiosity, I stopped a youth and asked him about their strange appearance. The School's first-year students spent the whole year marked as freshmen. *Burros* they were called, and donkeys they were to the senior students, the *sabios* (from *savants*—the know-alls.)

In order that the honest citizens of Ouro Preto should not fail to recognize the *burros* as the donkeys they really were, the *sabios* made them wear odd shoes, or a boot and a canvas boot, and in one ear an outrageous bejewelled earring. Round the *burros'* necks on a red ribbon a donkey-shoe was hung. It bore a card with the absurd false name awarded the victim for his year, with his real name on the obverse of the ungainly medal. But the worst humiliation of all was in the topiary wrought upon the poor *burros'* hair. Such channels were carved, such ridges raised, such bald patches left in such a variety of ludicrous shapes that it was a wonder the *burros* were not full of inferiority complexes. But they all seemed happy and resigned to their fate.

My new friend, Suez Rissi, was at school in Ouro Preto. He would not be a *burro* of the School of Mines until the following year. So for the moment he had his own natural head of hair, a normal pair of shoes and no earring. But Suez lived nevertheless in one of the student republics. The School of Mines itself occupied a building facing the square which had once been the governor's palace, built by O Aleijadinho's father. But the students lived scattered about the town in houses which they organized and ran entirely themselves. They made their own rules and regulations and maintained order under a leader. Suez's republic had ten people altogether and was in a house which they named *Mansão dos Dez Honrados*—House of the Honest Ten. From then on, the Honest Ten opened their house to me, for as long as I stayed in Ouro Preto.

I said a temporary farewell to Suez as I had still to settle in. My luggage was taken by some cheeky barefoot boys who shouldered the heaviest bags without a qualm and half-ran with them to the Pouso Chico Rei. I was going to stay at this beautiful old house which stood in a narrow street off one end of Praça Tiradentes.

Neither hotel nor pension, Chico Rei was perhaps more an inn. A high stone wall hemmed in the narrow way. And on the upper level was the splendid Carmo church which was also designed by The Little Cripple's father.

'Nothing has changed.' I said this aloud to myself, when I stood at Chico Rei's doorstep after booking in and having an excellent luncheon. I said it to imprint the little town's image indelibly on my memory. Every glimpse down steep streets between the white-walled houses, every aspect of mountain, every church on every hill, were sheer delight. I felt as though my eyes were too blunted by the ugliness of modern towns to take in the marvels of Ouro Preto. And it had not changed from the days when the goldminers built it to replace the wooden pioneering shacks. What I saw was what O Aleijadinho saw.

Almost nothing was altered. Donkeys and mules still clattered about the streets, the ring of their shoes on the stone setts making the only noise in the streets, for even cars were scarce in Ouro Preto. The animals wandered freely about the town, ignoring passers-by and standing solemnly near a wall shaded by overhanging trees or nudging each other against the parapet of the old bridge. Deep ravines traversed the town and were spanned by solid structures of wonderfully carved stone, perfectly in scale with the buildings. From the bridge carrying Rua Tiradentes over the stream, I looked into the extravagant riot of dense, green vegetation tumbling down to the water. A hill closed the view, crowned, of course, by another church.

From the old Contos bridge I looked on a scene unaltered for a century and a half. Unaltered, too, was the haunting of Ouro Preto. Its religious atmosphere was still powerful. Palm Sunday was the way leading to a week of intense emotion. In Ouro Preto it always had done, just as the donkeys had always been there as Palm Sunday reminders of the ass which Christ rode into Jerusalem. Palm Sunday was marked by a special event which happened once only during the whole year. The *passos* were revealed. These shrines, normally shuttered from view, were opened to the street. There were seven, representing stations of the cross. The worshipper could progress from one shrine to another, making a pilgrimage and an emotional journey through each of Christ's agonies. The culmination was the evening processions and open-air sermon near the *passo* up in the square.

I stopped by one of the shrines, a small room opening directly to the street. Fresh palms covered its floor like rushes, and there the faithful knelt to kiss the girdle of a plaster Christ in a robe as purple as Dona Olimpia's. The brown, thorn-bedraggled wig, however, was not like the old woman's hair, and made the figure a good deal more frightening than she was. The *passo* was tawdry, but the people of Ouro Preto doubtless found it moving enough.

I did not explore the other *passos*, but walked slowly up to Praça Tiradentes to get a good viewpoint for the processions. Climbing up the streets I wished that my own shoes had the nib fixed at the back like the donkeys' for gripping between the setts. From an old building used as a saloon and bar, which was shuttered coolly against the afternoon sun, there came the click of billiards in a green twilight room. Children played in the sun, and were watched from open windows or balconies by their parents. Framed by a few of the windows, beautiful black-haired senhoritas sat. Some smiled, others did not.

I found a comfortable seat on the Tooth-Puller's monument with a view over any heads which might get between me, the *passo*, and the procession. There were going to be two processions, the first of Christ carrying His cross and the second of His Mother. After starting off from different parts of the town they would converge on the square, and all being well, appear simultaneously. The *passo* on the square was no more than a small room on a corner. But now it was all done up with lace curtains and bare electric light bulbs, which more than adequately illuminated the interior. Outside, a temporary pulpit had been built and some youths were busy rigging up a microphone, a suitably male contribution amid the rather effeminate effects accompanying the rest of the proceedings.

Meanwhile the Sunday afternoon loungers in the square were joined by friends. Little knots of people grew into groups, and then into crowds. There were lots of Sunday suits with awkward occupants in them, just like a Sunday afternoon in an Irish country town. Students had come from their republics to meet girls, for they were not allowed to take them to their houses. But a man's a man, for all that he may only be a first-year *burro*. The students were not un-acquainted with Ouro Preto's prostitutes, and aptly called them 'moths', because the women flew by night and hovered round the bars' bright lights, though it was rarely the moths who were singed. Riders came up on mules to fill water-cans from the wall-fountain at the top of the square. It was built in front of the steps leading up to the ex-prison. Here, Tiradentes' gallows was on view, together with the chief conspirators' tombs. A collection of Minas Gerais's most beautiful carving and religious articles, oratories in jaspa, altar cloths in wrought leather showing a distinct Oriental influence in the elaborate design, sedan-chairs, costumes and capes once worn by the king of a so-called Black Brotherhood during Rosary Festivals, receipts and drawings signed by O Aleijadinho in frail even hand, was cleverly displayed behind the thick walls and barred windows built long ago by the sweat of slaves and prisoners.

Wandering donkeys drank from the museum fountain also, and then mixed with the crowd, although they had to be kept clear of the processional route. The crowd was thickening and at last signs of real activity appeared when a dear old priest tottered up the temporary stairs into the blaze of the *passo's* lamps. Though full of years and entirely unsure on his legs, he was quite determined not to miss a single minute of it. Being stone deaf did not help. The poor old thing nearly fell backwards down the steps when left alone for a moment by his two stalwarts. My eyes were glued to the bright *passo* as though it was a seaside-concert-party stage complete with a concert-party clergyman. Quite irreverently I forgot the evening's serious purpose. But the concert-party atmosphere was not easy to escape, for the angels appeared next.

They were rather young, even for angels, and looked more like giggly little girls in pink and pale blue satin frocks cast off by their mothers. They had haloes fixed behind their heads and enormous wings on to their backs, and were running about excitedly before joining their bit of the procession. Their older friends went with purple money-bags through the crowds. Then they returned to the *passo* to count the scruffy, dog-eared notes, near the old man who was still trying to keep himself from falling over while at the same time stopping the bolder donkeys from eating all the shrine's greenery.

I had been waiting for nearly two hours and was beginning to feel the hardness of Tiradentes' memorial. Darkness had come and a storm was gathering over the mountains. Silent flashes of lightning leapt up behind the clouds, adding just the right element of drama. But already the sound of brass bands came from streets leading into the square. The last late angels fled and I could see now that their wings were real goose ones, though decidedly shaggy and obviously used in every procession since last Corpus Christi. Still, goose wings could not be plentiful and Christmas, I supposed, came but once a year even to Ouro Preto. The angels' crowns had undoubtedly come from last year's left-over Christmas tinsel.

Then the processions appeared, late but miraculously both together. My best view was of Christ carrying His cross. Although I had been smirking over the angels and the old priest who kept falling about, and at the general atmosphere of a vicarage-garden-party pageant, the appearance of Christ's figure was another matter. The statue was robed in deep purple and was of a Christ stooping with the weight of a heavy cross. The stricken, condemned Saviour moved along at shoulder height. Round it was a posse of Roman soldiers, youths who were beating the ends of their spears in slow deadly time on the ground. In the darkened square, lit by the distant lightning, tense with expectation, the sight was blood-curdling.

For me, the effect was momentary. But for thousands of spectators it was a real projection of the historic crucifixion. I lived for a moment only in their haunted world, and then was back again amused by the young Roman soldiers' helmets. The visors were something between a mediaeval knight's helmet and the chromiumed front of an American car. They were preceded by the members of a religious fraternity in purple gowns and capes, who carried processional crosses shrouded in black, and tall candlesticks whose

179

flames fluttered in the evening air. The Roman soldiers had their own S.P.Q.R. banner and behind them came the satin angels, followed by a priest under a gold and purple canopy and the brass bands and choirs.

A negro priest climbed into the pulpit. He gave a fiery sermon with lots of arm-waving. During this the old priest in the *passo* carried on an amiable conversation with a much younger, shinier priest who was there to keep the old man from tumbling down the steps. Although the conversation was one-sided because of the old father's deafness, they chatted away and the old boy kept his eye on the stormclouds from which the first raindrops had already fallen. Something else had already fallen on me, not a bird's droppings but an angel's. Before the sermon began the angels scattered and some of them climbed on to the monument. I did not object too strongly to being poked in the eye by their wings. But I took the strongest exception to being spattered with drips from an ice-cream lolly which an angel on a higher ledge was loudly consuming.

The negro priest was telling the Passion story and gesticulated towards the statue of Christ and towards that of the Virgin Mother, both of them now being near the pulpit for this purpose. The lightning seemed to be timing itself to his words. And then at last the preacher came to his climax, for he bade the Mother behold the Son. Once again I had the uncanny sense that I was seeing an apparition as the two statues moved towards each other. I could have sworn, for a moment, that the figures were living. Then I dismissed the idea, not a little shaken by the powerful illusion induced and the hypnotism of an affair which looked so pathetic at the beginning.

With the sermon done, and the procession getting ready to move round the town, I looked across the square, peopling it in my mind with the crowds of the town's heyday. Perhaps then the difference between black skins and white ones was more sharply marked, though doubtless the old women had worn black, and muttered over their rosaries and thumped their chests as they were doing now. Doubtless, too, there were soldiers lounging about with eyes ready for the girls. But their uniforms were more colourful than the modern

Brazilian army's olive-green khaki, tiny forage caps and drastic haircuts.

But undoubtedly another figure had appeared in those days on the square. He went to watch the processions and open-air enactments of the last events in Christ's earthly life. Those events burned like fire in the heart of the mulatto artist. I could picture O Aleijadinho, following every move from his position at the edge of the crowd. He would not dare to show himself. Perhaps he wore the long coat of blue cloth which reached below his knees and the black shoes which were made so that his feet should appear normal. Or perhaps he was carried up to the square in a palanquin so that he could peep from behind the safety of its curtains. The figures of Mother and Son then might have been his own or a pupil's handwork. And O Aleijadinho almost certainly would have gone up to the square to see Tiradentes' head on display.

I did not follow the procession, but went back to Chico Rei for supper. The edges of what was real and what was not, were blurred. I closed the shutters over my windows. The Roman soldiers' spears had started beating on the cobbles again. The church bells began to toll as though it were Christ Himself going to the gallows. But at last the spears' beat faded as the Roman soldiers departed on their awful mission. The lightning was still playing when I went down for supper, and the bell from the Carmo church across the street still doled out its mourning.

9

Rococo Rodeo

If any dreams haunted my night's sleep at Ouro Preto, they had
evaporated by morning. I opened one eye to observe a chink of
light through the shutters. And I was still not sure whether Chico
Rei was real or not. I found myself lying in a four-poster bed of
turned jacaranda, and looking up at a panelled ceiling. When I put
a bare foot on the floor it touched wide boards polished smooth for
more than a century. When I opened the shutters I saw the bright
sun again, shining sharply on the little town, shining on the mottled
pantile roofs and glistening on the white walls of two hill-top
churches. But I would not have been surprised to have found it all
vanished like my dreams.

It was reassuring to find that Ouro Preto was solid after all,
although in that morning light it was looking like a sea town. The
blue and white colouring was like Clovelly, an impression confirmed
by the clatter of donkeys on the cobbles. Even nasturtiums hung
over walls, and only the sea itself was missing, and, of course,
Clovelly has no rococo churches, nor cacti as tall as that reaching
up from the garden to my bedroom window.

But Chico Rei was hardly the counterpart of a seaside boarding-
house. It was more of a miniature palace, and was certainly Ouro
Preto's most beautiful house. In fact, because of the antique
Brazilian furniture, carving and sculpture which filled its lovely
rooms the house could not be subjected to the hard usage of an
ordinary hotel. It had taken Dona Lilli and her friend Dona Ninita
a long time and a lot of hard work to collect the things and fit out
their home. Not that Dona Lilli, a broadminded Dane, cared whether
her P.G.s were the Duchess of Argyll or the German Ambassador.

182

But she had to be sure, before letting guests in, that they would not walk off with any of the baroque saints and Madonnas or the fine silverware.

When I had rung the bell and the maid opened the door, she took one look at me and said sorry but they were full. I looked scruffy, bus-weary after eighteen hours of travelling and she was not to be blamed. However, I wanted to see Dona Lilli, about whom I had heard much, and was finally admitted on the strength of a throaty Danish *God dag* and a relapse into English. Dona Lilli and I found topics of mutual interest to discuss about Copenhagen, though I found myself talking about Denmark with more nostalgia than she did.

Ouro Preto had an hotel which Oscar Niemeyer designed in 1944. It was a plain building, lost among the older houses in spite of standing on a prominent site. But being a glutton for old furniture and statues, I could not resist Chico Rei. Besides, the name of the inn itself had such romantic associations with Ouro Preto, for Chico Rei had been an African king sold into Brazilian slavery. There were old slave irons in the window ledge by the table where I ate breakfast. They were a cruel, hinged affair where the poor slave had been handcuffed and footcuffed all in one iron, doubtless for some kind of punishment.

Chico Rei and his fellow captive tribesmen were probably all too familiar with such implements. While I sat over my breakfast the great bell of the Carmo church boomed again over the town and reverberated through the house. Yet again I struggled to realize that the bell had probably been cast with the help of slave labour and certainly had been paid for by slaves' work. And when this bell first rang out from the church's Epistles' steeple it had been to the accompaniment of such leg irons and shackles as I found in the house.

To the boom of the bell and the clank of slave chains was added the chink, or the tinkle, or whatever noise gold made. Chief Chico Rei also knew this sound, for he worked in the goldmines. But the scene of his slavery became the cause of his later emancipation, a paradox which was carried further when the African slaves associated themselves with the church of Santa Ifigenia. And it was at this church that I proposed to begin my orgy of visiting in Ouro Preto.

Chico Rei and his family and tribe were captured, and, while crossing 'The Middle Passage' as the Atlantic was known, all the chief's family died of the terrible *maculo* fever, except one son. The tribe was quickly bought up for Ouro Preto's goldmines. Chico Rei was an exceptional man, and by one means or another saved money enough to buy his freedom. By prodigious work he also obtained his son's freedom, and then, striking gold himself, bought out his tribesmen and even other Africans. All these men clung together and founded a kind of principality ruled over by Chico Rei. They chose the dark Santa Ifigenia as the saint most likely to understand and pay heed to their needs. And into the church of Nossa Senhora do Rosario dos Pretos do Alto da Cruz (!) they placed a statue of Santa Ifigenia holding her model building, and the church was renamed after her.

So was the long street leading up to it out of the town. I walked down one hill, across another beautiful bridge, and climbed up what I was certain must be Ouro Preto's steepest, stoniest street. Every few yards or so I sat on the steps or stones giving access to the high shelf-like pavement. The church was at the top, but did not seem to get any nearer however much I climbed. This was the town's oldest part and aptly named Alto da Cruz. Single-storey houses stepped up each side of the way. The people were leaning out of their windows and watched me with suspicion and curiosity, though most of them said '*Bo' dia*' pleasantly enough.

The street was entirely a thing of the past. No cars had any cause to go there and probably would have got stuck on the hill anyway. Even the poor mules had to be beaten up it, as no doubt long before the slaves had been flogged up it. Negroes still seemed to be living in the tiny houses. Five young negresses struggled up the hill behind me, carrying heavy bundles of sticks on their heads. The bare feet they planted on the stones were like camels', big and spreading and sure. Between the houses tiny gardens bloomed with broom and dahlias, marigolds and oleanders, catmint and the exquisite fuschia which Brazilians call princess earrings.

Ouro Preto was free from the normal rash of advertisement signs and hoardings, and that in itself was almost enough to make it beautiful. However, there was one small notice posted on the walls of the Rua Santa Ifigenia. The university branch of the Belo Horizonte archdiocese anti-communist campaign had put it there. The poster warned the faithful to eschew Communism and to follow in the fight against it—led by no less a person than St. Michael himself. I was having enough trouble in following St. Ifigenia without fussing about St. Michael, too. And after my exertion I was not in the least pleased to find the church bolted and barred. Nor was I cheered to learn from a half-wit schoolboy playing truant in the churchyard that the sexton lived wellnigh inaccessibly across another monstrous valley on the opposite mountain flank. I gave up and went to sleep on the grass.

Ifigenia, I decided on waking half an hour later, was a tiresome saint. I gave this information to a cockerel with fantastic natural spurs as he pecked the whitewash on the church wall. In any case, there would not have been a great deal to see inside. The most interesting from a curiosity point of view would have been the holy water stoup where the negresses were supposed to have washed gold dust out of their hair when they came from the mines. The precious material was then collected and put towards the decoration of Ifigenia's chapel.

At my second church, the parish church of Nossa Senhora da Conçeição d'Antonio Dias, down in the valley, I was again confronted with locked doors. But this time I wanted no nonsense and went storming into the priest's house near by, for in this church O Aleijadinho had been buried. The priest was out. But the housekeeper, an old woman clad all in black, said I could wait and showed me into a parlour hung with horrible reproductions from Italian pictures of Sacred Hearts and dead popes.

Unfortunately, many Minas Gerais churches and presbyteries were getting rid of their original furnishing as they decayed, instead of attempting to repair them. In the place of the original native art and craftsmanship were plaster casts of the worst possible Fatima and Lourdes models kept under plastic protective sheets. An

185

Englishman, also staying at the inn, told me he had recently bought the whole altarpiece of a church besides other fittings and carvings, and later I acquired some of this from him in Rio de Janeiro to add to my other pieces of Portuguese colonial treasure trove.

In general, Ouro Preto was lucky in having expert attention focused on it as a national shrine. But many Minas Gerais churches in outlying places were beyond the scope of experts, and much art of value had already been lost through ignorance. I felt no guilt in removing part of the Minas Gerais heritage. My few *objets* would probably have ended on the scrap heap. President Kubitschek redeemed one of O Aleijadinho's most beautiful Madonnas. He had it enshrined as the principal object in Niemeyer's beautiful curved chapel at the Dawn Palace in Brasilia. The Little Cripple's work showed its own beauties against Niemeyer's plain yet subtle architecture. In the voluptuous curves of both, there was something akin in feeling despite the hundred and fifty years between them.

I did not wait for the tardy priest. Perhaps he would return while I examined his church from the outside. The first thing he ought to do, I decided, was to take down a gross Victorian cross studded with electric bulbs from the central pediment, and also remove from the main façade a chain of similarly naked lamps. After all, he had no need to advertise, and the conflict between *his* parish church and Ouro Preto's *other* one was over and done with two centuries previously. The church of Antonio Dias was sufficiently imposing without the need for vulgar lighting. It had been built on a triangle of sloping land caught between two steep streets meeting scissor fashion. The church consequently had a much higher base on one side than on the other. A symphony of colliding steps led up to it. At the tip of the triangle was a tiny sloping square.

To look at its slightly crumbly yellow stone, and at the rankness of the little churchyard in front of the west door, nobody would imagine that the church was once the centre of a bitter internecine struggle in Ouro Preto—part, in fact, of the violence that once ruled the town. It had been the parish church of the Brazilians from São Paulo, who had arrived first in Ouro Preto to exploit the goldmines. There were the same kind of tough Paulistas as those who first pushed into Brazil's interior. Not unnaturally they regarded Ouro Preto as their own. When immigrants from Portugal also arrived and, if you please, claimed the mines as theirs, not a little friction resulted.

There seemed to be enough gold to go round, and for a time at least the two groups restricted their enmity to bitter words, with perhaps an occasional skirmish. The rough-and-ready Paulistas with their lack of manners or refinements were looked down upon by the Portuguese. *Caboclos* the immigrants contemptuously called the Brazilians because of their admixture of Indian blood. But the pioneers cared nothing for this. Their retaliation was to call the dandy Portuguese *emboabas*—feathered legs. This was the name of a species of bird with long plumed legs and it suited the Portuguese, who wore long beribboned trousers and spats.

The two factions actually came to blows in the War of the *Emboabas* in 1708. The fighting went on for months, with the despised *Caboclos* emerging as victors. The fancy-pants *emboabas*, however, had the last word twenty-five years later when their own parish church of Nossa Senhora do Pilar was built. They put on a terrific procession to impress everybody, when the Holy Sacrament was taken to the church. From then on there was no doubt as to the Paulistas' inferior position. Ouro Preto had never seen a procession like it, either for richness or subject. The procession I had seen the previous evening was nothing compared with the four winds, the seven heavenly bodies disguised as Roman gods and godesses all decked with jewels and gold from head to foot.

But the days of extravagant demonstration were over for the little town. Such wonders now were reduced to the pathetic plaster casts of the Virgin factories and products from plastic rosary plants. However, Ouro Preto was not yet completely swamped with these hideous objects, and hand-carved things were still being made and sold in the one or two inconspicuous tourist shops. The hills of Minas Gerais were still studded with mineral deposits and many beautiful semi-precious stones could be bought. Then the soft steatite soapstone was still much in evidence. This beautiful blue-grey stone had become O Aleijadinho's favourite material, for it was easily worked, consistent in texture yet durable. Soapstone was the material used for Ouro Preto's churches more than any other. Not to miss their chance, the tourist shops sold ash-trays and beakers, poorly made Madonnas and crucifixes and small carved reliefs of famous people. I even saw one of Mozart, who was, it has to be admitted, O Aleijadinho's contemporary. The soapstone had also been used for making *figas*, the good luck sign of a clenched hand. I threw all my principles to the winds and bought some of the *figas* to give my friends at home, thereby encouraging the tourist trade, which one day will doubtless ruin Ouro Preto as it has ruined everything from Stratford-on-Avon to the pyramids at Gizeh. I crept in and out of that shop feeling guilty. But afterwards I consoled myself by thinking that, who knows, possibly Ouro Preto would produce another great sculptor for Brazil, and that perhaps he would start modestly by turning soapstone on a lathe for tourist drinking mugs.

I was certainly cross that Ouro Preto was producing no priest to open up the Antonio Dias church. But I refused to take *não* for an answer and climbed over the churchyard railing. I thought that further pleading with the lazy boys, who were lying under a red-parrot-flowered euphorbia smoking instead of cutting the grass, might get me in. The boys told me earlier that the priest had gone off with the only key. But I knew they were telling a lie. I proved this by giving them a packet of cigarettes. The oldest and surliest youth produced another key from his pocket, and in a trice the great panelled door was unlocked. I was in the parish church which The Little Cripple used to attend and which held his body.

All the trouble I had gone to in getting in might have been spared, for the church was a disappointment. Over the years it had been greatly changed, and the dim lighting did not improve its air of sad resignation. From its purple Passiontide hangings, its dusty carving and tarnished gilding Antonio Dias looked as though the *emboabas'* procession of 1733 had really dealt the Paulistas a final blow. Time, however, seems to remedy most things, including this superiority of the immigrants' Pilar church. Part of it collapsed during my stay in Ouro Preto. The sacristy just fell down. Its repair, or at any rate, restoration would be put in hand, no doubt as soon as possible—whenever that might be. Those churches required expert attention and, though nothing equivalent to England's Georgian Group and similar bodies existed to rouse a public conscience and interest, the Ouro Preto churches were at least cared for. The Patrimonio Historico was straining every muscle to cope with the remains of Brazil's past. Lucio Costa, Brasilia's creator, was a leading member of this association and had written papers on Jesuit architecture in Brazil. Unfortunately, the Patrimonio had all too little money to spend on its commitments.

The three youths who let me into the church had been joined now by a train of small boys. They all trooped up the nave when I asked to be shown where O Aleijadinho was buried. They indicated the side altar of the Hallowed Death, though I could not understand whether the sculptor's remains were in, under, or behind the altar. Perhaps his young fellow townsmen did not know. Somebody knew, however, for the body had been disinterred in 1930 for examination.

Admiration for O Aleijadinho's art, and curiosity about the nature of his disease had begun within a few years of his death. Neither the admiration nor the curiosity had ever subsided since, and in a way the one led to the other. Speculation about the disease would certainly not have occurred if the man himself had not been fascinating for other reasons. Among the slave population of Ouro Preto, and even among the masters, there must have been many people with horrible, and in those times, unaccountable tropical diseases. Even in the steep street I had just climbed to Santa Ifigenia's church there must have been many diseased cripples over the years. There were still, for I saw some that very morning, and even leprosy remains a major problem in Brazil.

Yet because of his sculpture, because he poured such energy and emotion into his work, and life into his art, *The* Little Cripple stood out. His disease has been discussed by many doctors and he has been given a posthumous diagnosis, but with varying verdicts. Some maintain that he suffered simply and solely from hereditary syphilis. Others say it was a rare form of leprosy. Yet another thought that O Aleijadinho suffered a heart attack in about 1770

189

with subsequent paralysis. Somebody else considered that it might well have been Zamparina, a virulent disease current at the time. It was rife in Portugal, too. The opera singer and courtesan, Anna Zamparina, sang in Lisbon while the disease was rampant in Europe. Her singing and beauty aroused an enthusiasm as infectious as the disease, the unfortunate symptoms of which were diarrhoea with subsequent paralysis. Ironically, Zamparina herself fell victim.

Curiously, another explanation of O Aleijadinho's misfortune was also connected with a woman. She was called Helene and had known the sculptor during his life. Four years after his death she told her story to the French traveller St. Hilaire. According to Helene, as soon as she heard that Antonio Lisboa was ill and what the symptoms were, she immediately knew the cause. He had been taking over-doses of *cardina*. Gypsies sold this drink at Ouro Preto's fairs. It was a most potent means of stimulating the brain, with heightened perception and intellectual capacity resulting from it. Also in some cases, the drinker lost control of his limbs, particularly the extremities.

That such a liquid as *cardina* existed is not at all unlikely. A preparation might easily have been made similar to the mescalin which Aldous Huxley took and approved or the magical Mexican mushroom which Arthur Koestler ate and disapproved of. And the wandering gypsies might quite well have known the formula for such a concoction. The sculptor had a highly strung nature in any case. It would not at all be out of character for him to have desired the bliss and vision such a drug might give him. He may even have been addicted, for his work certainly showed a more than normal degree of perception. But perhaps he merely had what Wyndham Lewis referred to in Augustus John as 'fits of seeing'. But apart from Helene's story to the Frenchman in 1818, there is mention of *cardina* or drugs nowhere else.

A little credibility might be attached to Helene's story, for so far as St. Hilaire was concerned, O Aleijadinho had not actually lost his hands and feet, but merely the power of manipulation. But the weight of evidence is that his hands were eaten away. When O Aleijadinho's tomb was opened with due solemnity in 1930, those doctors, scientists and priests present must have held their breath as the coffin lid was prised. By comparison with contemporary descriptions of the mulatto artist, the skull and frame were easily identified. But of smaller bones, which would have been hands and feet, there was no trace whatsoever.

Though Ouro Preto had no golden lads and lasses nor, presumably, chimney-sweeps either (though Dona Lilli's house had a fireplace), Antonio Lisboa had come to dust. Yet his creations would, with care, avoid a similar fate for many more hundreds of years. True, the Pilar church partly fell down more or less under my nose. Yet O Aleijadinho's parish church looked solid enough still, despite a certain mouldiness about the interior. Even less changed than the church, no doubt, was the street outside it. There might be horrid plaster statues in the church, and some reproduction pictures of stations of the cross in the worst of all possible tastes, yet outside, the winding, twisting narrow street looked quite unchanged. It might have come straight from one of those engravings of eighteenth-century Brazil I had seen, or even from the comical English ones illustrating, none too accurately, Maria Graham's journal.

Birdsong filled the street, though most of the birds were in tiny cages. Some houses had ten or a dozen wooden-framed cages hanging round the door or out of windows. The birds seemed content with captivity. Most of them were canaries, and were as green as unripe bananas instead of being yellow like ripe ones. The cages also held another favourite pet in Brazil, the crested cardinal. The cardinal was imprisoned more for his gorgeous scarlet hat than for any merit as a *castrato*.

But there was one singer finer than all the others. The Brazilians called it the *gaturamo*, a performer noted for his shimmering blue and yellow feathers. In England the bird has the misfortune to be called *violaceous euphonia*, a clumsy name in no way conveying the beauty of its singing. The *gaturamo* was native to most of South America and a favourite pet throughout the continent. I had first met the bird several years before in Trinidad, but there it was much smaller than in Brazil. And I could not remember that its singing was so fine either. The *gaturamo* often began with a running, continuous melody, like rhapsodic music wandering without pause from theme to theme. But all the time the pitch rose and the singing intensified until the bird reached the highest notes with its feathers shimmering, its body dancing up and down as though to help the sound out of its tiny throat. Like *Macumba* dancers, the *gaturamo* became obsessed, and repeated the whole ritual until it collapsed into exhausted silence.

It was not a streetful of canaries that I associated Ouro Preto and birds, but with a graveyardful of kiss-flowers. I found the humming-birds hovering in the burial ground of São Francisco de Assis, and I went there in the first place to escape the purple magpie —Dona Olimpia. She had descended on me four times so far during that afternoon, in search of cigarettes. As the church itself was closed until later, I was forced to retire behind the iron gates leading to the square funeral cloister. It was in a garden there that the *beija-flor* hung in the air or darted about, just like fishes in a pool.

Most of the tombs were built into the cloister's wall, and were sheltered from Ouro Preto's mild elements by a roof and a wooden colonnade. Not too securely in some instances, window-boxes and vases were fixed to various tombs like the birdcages were fixed to the houses down by the Antonio Dias church. Rich agapanthus lilies of blue and white leaned from many parts of the walls. As startling as false teeth were the white dog-daisies made of plastic, guaranteed no doubt to cut the number of cemetery visits for relatives by at least half. Being thus deceived by the daisies, many people would also have thought the anthuriums and their pools of crimson wax also made of plastic.

But decidedly not made of polythene or perspex were the humming-birds who came to attack me when I went near their nests while walking in the cloister. They stopped then their cicada whistlings and whirred near my ear with invisible wings, rushing in like dive-bombers. Brazil's ruby-and-topaz humming-bird, though very pretty, have been known to attack owls and hawks who ventured too near their nests. Those I found in São Francisco's churchyard belonged more to the green honey-creeper variety. These were different again from the Brazilian swallow-tail, which hovered round

Sometimes, gold or diamonds come out of the rivers . . .

. . . and sometimes oil. These river-boys were my friends on the Araguaia, proudly Brazilian despite European or negro or Indian origins

Fair winds for a north-east water pilgrimage

Figurehead and washerwoman of the São Francisco river boats

houses and even went into the parlours if there were flowers there—or even a queen eating bread and honey—for people hung up honey-pots to draw these large humming-birds into their gardens.

The church was opened at the appointed hour by an old negress with a fuzz of crinkly white hair. She bore the largest church key I had ever seen, as though it were the Host itself. The sounds of a samba on the radio issued from the open windows of a tall house by the church. Students had just come home from afternoon lectures. They leaned out of the windows, and while the old negress unlocked the church door, they beat time to the samba with their hands on the windowsill. This was the republic where my friend Suez and the rest of the Honest Ten ate their main midday meal.

Occasionally, one encounters art of utter felicity. It has a shining joy, neither heroic nor frivolous, sentimental nor superficial, but which by sheer delight carries the beholder away. Mozart could create such things at will, more or less consistently and repeatedly. Perhaps it was the special task of the rococo to shed a last golden light over mankind before the rumblings of romanticism and revolution darkened his sunny, albeit artificial, pastoral. O Aleijadinho created felicity, perfectly, at São Francisco de Assis.

Because it was so felicitous, it produced a kind of glow in me, not unlike the effect of the Brazilian wine I had been drinking at Dona Lilli's. I *enjoyed* São Francisco, a response to art not always condoned. The *terribilita* of Michaelangelo or the discords of the *Eroica,* or the neurotic, subterranean probings of Ibsen are safely beyond the reach of innocent enjoyment. In fact, enjoyment nearly always produces guilt feeling, as though it were connected with entertainment and not art. Perhaps that is why the rococo has never been popular in England and possibly even why England never had its own rococo. It was the period when John Wesley was already preaching a new puritanism. But then, we never had a revolution either, like Ouro Preto.

At Ouro Preto, when O Aleijadinho was working on his churches, the town was already economically declining. Through Tiradentes and his fellow plotters against Portugal, revolution and unquiet was in the air. Yet in such an atmosphere, and in spite of his personal sufferings, The Little Cripple created the entirely delightful São Francisco. By passing up and down the streets I had come to love the church. It stood on a platform cut out of a steep hillside. To pause at the church was like stopping at one of those shrines on steep mountain paths in Austria. In every direction from São Francisco the visitor had to go either up or down the violently tilted streets. Behind the church was a gaping green valley and beyond the great wall of the Minas Gerais hills.

I often sat on the low parapet surrounding the platform and gazed at the vigorous, boldly undulating forms of the façade and its two round towers. Invention had reached the peak of genius, yet still retained that rococo rare delight. O Aleijadinho worked at São Francisco on and off during most of his life, but somehow he never lost the pristine clarity of his first idea nor its unique kind of *naiveté*, an innocence not possessed, for instance, by the mundane parish church of Antonio Dias. The whole design was said to be his, much of it carved by himself, presumably with the devoted Maurício.

The sculptor used soapstone for the first time on this church and it was after this that the material became peculiarly his own. Many Minas Gerais churches had soapstone carving only as their western façade, but São Francisco was built of it entirely. The blue steatite shared some of the qualities possessed by the marbles of Pentelikon. On being quarried it was soft, easily worked, and could take fine and subtle relief without chipping and spalling. With age the stone hardened. This was its most valuable quality, for the work remained with the original crispness untouched by corrosion.

São Francisco's proportions were perfectly harmonious. Always, in the afternoon light, the stone glowed with honey and gold. The sun fell on its west façade, illuminating it sharply yet with mellowness, and making the whole surface alive by highlight and shadow. Bold columns and broken pediments and domed pepperpot towers stood yellow against a luminous sky which graded from light blue above the mountains' rim to a deep royal blue immediately overhead. In spite of his elaborate rococo line, the restless undulation and elaboration of surface, O Aleijadinho always kept a clear outline. Never was there confusion or ambiguity.

ROCOCO RODEO

I had come almost to speaking terms with St. Francis himself, whom O Aleijadinho showed receiving the stigmata on Mount Alverne in a great medallion of low relief over the west door. Every sign of nail and spear, every dice of the Roman soldiers, every thorn in their crown, every cord of the whip, was still as clear as the day it was carved.

An angel holding up the medallion had, in fact, lost one leg which nobody had bothered to replace. But then, in my wanderings round the flat grassy precinct I had discovered one or two bits of broken sculpture lying about, though whether they belonged to São Francisco I could not tell. There was nobody I could ask, certainly not the wizened old negress with the key, who looked rather astonished at the way I bolted in as soon as the door was open. She would have known as little about it as the drunks who slept against the shaded wall outside, using the fragments as pillows. These sleepers were well protected against the sun by a high bank of Brazilian pines, mimosa trees, and an orange grove weighed down with fruit.

The church's inside was cool, too, but the drunks could hardly have slept there. It was true that a cloister-like side aisle, shut off from the nave and sanctuary, was provided with stone window-seats and a view of the breeze-stirred pines, but they were doubtless intended for the sober faithful. The peace was unbelievable. While I sat there, mooning idly at one of the windows, the old negress came from the church to keep her eye on me.

When she was not looking I flew up a broad flight of stairs at the back. It led to a gallery which looked into the church and, from an external arcaded balcony, over the town and the mountains. Presumably in the old days, the wealthy miners and privileged among the congregation had sat up there, carrying on in a thoroughly shocking fashion, with their courting and singing, dancing and eating of bread baked in curious shapes, though to be sure one could not wish for a lovelier place in which to be merry unto the Lord. And since São Francisco, like most Brazilian churches, was more like a rococo palace ballroom than a house of prayer, it is not altogether surprising that the congregation behaved as they did. Through the church's

195

open doors and windows I could still hear sambas from the student republic, but it did not seem out of place when I thought about the wildness of the old days both in and out of church.

Being alone, I felt sure that there was nothing I could do up in the gallery in any way to approach the eighteenth century's licentiousness. The negress had other ideas, however, and stood at the bottom of the staircase eyeing me with the greatest suspicion. She may well have been afraid that I would steal the Roman soldiers' armour which had been used in the previous evening's procession. It was stored in São Francisco's gallery with the painted brown spears standing in a corner waiting for Good Friday's procession and actual burial service. Their bases were tipped with metal, so that they would make that slow-march metallic clatter which persisted so long in an inner ear. The spine-chill was somewhat lessened when I discovered that the macabre effect was partly obtained by the tops from Coco-Cola bottles. They had been flattened with a hammer, painted silver and nailed on to the spears to rattle like the metal discs of a tambourine.

But illusion was the artist's principal business in Ouro Preto's churches, and O Aleijadinho was the chief illusionist. He and his assistants modelled São Francisco's interior so that the main concentration, the rush-hour, so to speak, of this commuting between heaven and earth was over the high altar, where in fact the Trinity itself presided. No mistake could possibly occur as to who was who.

God the Father, besides having a distinguishing halo in the form of a triangle, held a blue sphere representing the world in His hand. He also had an enormous W. G. Grace kind of a beard, quite a different affair from the small, curly wisp on the Son's chin. God the Holy Ghost, who hovered over Father and Son, looked like a hybrid between a Roman and a German eagle. Beneath, to complete the composition, was a figure of the Madonna. She had a decided touch of goitre, not altogether unattractive, as though the sculptor had looked to African primitive art for his models, like Modigliani. What pleased me most in this ensemble was a beautiful man-in-the-moon. He was the Virgin's footstool, a white horned moon like a slice of melon, and he had the lugubrious face which all men-in-the-moons have had ever since there were fairy-stories.

Not all the carving at São Francisco's was O Aleijadinho's. Yet the quality was consistent. From where did these men, hemmed in by the gold-riddled hills, get their extraordinary wealth of ideas? How was it that they kept so close to other beautiful work in Brazil, in Portugal, and indeed in a Europe which they almost certainly never saw? Most of them probably never travelled even as far as Rio de Janeiro, for the style of Minas Gerais was local, by local men in local materials. So centralized did the Minas Gerais church building become that it was eventually known simply as the *estilo aleijadinho*—The Little Cripple's style.

O Aleijadinho is supposed never to have had an artistic training. He may have had some tuition in figure drawing from the man who cast coins for the royal mint at Ouro Preto. Another source for The Little Cripple's extraordinarily wide vocabulary of decorative motifs and physiological types for his statues is thought to have been from books and prints, especially those illustrating the Bible stories with which he was very familiar. And he would certainly have seen those elegant, delicately coloured rococo groups of figures in porcelain which the wealthy miners imported from Europe for their homes. O Aleijadinho probably also saw biscuit *maquettes* for similar groups. Various people have even found traces in his work of Gothic, Byzantine and Oriental art. That a number of different influences came into play was no doubt true. Certainly O Aleijadinho never went directly to the source of great works of art. He never visited France or Italy. He began, no doubt, by looking at wood engravings and ended in the fantastic realms of his own imaginings, where, ultimately, every artist is alone.

By the last years of his life, when he was an octogenerian, O Aleijadinho was a mighty artist. He was not without faults, but was nevertheless capable of producing a *tour de force* every time he put chisel to stone or wood. The twelve prophets at Congonhas do Campo tower above any other work of his. Nothing in the São Francisco church at Ouro Preto compared with the drama of those figures. But the aim was different at São Francisco. Even when dealing directly with Biblical subjects which he carved in panels on the two wall pulpits, O Aleijadinho kept to the building's predominating spirit of gaiety.

Both pulpits presented a highly stylized version of the sea, which in all probability The Little Cripple never actually saw. One was a watery story from the Old, the other from the New Testament—Jonah and the whale, and Christ speaking to the people. When you do not know what a whale looks like, and cannot find anybody who does nor any wood engravings, then you are obliged to make up your own whales. O Aleijadinho did this and the result was most un-whale-like, being more of a dolphin-cum-porpoise. But as the Bible story does not actually specify that it *was* a whale which swallowed Jonah, perhaps the sculptor can be excused. Jonah was one of the prophets at Congonhas do Campo, too, and the whale there had a splendid tail ending in a forked fishy acanthus form, not unlike celery leaves. São Francisco's pulpit Jonah also had a curious whale wallowing in waves which were no rougher than those of a goldfish pond.

In the left-hand pulpit, Christ was also in a boat and talked to the people on the shore. In spite of being conventionalized the whole scene was so lively that I could almost hear the waves breaking, Christ's boat creaking and a pug-like dog lapping at the edge. O Aleijadinho's eye picked out incident and he portrayed narrative as vividly as possible. As with Bruegel, inaccuracy of human anatomy was no hindrance to O Aleijadinho. Possibly, it was an advantage for, as with his whales, what he did not know or could not see he had to invent.

But the interior of the church was bright with white and gold. The high altar in the sanctuary and six altars flanking the nave were exceedingly gay with profuse yet delicate decoration of gilded foliage against white columns and arches. It was this splendour of white and gold set within the plain, nobly-proportioned space, which gave the church its rococo felicity.

Strangely oppressive by contrast was the sacristy, a low long room in the usual position for sacristies of the Minas Gerais churches, across the extreme eastern end. The room contained a lavabo carved by The Little Cripple, a stone affair set in the wall and decorated again with angels and medallions of the stigmata, saints and scrolls bearing Biblical verses, enough to make the pilgrim wonder once again at the amount of work that pair of crippled arms got through. Yet the lavabo was not enough to redeem the room's heaviness. The huge sideboards for vestments and relics, made of dark rosewood, and solid benches and dark oil portraits on the walls and the luridly painted ceiling seemed so earthy after the airy brilliance of the church. But perhaps the contrast was deliberately contrived to enhance the church.

I did not like the sacristy and escaped into the sunlit precinct, leaving the old negress talking in whispers to a child who wanted to kiss the relics. But leaving the church was not to forsake the past for the present. Clattering up the stony streets were donkeys and mules and men with wide-brimmed hats on horseback. And even the students from the School of Mines could not upset this ancient air. They were the sole surviving element of the noisy and the wild which had always been Ouro Preto's character. With its population of 100,000 it has been anything but sleepy, so the presence of Brazil's young twentieth-century blood in no way contradicted the eighteenth-century surroundings.

I think that my friend Suez Rissi and his fellow republicans secretly believed I raved too much about O Aleijadinho and the churches. They thought Ouro Preto would be improved out of recognition by importing a little of Belo Horizonte's liveliness. They were right, of course, about such an influx changing the town beyond recognition and wrong about it being an improvement—at least, I considered them wrong. But it was they who had to live there, between school and republic, between study and any amusement they could provide themselves. While I stayed in Ouro Preto, Suez and his friends dragged me off to the House of the Honest Ten and made me share their amusement—often as not out of a *cachaça* bottle. Any suspicions that I was a church-haunting fogey could only be removed by making sure that I was real flesh and blood ready to be set on fire with *cachaça*.

Despite what was perhaps a legitimate grievance for teenagers about being cooped up in a museum town, I was sure that no students ever had such pleasant lodging as at the Honest Ten. The house was approached from a road along the mountain flank, and a suicidally steep path led down to it. Heavy greenery grew over it like a tunnel, and near the house a wooden bridge crossed a deep gorge which the students called the Grand Canyon. The Ten had fixed a wire from a tree to the bridge to stop any Honest drunkard from pitching into the gorge. The wire was necessary for me, even when sober.

But after sundown, when their view across the valley to São Francisco and the further hills was lost, I was not often completely sober. At Dona Lilli's table there was sure to have been another bottle of nutty Brazilian wine. Then, at a prearranged time, one of the Ten would meet me with an electric torch and conduct me down the perilous path. And then, in one of the student's rooms, the effects of the wine would be augmented by those of the *cachaça*. The rosiest of all rosy moods settled on me then, and an amplitude of feeling, a warmth which told me how much I loved Brazil—or rather, the thousand different Brazils I had encountered so far. It also told me I had to be careful going home.

Sessions in the Honest Ten's *mansão* did not create this mood out of nothing, but merely, as it were, varnished and glazed the colours which the picture already had. I had no need to be in such a mood to see how the old house was beautiful on its precipitous site with an overgrown, neglected orchard tumbling all about it, cascading with a green profusion right into the valley below. All sorts of exotic Brazilian fruits grew on the abandoned trees, or lay rotting on the ground. Most prevalent was *caqui*, a full, round red fruit like oversized tomatoes. Street vendors sold the fruit everywhere in Brazil. The boys and old women who sat on pavements with trays of them wrote the name phonetically on the price-card—*kaki*. *Caqui* was no particular love of mine. I much preferred the sweet and succulent chrome orange papaya which I often had at breakfast, or avocados mashed with cream and sugar.

But at night the orchard was only a dark mass beneath the balconied windows. The only fruit I thought of then was lime to squeeze into the *cachaça*. Without fruit and sugar I could not swallow the firewater. When neat, it had a raw, oily taste as though made of poteen mixed with methylated spirit. In fact it was a cheap extract of sugar-cane, not dissimilar to rum, though far cruder. As a stimulant for students jaded by ennui or as a dose of hope for dispirited gold-diggers, nothing could be better—at the price.

The price could be a thick head next morning or, in extreme cases, temporary trouble with the bile duct. But at the time, during the golden moments of talking and singing, or recalling the past and of shaping the future beyond the bounds of possibility, who cared about hangovers? The Ten and their guest certainly did not. As the hours passed, the students remembered more and more stories of their farms and villages scattered widely throughout Brazil. Or, pausing in the middle of high spirits, they might stop to recall a nostalgic moment and perhaps quote the beautiful words of the nineteenth-century Brazilian poet, Casimiro de Abreu,

> *Oh! what memories I have*
> *Of my life's aurora,*
> *Of my beloved childhood,*
> *Years which will never come again.*
> *What love, what dreams, what flowers*
> *In those drowsy afternoons*
> *In the shade of the bananas*
> *Below the orange trees!*

Then pushing nostalgia aside, the Ten would ask me for the hundredth time what I thought of Ouro Preto's 'moths' and were they better than those of the Dublin bars or the far-away streets of London. How can questions like these be answered, when one is torn between truthfulness and a desire to please one's hosts? But when we climbed and slipped up the path, breathing in the pure mountain air, and made our way back to the Praça Tiradentes, we could laugh about any moths who still found the street-lamps irresistible. It was usually so late, however, that most of the moths had fluttered away to bed long before. In the square, my friends left me, and I walked alone except for donkeys and mules which still looked for stray blades of grass between the cobbles. I went through the silent streets, perhaps making a detour to see a fountain or a bridge by starlight, and so to the night-muted flourishes of Carmo church and a darkened Chico Rei where only the statues' eyes were still open.

Some late riders might be watering their horses at the wall-fountains by the museum. They were passing through the town or had just returned after a long journey to one of the villages around the hills. In the light of street-lamps it would be difficult to discern the fine tooling of the saddles and elaborate leather coverings and stirrup flaps. I never knew whether this leather was for protection against the bushland's thorns, or against the mountain cold, or even just for the effect of grandeur. In Ouro Preto one expected even saddlers to be artists as well as craftsmen.

Most craftsmen of the mountain town will remain without a name. For them, the rococo glories, in this place of black gold rivers and soapstone churches, must be the memorial. The name of the greatest among them, the man who won for Ouro Preto an honoured place in the world of art, Antonio Francisco Lisboa, must stand in the stead of each. It was not necessary to go in the Antonio Dias parish church and find the altar of the Hallowed Death in order to see the monument to the mulatto genius. Ouro Preto's churches, the twelve prophets and his whole influence on the rococo art of Brazil were monument enough. The one name must suffice, that of O Aleijadinho, The Little Cripple, who will live in the history of art, the man who made stones speak, and who seared the lips of the prophets with live coals.

10

Moto Perpetuo

Though intensely moved after five hours of Wagnerian subli-
mity, I am always secretly glad when Tristan dies and Isolde
evaporates and joins him, and I can get out, stretch my legs and
have a refreshing drink. But I did not feel at all like that at the end
of my stay in Ouro Preto. I have been pining for it ever since.
Provocatively, the great tree shading the façade of the Carmo
church had suddenly burst into a firework of pink blossom, a
shower of flowers shining with colour against a sky enamelled by a
blue morning. The sun smote the white church walls, and the
barriguda's flowers picked up a pollen of reflected light.

It seemed like springtime in the mountains of Minas Gerais. But
I could not remember the blossoms being there on the previous days.
Yet they could hardly have sprung out overnight or that morning.
Not that I would have been surprised if they had, for this was Brazil,
where the impossible frequently happened. Beneath the froth of
flowers the *barriguda* (or *paineira*) had a thorny trunk, with sharp-
pointed knobs like some absurd article of mediaeval armour. Yet in
spite of this, the tree was associated in Brazilian minds with beds,
for when the flowers dropped leaving seeds behind, these were
surrounded by a white kapok, which was then harvested for pillow
stuffing. Such a pillow was, at that very moment of saying good-
bye to Dona Lilli and Dona Ninita on the steps of Pouso Chico Rei,
waiting for me on the fourteenth floor of a noisy hotel in Rio de
Janeiro.

By telepathy, my departure was broadcast to Ouro Preto's streetboys and they were outside ready to take my luggage on their black,
fuzzy-haired heads down to the bus. Though not the acme of

comfort, this bus at least had the virtue of avoiding Belo Horizonte altogether by dodging along some country roads, and then of going direct to Rio by the main highway, with no changes *en route*. This country bumpkin of a bumpy bus looked rather slow-witted amongst the cheeky, fly *lotacões* of Rio when we got there twelve hours later. Yet our driver, who was so happy along the empty country roads, was just as fresh when we got to the lamplit city in the evening.

The transition from Ouro Preto's other-worldliness to Rio de Janeiro's worldliness was done in gentle stages, which lessened the shock. Before striking the Belo-Rio highway we passed through a countryside quite unlike any other I had seen so far in Brazil. And it helped a little more to break down any preconceived notion I may have had as to what was 'Brazilian'. I was rapidly discovering that the usual European conception of Brazil being a vast land occupied by wealthy playboys in luxury hotels on the one hand and savages in steaming jungles on the other was about as accurate as, say, the Russian idea that Dickens's London is today's London. This soft, pastoral country that I passed through surprised me by its human scale. In a way it reminded me of the Swiss Jura near Basel, perhaps the loveliest of Europe's landscapes.

The bus ambled along winding, dusty roads between the neat fields and plantations of *fazendas*, slowing now and again while lazy zebus picked themselves up from the middle of the road and stood aside with an offended air to let us pass. There were men and boys on horseback or riding donkeys. There were little painted houses standing among trees, and dark green trees dotted the green hills. Once or twice we passed through the old mining villages, as quiet and as beautiful as the rococo citadel itself. Most were single-street affairs, and one was just a great bower of datura bearing white or pink-tinted trumpets of fantastic size.

Although it was officially approaching winter, the flowering trees and shrubs obeyed no apparent season. During each month I had been in Brazil new splendours appeared, a new range of strong and often strident hues. Flowers ran amok in clumps or plunged themselves over walls or sprawled in the sun on rocks or city waste lands. Blobs and splodges of colour were everywhere, in a careless prodigality which mocked the painter's careful palette and shocked the eye accustomed at the most to a profusion of gorse on a Devon hill or the wildness of rhododendron excesses on Howth Castle hill.

Goethe's solitary rose on the heath and even Housman's loveliest of trees seemed pretty poverty-stricken besides the extravagance I saw everywhere. Brazilian poets almost had no need to be poets at all. To make a dazzling effect they had simply to describe what was around them. Yet before going to Brazil I was surprised at the number of writers who singled out individual trees for attention, such trees as *juazeiro* or *mangaba* or even old cocoa-trees. But then, nobody who did not know could have expected the ugly *barriguda* to have put up an umbrella of flower that outdid even the camellia or magnolia.

I could never be certain, either, when particular trees had their flowering season. On arriving at Salvador in December I had found the big flamboyants already heavy with seed-pods. Yet by the beginning of April, on leaving Ouro Preto, I went through villages still blazing with the flamboyant's red and still sumptuous with the fires of cockspur coral trees. After the first village drowned in datura, I gave up trying to cope with the continuous unfolding of new sights. For hundreds of miles, right into Rio's traffic-bound streets, there was something gorgeous, something spectacular, more and more *barrigudas*, and even some of them waving their pink lace above the city's telegraph wires.

The bus did not stop, though a hundred times I wanted to pull the cord, so that I could get out and stare, if only for five minutes. But we rolled on. Every valley had a white ribbon or a score of ribbons where mud-lilies choked the drains and rivers. Some villages had kept their palm arches from the previous Sunday. Men stood in the shallows of the bigger streams, panning for the elusive gold sand. While climbing out of Ouro Preto's amphitheatre site in the mountains, we had run through patches of mist, and loose cloud was floating over the highest ridges. But now the sun rose up higher and an altogether Arcadian morning set in. The little blue and white houses and pink-painted farms, shaded by their banana groves or fountains and plumes of bamboo, shone and sparkled in the bright, clear light. Birds darted and swooped across the road in front of us, or sat, their plumage as brilliant as flowers, in the trees.

Occasionally the bus went over a railway line at level-crossings guarded by wizened brown men in caps far too big for them. But what was a railway doing in this land of nymphs and fauns? I soon found the answer. A few hopeful men still took to the hills of Minas Gerais for gold, but machines went there for iron ore. Before coming out on to the main Belo-Rio highway we passed through one whole settlement whose business was the extraction of the ore. So much for Arcadia.

But after that the landscape changed anyway and a great up-thrust of rocks in a sheer precipice stood frowning over the land. And then we turned on to the highway. A twinge of homesickness for Ouro Preto touched me when I saw all the signs of modern life again, petrol stations, power pylons, giant hoardings. Our first halt on the journey to Rio was not encouraging either. We were at Conselheiro Lafaiete. It was no better than Swindon. Even the sunshine did nothing more than show up its grey and grimy ugliness. Being a railway junction, Lafaiete dealt with the region's iron ore. Its street too was jammed with enormous lorries heaped high with the brown ore.

The station was dirty and hideous and full of black, smoking goods engines and all the other accoutrements of railways. They ran at a slightly higher level and parallel to the main street and belched filth into the air, vying in this respect with the heavy lorries pounding through and turning the air blue with exhaust. Then I found that after all the town was not Swindon for, of all things, I saw for the first time a big team of oxen drawing a wagon. Eight gigantic, docile beasts were pulling quite a small load of coffee beans, as though all the engines and lorries around had never existed. From the solid wooden wheels came a long moan of unoiled axles. Then the sound changed key for another long moan which set my teeth on edge.

I was not so deluded by the idea of a romantic past that I would have liked to travel by ox-cart to Rio. This was particularly so now that stretches of the road belonged itself to the past, and became an affair of ruts and pot-holes which sorely tried even the springs of our bus. I thought then of the long snaking and snake-smooth roads from Brasilia. Going down to Rio the worst parts were always near towns, as though the likelihood of heavy traffic had never entered the road engineers' minds.

We came to Santos Dumont. Here was another unfortunate-looking place, a suburb looking for a town. We had to crawl in at one end, through the long ribbon of main street, and out at the other end, at five miles an hour, often in single file to avoid the worst holes and subsidences in the road. I presumed that the Brazilian father of aviation, Santos Dumont, had been honoured by having this town named after him, like Rio's seaside airport. But I am sure, had he been in my bus and forced to suffer the roads of his name-sake town, he would have screamed for a helicopter. Two students from Ouro Preto's School of Mines sat in front of me, and they pointed out the bus's broken window-frames and catches. The vehicle was less than a year old, but what else could be expected, they said, on such roads.

Nor was Juiz-de-Fora, our next stop, much better. This town's most interesting part, and a welcome relief from the monotony of the rest, was the cemetery—a scar of white marble, strategically placed so that the inhabitants should never lose hope that one day they would escape from the town. We stopped for refreshments at a typical roadside café-bar of chromium, neon, and plastic, where, of course, a juke-box was playing sambas so loudly that I had to shout at the man when I ordered a *guaraná gelada*. This cool apple-tasting fruit juice was the reward for another two hours' driving.

Afterwards, in the bus, I was joined by a teenager who wanted to know what I thought about Juiz-de-Fora and then my opinion about Brazil. I lied about the first and told the truth about the second. He was pleased that I liked both and promptly turned up the volume of his pocket transistor radio so that it drowned the one in front, for he was sure I wanted to hear some new Brazilian sambas. Brazilian ears, I was sure, were fitted with special filters which eliminated the advertisement propaganda in between broadcast music.

The afternoon was warm and humid, but when I dozed my new

friend woke me to hear yet another samba number, one of the best that had been composed specially for that year's carnival. Not being a samba connoisseur, and being always unable to discern music in the squawks which those pocket radios produce, I made at least a show of enthusiasm. Had Suppé been Brazilian, I am sure he would have written his *Morning, Noon and Night* overture as a samba, for wherever I went in Brazil, the air was filled with sambas. At morning sambas were already going when I woke. At noon I ate and took a siesta to the sound of sambas. And at night, when the lights were on, the streets noisy with life and the southern wine bottles open, it was the samba which came from radios in the public gardens, or from country boys' guitars under the *fazendas'* trees.

It had been almost a relief when *Onward Christian Soldiers* saluted my first Brasilia happy morn. Yet, whether in the heat and dust or under the shade of great trees, whether high on the inland plateau or down by the Atlantic, sambas at noon *were* Brazil for me. It was the same in black and golden Salvador or in the vineyards of the south, it was the same with the gardeners of Brasilia's water-meadows or Rio's carnival bands, it was the same whenever the happy Brazilian needed music. And that was always.

So the little hills were skipping in time to sambas, and so were the green peaks. The river we followed for hours seemed to fling itself over rocks and weirs in time to the music. Then it vanished and reappeared on our other side, still flooding round islands, over miniature rapids and between giant boulders to some unknown outlet. We passed through places with unlikely names—Ressaca—Hangover—to Ressaquinha—Little Hangover. We sped from one state to the next, from samba to samba, from Japanese cedars to golden cypresses, from another vast precipice, a sheer wall of rock, and up a long winding road to the heights above Rio de Janeiro, and through the forest glades that helped to screen the architectural sins of Petropolis.

When we reached this imperial morgue nightfall was complete and rain buffeted the bus in squalls. Through the windows I saw shiny pavements colourful with reflected neon signs and shadowy with figures hurrying along under umbrellas. This suburb of

There's a kick to *capoeira*—the foot-fighting of north-east Brazil

Open wide! Venom is 'milked' for anti-bite serum from a poisonous snake at São Paulo's Butantan Institute

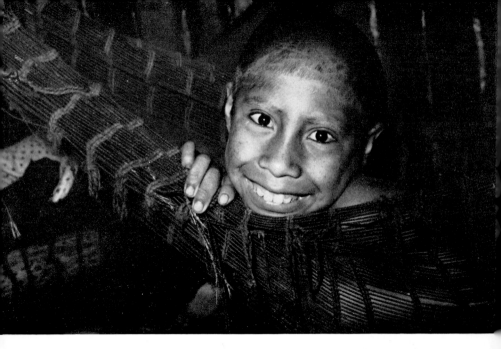

Mischief in a hammock—but his head is shaved in mourning for his father

Long ago and far away there was magic in Brazil

hydrangeas was the haven to which tired bank managers rolled up from Rio behind their chauffeurs, and where, according to my French guide-book, dear things 'flee the sultry heat of Rio', presumably to relax behind their old wrought-iron gates in the pine-scented air.

The heights of Petropolis no doubt looked most imposing by day, quite different from the quieter landscapes I had seen earlier. But we crawled through the town, stopping every five minutes for traffic-jams, and at last broke free and on to the descending road. The rain had cleared, but it was now too dark for the sheer drops beside the road to be seen. I could just discern a wire rope at the road's edge, which was supposed to hold us from going the shortest and quickest way down the 2,500 feet to the twinkling lights below. Any sense of security the rope might have given was much reduced by noticeable gaps in it.

Rio's rush hour was still in progress when we finally arrived. I deposited my luggage and went straight for the Niteroi ferry. I had all sorts of things to do across the water besides seeing queens-of-the-night in flower. A phenomenal crowd was waiting with model patience for the ferry—until it actually came in. Then there was a wild stampede down the wooden jetty. In a moment, the ferry swarmed with people. Plimsoll would not have approved, because the boats were designed for eight hundred passengers, but carried twice as many in the morning and evening rush hours. Not only were commuters sitting on the benches inside, but crowded on the decks outside. There were even some outsiders, as on Rio's trams. They stood on the bumper round the boat, with the water beneath them. But sitting under the stars to the sound of waves in Guanabara Bay and in the light of many anchored ships lying all around, was preferable by far, rush hour or no, to London's Underground rush hour.

I could hardly wait for the ferry to reach Niteroi, for I was burning with curiosity to know the fate of the fakir Zamor. Ever since I had left Rio three months before he had been sitting fasting in his glass box, being gawked at by hundreds of people and presumably growing thinner but richer every day. His one hundred and twenty days of fasting on a bed of nails was not yet expired. With the entrance fee ready in my hand I went to the booth. But it was deserted. The signboards had gone, the entrance was barricaded up and a few bold weeds grew on the temporary doorstep. *Quo vadis,* oh Zamor? Well, he had gone to hospital, I learned afterwards, at the end of a hundred and two days, because of weakness. But this was a record fast for South America and entirely certified as genuine by the military police who guarded him day and night. In this Zamor was well pleased. What did not please him, however, and what, in fact, led to his capitulation, was the fact that his impresario cleared off with all the money leaving not a trace behind him.

Not all fakirs, of course, are as longsuffering or suffer as long as Zamor. Brasilia had a fakir, too, but he did not come anywhere near Zamor's record. This was not his fault, for somebody made faces at him through the glass and he crashed through and chased the offender.

Like people the world over, the Brazilians were fascinated by bearded ladies and fakirs, although they also had their own special oddities to enjoy. The bandit Lampeão was one of these, and at Niteroi, as elsewhere in Brazil, he was in demand as entertainment. Yet another film about the outlaws was currently running when I was there. The cold facts of the matter were that the gangs of thugs and thieves who roamed and terrorized the wild, inaccessible regions of north-east Brazil were far from romantic. Yet although the outlaws were still at the height of their power thirty years ago, a myth had already grown up about them. Perhaps the Brazilian heart hungers for romance no less than the British one. We have Robin Hood, they have Lampeão. Now that history is giving King John a face lift, Robin Hood will no doubt get a new look too. It may even turn out that he was a villain who robbed the poor to give to the rich. Lampeão robbed everybody, besides burning them or their property and torturing his prisoners.

Robin Hood is at a disadvantage, for there is nobody alive to-day who knew him. But in Brazil I met people who had known the dread shadow of Lampeão, either from those who came against him, or from personal experiences with his or other gangs. Ignoring the fact that the outlaws made excellent entertainment in the cinema, the man Lampeão himself in real life was a wild animal, totally devoid of the qualities which make human beings human. His followers were little better. Of all the accounts I heard since I first saw his severed head in the Salvador museum, only one had any good to say of the bandits. A typist in Oscar Niemeyer's office told me the story. When she was a little girl the outlaws fired on her father's pony and trap as she was riding home one day. Fortunately, the only casualty was her pet caged bird. The little girl broke her heart over this. But next morning, outside her home, was a much larger cage full of singing birds. The outlaws had stolen up to the house and left it for her.

But equally true are the reports of Lampeão's sadism. He was nothing if not inventive. For ingenuity his tortures were second to none. The branding of women was a mere diversion for Lampeão. He really enjoyed himself with his men prisoners. He had them fixed in a most unfortunate manner into the drawer of a table. The drawer was shut, the table soaked in paraffin, and then set alight. The victim then had to make a choice between being burnt alive or of castrating himself. Lampeão was not alone, of course, in his grotesque enjoyments. It was the 1930s, and across the Venezuelan border Gomez was hanging up political prisoners by the same means of suspension, and women by their breasts. Nice work if you can get it, but by no means a South American speciality. By 1940 Europe was doing worse things wholesale.

Nevertheless, I saw the new outlaw film and went in the company of an architectural student. His first name, perhaps not unsuitably, was Archimedes. This was no isolated extravagance, for I also knew an Aristoteles, a Demetrius, a Demosthenes, and in Brasilia I heard of a girl called Erotildes. With no holds barred so far as Brazilian names were concerned it ought not to have been, but *was*, startling to hear of new-born babies being called Chessman. There were also smart clubs having the name of that unfortunate North American, who had become something of a martyr in Brazilian eyes.

Archimedes was vivacious, and walking back to the ferry after an hour or so of outlaws he was excited. He gave a jump, a quick turn, and nearly knocked me down with a sharp, well-placed kick behind my legs. I wondered what had hit me. But Archimedes laughed and said surely I had seen *capoeira* in Brazil. I had not, and apparently had missed a form of fighting peculiar to Brazil, but originating in Africa. It amounted to boxing with all four limbs at once, and *capoeira's* devotees had developed their legs to move just as fast, as accurately, as dangerously as fists. By leaping in the air, or falling suddenly to the ground and striking upwards with the feet, the *capoeira* man could take an opponent by surprise. And his, of course, was the advantage over an opponent who knew nothing of *capoeira's* wiles, just as the man who knows judo has an advantage. In some ways, *capoeira* was not unlike judo. Training schools for *capoeira* existed, mostly in the north and notably in Salvador, where the old African traditions still remain.

Rio de Janeiro's climate was in its usual sultry mood. For a month now I had been waiting for the rainy season to end. But the city was still alternately wet and dry, the rain holding off cunningly until I was actually in the street. The heat was bearable, just, and certainly an improvement on December's hothouse. People were saying they could not understand the weather, and added in confidential tones that if you asked *them*, it was the delayed effects of atom-bomb explosions. This under-the-Geiger-counter information may, for all I knew, have been perfectly true. I certainly felt exhausted by the humidity as I slouched along the Avenida Rio Branco in my sandals from one news-stand to the next.

It seemed the most natural thing in the world to stand and read the magazines pinned open at certain pages on the news-stands, and I had become completely Brazilian in that respect at least. After all, the juiciest of the articles were displayed, and at that particular time there were really choice tit-bits to gobble—the Bishop of Maura and the 'children of incest'. The bishop had died, thereby providing magazine photographs with excellent material straight, so to speak, from the coffin. The delighted public thus fed with this heavily morbid example of the mortician's art were able to stare, through the medium of printer's ink, at the famous bishop lying, becoped and bemitred, in state, without going all the way to view him in person.

I liked him. He had a big-boned face, just the right sort of thing for showing determination to Rome, which he had done when he broke away from the Holy See to found the Brazilian Catholic Church. The Bishop of Maura was a much-honoured and revered person during his life. At the time of his death the national Church was flourishing and increasing in number. I had met some of its priests in Oscar Niemeyer's office when they came in to sell raffle tickets.

Anglo-Saxon stomachs, on the whole, find it difficult to digest Latin dishes of death. No less than Latins, we *know* we have to die, but feel perhaps that there are subtler ways of contemplating this. It is not necessary, when all is said and done, to use a steam-roller for cracking nuts. But perhaps this morbidity is the inevitable complement to the high spirits which produce carnivals and non-stop sambas.

So, only just on this side of death were the 'children of incest', the magazine's other big draw. There was a series of photographs showing some hideously deformed, skeleton-like creatures with hopelessly contorted limbs who were the results of incestuous intercourse. These unfortunate people lived in poverty and near-starvation in Brazil's remoter parts. There could hardly have been a better exemplar of the dangers of incest. And on the heels of this thoroughly gruesome display, which attracted so irresistibly, came the trial of Adolf Eichmann with *its* accompanying horrors. Whole shop windows appeared this time, given over to the display of concentration-camp cruelties and that excess of horrors which was incomprehensible, even, or perhaps especially, to Eichmann. Compared with this expert exterminator, Lampeão was as tender as a wet-nurse.

I was not done yet, however, with the grisly, because before leaving the city I had to see the São Bento monastery. Rio de Janeiro was not overcrowded with remains of Brazil's early days, but the São Bento monastery had been there more or less from the start. By 1589 the church was started, although the one I went to see was a seventeenth-century building, complete with French cannon balls buried in the thickness of its walls in the best swashbuckling tradition. São Bento overlooked Rio harbour and sprawled on a rocky

213

eminence commanding a wide view of the coming and going of ships and the further side of the bay. It must have been an easy target for the marauding Frenchmen.

Having such excitements without their doors it might be thought that the monks were glad of the quietness within. Architecturally, at least, this was not the case, for the church interior was far from restful with its jungle of carved and gilded acanthus foliage. The walls were completely smothered and groaned with the weight of all this dark, tarnished stuff. After the rococo lightness and gaiety of Ouro Preto's churches, São Bento seemed oppressive and as heavy as plum pudding. But the plums were elsewhere in the monastery, as I found when a brother took me round. Here were the high rooms, beautiful woodwork, cool corridors and fine native furniture which I had come to expect in old Brazilian buildings. At São Bento, however, an added loveliness was an occasional balcony opening unexpectedly from a passage, and giving a splendid panorama of the harbour.

On an upper floor was the fabulously and richly wrought chapel of relics. The room itself was small, but beautiful with its gilded and painted panelling. It appeared to have been made specially to house the monastery's extensive collection of relics, and did so in a series of little glazed recesses set in the panelling. There were so many relics and bits of human beings that it looked rather like one of those bewildering shops which sell motor-car spare parts. One tiny framed picture alone would contain half a dozen specimens of saints' beards, a few threads of shirt, toenail clippings, or a brown stain that had once been blood. And there were scores of these pictures apart from the recesses. The greatest haul was undoubtedly the stock of shank bones, which showed that not a few of the saints had been tall men.

Long ago somebody must have had a nice time sorting out all the relics. My companion obviously knew most of them, and smiled over them, and showed that he felt at home with them. His genuflection when we left the chapel was full of fond affection rather than cold reverence. The courtyards round the monastery were shaded by thick spreading trees, and I sat on a wall over the harbour for a while, enjoying the comparative coolness and the shade. It was not likely that I would find anything so romantic among São Paulo's skyscrapers. My bus journey south to São Paulo was due on the following day, and I did not feel enthusiastic over what on one hand I had been told was the 'Chicago of South America' and on the other the 'most European' of Brazilian cities. In the event, it turned out to be neither, but I was not to know this as I descended from São Bento to the petrol fumes of Avenida Rio Branco again.

The bus down to São Paulo was air-conditioned, superbly sprung, and had green anti-glare glass in the windows, so that the passenger's eye view of the world outside was a strangely distorted one. It was clearly going to be another stifling day when we pulled out of Rio's bus station, yet we inside were fresh and not even perspiring, certainly not as much as the footballers. All along the way, until we got well clear of the city, I saw football teams rushing about with mad energy in the sun. Some teams were smart in brilliantly coloured (at least they looked brilliant through the green glass) shirts, shorts and striped stockings. But others, with sweat gleaming on shoulders and backs wore nothing except swimming trunks which also served as underwear. For the whole stretch of Rio's seaside industrial areas the teams were playing on waste lots, exactly as others would be doing on the burning beaches of Copacabana.

Travelling out of Rio de Janeiro by road was to go out by the city's back door, so to speak, passing the dustbins and coalhole on the way. The front door, of course, was the sea approach. But at least the back door showed something of Rio's kitchen-sink department. Miles of factories hugged the sea. There seemed to be vast patches of slobland, as though much of the land had been reclaimed from the sea. This was not at all unlikely, as reclaiming was being done in the city proper, noticeably where Affonso Reidy's new Museum of Modern Art was being built. The urubu vultures had taken a fancy to Rio's factory sites and sat about in great clusters looking like a conference of Lutheran clergy. Where the factories ended, home-made shanty villages appeared, also with their expert looking football teams. But eventually we dropped even these behind and had banana and orange groves as we began to climb into the mountains.

A journey of nearly four hundred miles lay ahead now. This was a mere jaunt which would not even involve sleeping overnight in the bus. São Paulo was always considered to be near Rio de Janeiro, and certainly was its nearest big neighbour. But we travelled in that luxury bus most comfortably, taking long, and good, mountain roads in our stride, and in consequence four hundred miles did not seem at all formidable. I did not think the landscape so fine as that of Minas Gerais between Belo Horizonte and Ouro Preto. We saw mountain ranges and vast areas of wildly undulating land where lakes and farms were held captive in the valleys. But it was repetitive and without the startlingly clear profiles of Minas Gerais.

The bus stopped at several roadhouses, including one for lunch where I ate *canja*, a delicious thick broth of chicken and rice which could be got everywhere in Brazil. The driver ate enough for ten men, and I was afraid lest he should fall asleep over the wheel and we should crash over a precipice. But I need not have worried, because from then on there were no more precipices and we bowled along smoothly on our superior springs to Guaratinguetá. This was Black Virgin country. The road followed the River Paraiba for some distance. It had been from those waters, of course, that the negress Our Lady of the Apparition had been rescued. Her actual shrine was the cathedral a little further along the road in the town named after her—Aparecida. At Guaratinguetá only one thing impressed me and that was the colour of the flame trees by the hotel gates. Each of the thousands of Roman-lamp blossoms looked as though a flame burned inside it. The cloud of colour was the most intensely orange I had seen anywhere in Brazil.

Until the bus was ready to leave again I sat near the flame trees. They were worth looking at, which was more than could be said for the trash on sale in the roadhouse. The dark Virgin was certainly done proud in there, by all the plastic figures of her in tiny plastic shrines, to say nothing of pocket-knives with the Senhora da Aparecida on their handles, and ash-trays with her on the bottom, and key-rings and cigarette-lighters. However, I did learn from all the souvenirs that in some way a horseman hunting a stag over a high bank into the river was another part of the miraculous event.

The town of Aparecida was perhaps rightly named apparition, though rushing through it in an express bus probably did it less than justice. The town had no skyscrapers, but only low buildings and a number of churches. Their spires pointed above the roofs like London's towers in Canaletto's paintings of the Thames. And greater than any of them was the new cathedral under construction. Only a slice of it had been attempted so far, an affair of piled-up, round-headed arches, sticking up vertically above everything else, as Gothic cathedrals did when being built bay by bay.

But we were through Aparecida in a flash, leaving behind its footballers and Sunday fishermen in the marshy lands around the town. Gradually even the peppering of roadside shrines, all to the Black Virgin, began to thin out, and the last one I saw was wreathed with orange neon-tubes, so that for a moment I mistook it for a petrol station. Rain set in again, for the coming of the dry season still delayed. The tops of mountains beyond the river had been lost in mist most of the way, and now the rain swept down over the plain.

And then we came to the first indication that São Paulo was no more than forty or fifty miles ahead. Giant advertisement hoardings appeared again, spaced along the road on vantage-points. When they began to stand closer together I knew that the small towns, the groups of mud huts, the isolated modern bungalows built like miniature Palaces of the Dawn, were all left behind. Then the first factories flitted by our green windows. We still were twenty miles from the city. But, in a sort of long-drawn-out Great West Road, the factories stayed with us for the rest of the way. In many cases, surprisingly, the buildings were not at all displeasing, and at first were dispersed among hayfields and market gardens. São Paulo's industrial tentacles possessed a trim kind of efficiency rather different from Rio's factory sprawl. I felt almost at home when I saw the neat white buildings of Johnson & Johnson and I thought of baby's bottom.

There was never any twilight in Brazil, but if there had been, then that was when we hurtled into the city, just as the skyscraper cliffs of the centre were vanishing in gloom. My companion on the journey had been a dried-up old lady who slept the entire way. Now she woke, thanked me for an enjoyable time, and would I be so kind as to get her bags from the rack? For my pains I was given a small religious medal bearing the Black Virgin.

11

Paulo-Post-Future

São Paulo had everything against it. Despite being founded in 1554 by two Jesuit priests, São Paulo belonged entirely to and owed its continued existence to modern commercial and industrial life. You would see nothing in its streets older than its trams, people said, for buildings, apparently, were the more expendable of the two. São Paulo had no special beauties of landscape, was overcrowded by four million people and choked at its heart with motorcars. And the people with whose views and tastes I most disagreed had all said that São Paulo was wonderful. There was, then, no reason why I should fall in love with the city. But I did. Whatever else it had or had not, the city was filled with an abundance of human life. It was the most vital city I had ever been in.

I arrived just as Sunday evening was getting under way. Just as the city had grown from the Jesuit settlement, so now the quiet evening *paseo* of those days had become the tremendous ceremony of flocking to the centre in smart clothes, drifting along the pavement, strolling under the dark trees in the *praças* and making headlong, sudden flights across wide avenues before pent-up floods of traffic, drinking at the bars and coffee-houses, going to the cinemas which *started* their last Sunday performance at 10 p.m. The lights were dazzling and the pavements jammed full. São Paulo's downtown Sunday night was like Southend seafront on a bank holiday, with all the same noise, colour and excitement. But there was much more elegance and, in spite of the numbers, a sense that everybody was a Paulista and belonged to this town and that it was *their* town.

It was obvious that I was going to have a rowdy and boisterous time for as long as I stayed, and so I found a small hotel right in the middle of the *mêlée*, in fact in the heart of '*cinelandia*'. But I managed to get a reasonably quiet room facing a high wall at the back. A room without a view was the only way to escape the growl of car engines and the blare of loudspeakers. The hotel, for better or worse, was situated between two gramophone-record shops which had to outdo each other in the loudness of their relayed music in order to get the more customers. They were open and doing a literally roaring trade on the Sunday evening. But provided you did not stand immediately in front of the hi-fi cabinets, the noise somehow got absorbed in the general hubbub. They were still booming out sambas at midnight.

Sibelius once said that other modern composers gave their audiences rich cocktails, but he gave them pure crystal water. I had taken my crystal water of Brazil's cities by staying at Ouro Preto. Now I was going to enjoy my cocktail, sickly, sweet, and a quick intoxicator—the São Paulo sizzler made of one part Brazilian passion, one part Brazilian gaiety, and two parts Paulista energy. This recipe was not so bland as would appear, for the Paulista ingredient was itself a highly spiced international mixture. São Paulo's largest colony of foreigners was Italian, though in bars and buses I frequently heard German being spoken, then there were Spaniards, and more than a sprinkling of almond-eyed Japanese and swarthy-skinned Middle Easterners—all Paulistas. São Paulo was justifiably proud of itself and if you asked anybody if he was a Paulista he would say: 'Yes, and a Brazilian, too.' This was more than a cocky answer, for many thousands of Paulistas only one generation back were not Brazilian but belonged to any one of a hundred less fortunate lands. To be a Paulista *and* a Brazilian was an accomplishment worth being proud of.

Energy was perhaps the key, for you could almost see the Paulistas flinging themselves with fantastic energy into whatever they were doing. Sleep was obviously not part of Sunday night's entertainment. Although the party, so to speak, was still high at midnight, Monday morning's first traffic already woke me at 5 a.m.

It did not take me long to decide that I not only liked São Paulo, but liked it more than Rio de Janeiro, and not simply on account of it being cooler. Rio's chief glory was its setting in the incomparable

Bay. Remove the city and its flat streets and undistinguished architecture to the banks of the Thames, and put Copacabana's urbane
hotels along Brighton front, and the gilt would be off the ginger-
bread. But put Ouro Preto's churches on any other hills and the
town would still be as beautiful. So with São Paulo; it had nothing
to boast but its life. It would be highly successful beside the Thames,
except perhaps the Paulistas would be depressed by fogs and rain.

I soon made several discoveries about the city. The first was when
I took my supper of big prawns á la Bahia and a bottle of Brazilian
Liebfraumilch and found that it cost me less than anywhere I had
been so far. This sent me flying out to look in the shop windows, to
see if everything else was correspondingly cheaper. It was, and this
led to the second discovery—that São Paulo's shops were better
than Rio's, with goods of better quality and of more variety, shown
in more ingenious and certainly more up-to-date window displays.
I passed some of the world's most beautiful flower shops overcrowded with the world's most exquisite orchids and bird-of-paradise
flowers.

There were wonderful pastry shops selling things almost as
beautiful as the orchids. There were inventions in sugar, mouth-
watering flans and cakes decorated like elaborate flower gardens. It
seemed as though the European immigrant bakers and confectioners
had all settled in São Paulo to add the Brazilian art with sugar to their
own craft. Being full of prawns, I could eat no more, but stood with
my nose pressed against the glass. Not the least part of the uncanny
mesmerism those windows exercised was the complete absence of
flies, a new experience for me in Brazil. I well remembered a rather
appetizing cake I had seen in a restaurant in Brasilia. Aha, I had
thought, licking my chops, a currant cake just like mother makes.
It was cake all right, but plain cake covered with flies. But not a one
stalked across the shelves or windows in São Paulo. It was also
possible to eat a meal, too, without waving one's hands over the food
like a flustered penguin.

Penguins could actually be bought in São Paulo, the kind with
glued spines and paper backs. The bookshops were as good in their
own field as were the pastry shops in theirs, in fact probably better.

Not only were the bookshops numerous and well laid out, but they were also, like everything else, open until very late at night. After all, although this was downtown São Paulo, full of cinemas and bars and night clubs, there was just the possibility that one would be out with a girl who liked good books. Instead of buying her orchids, what could be better than to pop into a bookshop and buy a parchment-bound 1655 edition of Gottfriedt's *Newe Welt*?

A fine shop called Livraria Kosmos had just obtained this single copy while I was in the city. Its ancient paper was beautifully preserved, the fascinating engravings still clear after three hundred years. This traveller's book was one of the earliest to be published on Brazil. Livraria Kosmos also had many beautiful books on art, including some new facsimile reproductions of other old books about Brazil. But then a number of São Paulo's bookshops were publishing houses, too, and made a point of resurrecting old books and engravings about the early days of Brazil. Indeed, many of those books and drawings were the only surviving evidence on the now-remote colonial times. Similarly, drawings and accounts preserved in Rio's Military Archives were almost the only record of the great Jesuit colleges and churches which fell into decay following the order's decline in the eighteenth century.

Although beautifully produced books on art are certainly among printing's finest achievement in this century, they always leave me feeling irritably frustrated, for there is no substitute for the original. And it was this thought which led me to another pleasing discovery about São Paulo, or rather which reminded me of something I had forgotten—that this rip-roaring city ripped and roared about art as much as it did about other things. And not only was it a repository for as many canvases of past masters as the city council thought it ought to afford, but it was a city in which art was actively being produced. Along with all its factories and salesmen and high-pressure business executives, there were real, live artists and, just as importantly, enough people to take them seriously. This looked more like culture of the many than cult by the few. Perhaps, on the other hand, it was only as things ought to be in a city with a population as big as the whole of Denmark's.

The pictures, however, unlike the pastry and the Penguins, were not available late that Sunday night (how nice to see British books generally predominating in some of the shops over the American paper backs whose garish covers are never related to the contents). I had to wait for a weekday before I could go and see São Paulo's collection of Impressionists hanging far from their native France in the city art gallery. This building was quite distinct from the famous Museum of Modern Art. The one gallery was in the centre of town and the other a short way outside in a great public park called Ibirapuera. The city gallery had a fascinating selection of paintings. Over the years, various directors must have been most astute and assiduous in making purchases. Amongst the classics was Velazquez, but that was going back into time—even beyond the gallery's other patriarchs such as Cézanne and old father Renoir, one of whose pearly-fleshed nudes which dissolved light and colour into almost a new element was worth, in my opinion, twenty nudes by anybody else, including the fat ladies of Rubens. Also in town was the always elegant Degas, seen in company with that rough, wild-eyed van Gogh, and Picasso.

If hopeful travelling is better than arrival, then all the painters in the city gallery might be said to have arrived. The hopeful travellers had the other museum where they could display their work. How different it all was out there at the Museum of Modern Art, for painting and sculpture could be shown there which was so new, so revolutionary, that nobody could tell whether it was 'good' or not, and definitely could not tell whether it would still be looked at in fifty or a hundred years time. Larger numbers of people are beginning to understand that art does not necessarily have to look like something else, flowers or faces, for instance, in order to be art. There are comparatively fewer who understand that it need not even look like art. But the museum understood, and this was its great gift to artists—unconditional freedom from the need to conform. And having no obligations other than to paint or sculpt as the spirit moves is and always has been essential to the continuous evolution of art through the centuries. So, by actually showing new works, São Paulo was making a tremendous contribution to civilization. Art is not like pigeons—meant only for fanciers—it is the most subtle, most precise instrument for measuring a nation's feelings and degree of civilization. It was not simply pictures that the thousands of visitors went to see when they flocked to the recent exhibition of Russian paintings at Burlington House. They went to look in the mirror of Russia itself.

The Impressionists themselves, now accepted and hung with the classics, only created because they freed themselves from what their contemporaries thought they *ought* to be painting. Had the Paris of the 1870s had an institution like São Paulo's Museum, the Impressionists could have shown their work and spent more energy on painting than on fighting for recognition. No need for a *Salon des Refusés* would ever have arisen.

So São Paulo's great building out at Ibirapuera was devoted to the artists who, according to their lights, were hacking their way through to a new visual experience. The museum not only gave voice to Brazilian artists but, in its biennial exhibitions, to experimenting artists from the world over. The Paulista could go and see what was happening in Italian studios, on German canvas, to American bronze.

While I was in São Paulo, the museum was showing some remarkable paintings by Arcangelo Ianelli, a Brazilian painter born in the city in 1922, and who indeed painted like an archangel should. His canvases were large noble panels glowing with sombre colours as though he were sounding previously unexplored depths of tone and charting his soundings more profoundly than any other artist ever. His pictures were not *about* anything, but existed solely in their own majestic beauty. In striking contrast was the work of another Brazilian artist also on show. He was of Japanese extraction, a fact reflected in his delicately coloured wisps of pattern—as though *he* were experimenting with the absence of darkness as Ianelli was with the absence of light.

There was also an extensive display of sculpture by Felicia Leirner, again unique, experimental and symptomatic of a vigorous artistic mind. And this exhibition of three men of widely diverse methods and views was by no means an out-of-the-ordinary show for the Museum of Modern Art. I saw catalogues and photographs of many similar past exhibitions and plans for those in the immediate future. If the word 'museum' does not signify a morgue of art but a place where the muses put fire into life, then São Paulo's was certainly a museum.

On the ground floor, in a more or less permanent display, I spotted a John Piper picture of a stone wall which recalled the crumbly walls I had seen near Swansea docks at the very beginning of my journey to Brazil. There was also a purple pianist by Ceri Richards, and a sad-looking Michael Ayrton shepherd and one or two other works by contemporary British artists. The British Council had distributed these visible exports. Somewhat more difficult to transport but in great demand (or at least in the fashion) were those polished monoliths by Barbara Hepworth.

A further discovery I made during my first days in São Paulo was that the fever of life was never over, nor the busy world hushed. You could linger in the museum until ten o'clock at night and still find on returning to the centre that the city's night life was only just beginning. This pitch of living was an intoxicating cocktail indeed, following so closely on my retreat at Ouro Preto. Yet even there, of course, O Aleijadinho had devoted himself with demoniac energy into his work, stopping at nothing, in the way that did Renoir a century later, an artist who also worked with his tools fixed to his crippled, arthritic fingers when he grew old and could no longer hold the brushes.

But the ordinary Paulista, far from being driven by creative urges or by neurotic tendencies, was merely living at his own normal Brazilian rate, extracting the last drop of pleasure from every minute of existence. The Londoner had just the faintest whiff, the merest breath of a similar atmosphere during the 1951 Festival of Britain. Since then he has succumbed again to the inbred guilt-feelings that anything done after eleven at night in public must be immoral.

São Paulo, as a place, was eminently suited to the entirely delightful habits of the Paulistas. But the photographs I had looked at before going there showed only a nondescript town with random skyscrapers of doubtful architectural parentage, and a few public

gardens wedged into whatever spaces were left between the buildings. Yet though this might be true in some ways, São Paulo's
centre was in reality curiously spacious. The skyscrapers did not by
any means scrape the sky and consequently did not dwarf everything else. And the sense of spaciousness might also have derived
from the city's considerable differences of level, which gave changing, and therefore seldom tedious, viewpoints.

The most important amongst these changes of level was the
wide avenue which cut through the city like a canyon. Other
avenues on bridges crossed it at a number of places, adding still
more to the amount of movement to be seen in any one place. I was
told that the canyon's name—Anhangabaú—was Indian in origin,
but it sounded German to me—as Teutonic as the handsome blond-
headed and blue-eyed people who caught buses in Anhangabaú, or
walked briskly over its bridges.

Although it was on a considerably greater scale, Anhangabaú
reminded me strongly of Brasilia's centre. I wondered if São Paulo
had perhaps subconsciously influenced Lucio Costa's ideas for the
great axial crossing of Brazil's new capital. In both cases the fast
traffic road sweeps under a series of bridges and both are in the
thick of the business and entertainment areas, and both are surrounded by multi-storey towers. The similarity was too striking to
ignore and it pleased me, for I could wish nothing better for
Brasilia that it should be, when fully grown, as lively as São Paulo.

Because of the cooler climate briskness was possible in São Paulo.
Instead of drooping every half-hour, and stopping frequently to
drink gallons of orange juice, I found that less energy was sapped at
the end of a whole day than in half a morning in Rio. No doubt
these factors had a great deal to do with São Paulo's popularity as a
settling-place for foreigners and also with the development of industry. It may possibly have had something to do with the founding in
1902, by São Paulo State, of the Butantan Institute.

Although the snakes in the glass case with him were sleepy, I do
not know whether Zamor, Niteroi's fakir, included snake-charming
among his other accomplishments. But the Butantan Institute
certainly did, and by every scientific means at its disposal, for this

was Brazil's famous establishment devoted to the study of venomous creatures, snakes, spiders, and scorpions. It was a place of pilgrimage for people professionally concerned, and they travelled to São Paulo in many instances solely to visit the Institute. But unlike so many other scientific establishments, Butantan had considerable fascination for the layman as a sort of snake zoo, in fact was the city's biggest tourist attraction. Besides its work with viruses, bacteria and the preparation of serums, the Institute maintained a fantastic collection of snakes whose venom was extracted and used in anti-snakebite serums. The snakes were sent to Butantan from all over Brazil, as I knew from seeing some dispatched from various places in the interior. The people who caught these live snakes for the Institute knew the value of its research and products. Working in the interior meant working in snake country. Thousands of lives had been saved by injections from the small phials of Butantan.

From the Garden of Eden onwards, snakes have exerted a horrible fascination on mankind. So has poison. There is always a hush in *Hamlet* when the sleeping player king has poison poured in his ear. With such excitements alone, Butantan would have been an enormous success, but the Institute was far from being a bare laboratory. Butantan was out in the suburbs, and the many buildings stood among lawns and flowering trees and brilliant shrubs. And there, in the open air, were the snake pits. Some of the Institute's specimens lived grisly lives here in full view of visitors who knew they felt safer on their side of the seven-foot drop into the pits. A vertical concrete wall lined the pits. There was grass at the bottom and here the venomous, mottled coils lay like cow-claps in the sun, or slid evilly over the grass or even tried to climb the walls. One of the pits was devoted to huge poisonous frogs whose bite was death for certain types of snake which attacked them. As in the case of 'man bites dog', 'frog bites snake' was news, for the reverse was normally the case. Little houses like miniature igloos had been built for the snakes to snooze in with comfort and darkness, rather like the five-foot-high anthills of the interior which snakes liked to take over when the ants abandoned them. Hundreds of snakes lived in the pits, including some enormous rattlesnakes, and all were as poisonous as a brood of Borgias.

Naturally, the Institute's staff were on more intimate and relaxed terms with their dangerous captives than were mere visitors. I was not prepared, however, to come face to face with a fourteen-foot boa-constrictor. He was living in a corner of Dr. Hélio Belluomini's office. Dr. Belluomini was kind enough to stop his work to take me round the Institute and we began in his office. The boa-constrictor was quite a new acquisition, one of the finest the Institute ever had. Nobody knew exactly when he had last eaten, and although I did not say so, I thought that he looked at me in a hungry sort of way. Only the thinnest sheet of glass separated this massive snake from us. But Dr. Belluomini said the boa-constrictor did not actually *know* it was only thin glass. . . .

It had a rather nice face, not unlike a fox-terrier puppy, without ears, of course, and with black boot-button eyes. For company the boa-constrictor had a two-foot-long scaly lizard, a companion which it was later expected to devour. I asked Dr. Belluomini if I might touch the snake, and he said yes but it was dangerous and I would have to do it quickly. He opened the glass door and I put my hand in and touched the beautiful creamy, greeny body. It did not show the slightest sign of life. Even when Dr. Belluomini scratched the snake's head with a steel ruler, nothing more than a convulsion shuddered through those powerful coils of muscle. All the same I wished that he had closed the glass door when he went to another room for a telephone call.

With some trepidation I watched the lizard walking over those tubes of greenish, cold skin and was glad when Dr. Belluomini returned and took me to the laboratories where the snakes were 'milked' of their venom. The walls were stacked with ordinary wooden boxes and the effect was that of a market-gardener's store with boxes of tomatoes waiting for dispatch. To show me the milking process Dr. Belluomini asked an assistant to get out a rattlesnake, there and then in the room. I still could not get used to the idea of being so near the snakes. I felt naked without protection. However, nothing daunted, the box was unscrewed and a long thing began immediately to slide out of it, to be picked up by a hook in the end of a pole. The rattlesnake was put on the floor, the hook was put behind its head. The assistant bent down, took hold of the creature with forefinger and thumb behind the head. Then, like some busy district nurse, he squeezed. The mouth opened wide, two great fangs appeared. They were pressed against a small glass jar. Three drops of an amber liquid like honey ran down and settled at the bottom of the jar. Far from being honey, it was enough venom to kill three people.

The snake was put back into his box to rest for twenty days until more venom had been built up. This matter-of-fact attitude towards the snakes only added to the cold horror. But I tried to make intelligent remarks as Dr. Belluomini cheerfully brushed up his English and talked to me about the Institute's varied work and his own specialist interests. Amongst these was serpentine surgery. He even knew his snakes so well that he could, and did, perform Caesarean operations on them. He showed me the horses used in the production of serum, the small hospital for snake, spider and scorpion bite victims, and the helicopter landing area where those unfortunate people arrived. Every case was, of course, an emergency. He thought that an average intake was one patient a day. To show me the variety of snake specimens Dr. Belluomini asked the pit-keeper to bring out his special charges from their glass cases in a small kiosk.

On his pole and hook the man then brought out an astonishing number of different snakes, including some, notably the coral and jararaca, which I had encountered up in Brasilia. The talk was all very well about there being only one poisonous snake in Brazil to every eight non-venomous ones, the reverse case from Asia and Africa, but nevertheless the most widely scattered species in Brazil was the jararaca.

I was given a non-poisonous coral snake to hold, a most ungratifying experience, particularly as I had my eye on the venomous one squirming at my feet. The keeper teased his snakes, as he had done earlier in the pits, to make them strike, which they did with the power and speed of released springs. But he kept always just out of reach. Dr. Belluomini ruefully showed me some fang scars on his fingers, souvenirs of the occasions when he had not been just out of reach. More horrifying than these *serpenteiras*, however, were the two huge, hairy spiders which the keeper brought. One was simply crawling in a half-hearted way on a piece of glass. It was as big as my hand. The other, a type of tarantula, was considered dangerous enough to be kept in a jar. And when Butantan considers a creature dangerous, you can rest assured it is.

Samuel Johnson's verdict would undoubtedly have been that when a man was tired of São Paulo he was tired of life. I was tired of neither, but nevertheless had to pack my suitcases and once again think about transport, this time to the deep south of Brazil. Flying could not be considered, as by now I had accumulated an embarrassing amount of luggage. The excess baggage charge would have been crippling. I had decided also to nurse my most valuable Madonna on my knees as well as my typewriter, to protect them from further damage, and this might have been awkward in a plane. So I was left with a choice between train and bus. The train took four uncomfortable days, and the bus thirty uncomfortable hours. My dilemma was eventually resolved on learning that the train ticket had to be booked at least a month in advance. Without the least shame I tried to get my name at the head of the formidable waiting list, but to no avail. I steeled myself to the long drive by road down to Porto Alegre. Losing yet another night's sleep, I supposed, would not matter, since in São Paulo I seemed hardly to have slept at all. Rarely before eleven at night had I started my hunt for unfamiliar restaurants among those of a score of different nationalities. Having eaten perhaps a Russian meal I would begin a series of nocturnal adventures the like of which I would never have dreamed of in Europe—or at least, not on every night of the week.

So, loaded with my baroque Madonnas and crucifixes, with other bits and pieces of carving and the surprising number of books I seemed to have collected on my way through Brazil, I arrived well in time at São Paulo's bus station. It was new-pin and whistle clean. It positively shone with polishing and sweeping. Any other station of any sort I had seen anywhere was put to shame. Even the lavatory seats carried paper seals which said that they had been sterilized since the last occupancy. In the refreshment bar I drank a Coca-Cola, feeling as though I was in an operating theatre.

If you are going to travel and see things, this is the way, I kept telling myself in an effort to exorcise regrets that, after all, I had not taken the plane. The worst moment, however, was in a traffic bottleneck over a bridge on the way out of São Paulo, where we had to wait half an hour in a fog of exhaust. We also put all the windows up because the lorry waiting next to us carried a load of cow heads complete with horns and the stench was a killer. After that our bus fairly leapt ahead, so that the afternoon and evening passed sur-prisingly quickly. We rushed through São Paulo State, and I barely had time to see the strange blue beauty of its eucalyptus woods. The trees were sometimes islanded in a sea of freshly-turned ploughed lands and pasture where the Hereford and Polled Angus, the Devon and Jersey had replaced the zebu and Chinese cattle of the north and central plains. But here the landscape was on a different scale. The whole region looked as though its wildness had been conquered long ago and that it was many years since the wide, placid fields had last seen tangled, matted undergrowth.

Porto Alegre was the capital for the state of Rio Grande do Sul, and to reach it we had to get free of São Paulo State and cross the states of Parana and Santa Catarina. The *Rubens's* crew had talked about Porto Alegre soon after the ship had left Swansea. You wait, they told me, until you get to Porto Alegre. But at last I was to taste the paradise for myself, though realizing that easy girls and cheap waterfront bars do not necessarily make perfection. On that bus I had a lot of time to speculate about Porto Alegre, for my seat was next to the corridor and I could not look out of the window all the time. I caught only occasional glimpses, perhaps of Protestant mis-sion churches in small villages, with the Assemblies of God always well in evidence, alternating with garages given good Brazilian names such as 'The Good Jesus for spare auto parts'.

We ate supper at Capao Bonito in an extraordinary room like a film version of a mediaeval banqueting-hall. Each of the twenty or so tables had the traditional block of wood in the centre, pierced by swords on which roasted meat had been spitted. I almost expected some of the guests to jump up swearing frightful oaths and begin running duels with the swords, jumping on to the tables and swinging from the lamps in the best Hollywood manner. Unfortunately nothing so exciting happened, though there were dogs lying about waiting for morsels to be thrown. It was an extraordinary sight, especially to see rather dainty women carving away at an enormous hunk of meat on the spit in front of their noses and devouring unbelievable quantities. The swords sprang to and fro in their blocks as the women sliced away at the meat, so that the whole room quivered like a bamboo clump in the wind.

Dona Isabel was amongst them, a petite creature who, you would have thought, lived on nothing but tea and toast. But while I watched she got through enough meat to keep a circus lion happy. Perhaps she did feel guilty, for she kept reminding me that we were in 'beef country' now and must eat lots. But Dona Isabel was in an elated mood, as I well knew from her story on the bus of the family's trip to São Paulo. They were on their way home again to Porto Alegre *now,* and she felt triumphant, for in São Paulo her son had become a man—at last, she added darkly. In Porto Alegre she had employed various girl servants to help precipitate this happy event, but it had taken her sister's coloured girl in São Paulo to do the trick. And about time, said Dona Isabel indignantly, for her son was already sixteen.

Like dentists, Brazilian bus companies did everything they could to make the customer feel at home. Even the bus seats were like dentists' chairs, fully adjustable and provided with a head-pad. One immense blessing also was that after sunset no lights were switched on to glare into the passengers' eyes all night. The darkness, the motion, the half-prone position of the seats were all conducive to sleep. But as always, of course, the human element upset calculations, and I found myself wedged into position by the lowered back of the seat in front of me, which forced my typewriter and Madonna into my stomach. The man next to me against the window was suffering from *grippe* or some other kindred influenzal infection. For thirty hours he sneezed with no attempt to cover up. In an agony of nerves, I thought of the millions of germs. He also made frequent and urgent trips to the lavatory rigged up at the back of the bus, which meant I had to unload my Madonna and typewriter into the gangway, and then stand up to let him get in and out.

All through the night Dona Isabel, my neighbour across the gangway, fluttered and twittered occasionally under her blanket like a canary in a cage with its cover on. But whenever we stopped, and the relief driver took over, Dona Isabel emerged as bright as a morning lark, trilling melodiously about her family and the São Paulo sister and the maid. At Apiai, when we stopped at some forsaken hour of night or early morning, Dona Isabel had to have a chair brought because she laughed to the point of convulsion when I knocked my head against a large chocolate Easter egg hanging from the cafe's low ceiling. It broke, much to the proprietor's distress and Dona Isabel's delight, and I bought the pieces. She was still laughing when we settled under the blankets again.

I would have been most pleased to have found amusement so easily, for the journey was becoming tedious to a degree. Besides my neighbour's influenza I now had the tangerines. Until that journey to Porto Alegre, the smell of tangerines always reminded me of Christmas. Unfortunately, now Christmas will always remind me of the tangerines on that journey. Of course, it was understandable that the poor fellow should want to boost his resistance with vitamin C. But there must have been some other way of doing so without showering peel all over the floor and bombarding my Madonna with pips.

But how pure was that night air outside and how cold. We drove through patches of mist. Since sundown, a continuous procession of lorries going towards São Paulo had passed us. Their loads were piled high and covered by tarpaulins and ropes, making them look like camel caravans going through the Khyber Pass. And after we left Apiai the lorries were camels indeed, for the road was the old mountain trail, an unsurfaced affair of rocks and ruts which threatened to shatter the bus to pieces, and make the top-heavy lorries pitch and roll like caravan camels. My neighbour had retired under his blanket with the tangerine bag some hours before. But occasionally he popped his bald head out like a tortoise from its shell, when the

232

bus leaned at a more than usually alarming angle, or when the flickering light of flares, set to warn of new landslides, shone in the windows. He seemed to have a sixth sense which told him when we were passing a roadside shrine, for his blanket went down and he crossed himself as though it were for the last time on this earth.

He had some cause to be alarmed. Often the grinding, lurching procession of lorries almost scraped the bus. We saw several heeled over, the outside wheels sticking up in the air like helpless legs. And after seeing a purple glow in the sky for a mile or so, we crawled and slithered towards a pyre of leaping flames. In the middle I saw the black skeleton of another lorry, all but burnt out. Keeping their distance from the intense heat, drivers were standing round, and across the road others knelt in a wooden chapel where dozens of candles rivalled the lorries' flames which writhed and surged up to thirty feet or more. Our own drivers got out to see if there was room for us to squeeze by, and luckily the old trail was wider at that point. The sneezer would not countenance going past in the bus and to the driver's and my annoyance insisted on getting out with his string-bag of tangerines and walking by the burning wreck. When he climbed aboard again and had settled, he crossed himself and we left the arena of fire and shuddered on into the darkness.

All along the road lorries were parked in groups of ten or more. Each was without lights. Fancy curtains and fringes were drawn across the cabin windows, for the drivers slept inside, oblivious of passing convoys, stretched on the beds let down from the back of the cabins. Two o'clock came and went, the rocky trail showed no sign of ending, and the night outside alternated between blank blackness and the outline of yet another caravan of lorries and clouds of dust pierced by the headlamp rays.

As at Apiai, a small village called Ribeira was lined with dozens of parked lorries. We drank more coffee in the crisp air and listened to a huge, fat negro yodelling. He looked as though he was in a trance, possessed by the spirit of a Swiss mountaineer. His yodelling carried, as yodelling should, far beyond the little café, but the good burghers of Ribeira were apparently used to *eine kleine Nachtmusik.*

They might even have called it that, for now we were well into the south's German-speaking areas. The houses we could see were beginning to assume steep roofs with overhanging eaves and have carved balconies all in the best cuckoo-clock style.

The yodeller (he was a negro edition of Burl Ives) accompanied himself on a small guitar. Percussion was provided by a boy with a tambourine and a garage-hand taking a few minutes' break to play a tiny drum called a *borracha*. He held it between his knees, and with his hands produced an astonishing variety of sounds, ranging from sharp staccato plops to a kind of caressing ripple.

And so on to a village called Tunas, still by the terrible road, and still creeping through narrow cuttings where the rocks almost touched the bus, rock which glinted in the headlamps, but whether with water or mineral deposits I could not tell. Black pigs ran around the petrol pumps at Tunas and came grunting after Sneezer's tangerine peel and such crumbs of biscuits and chocolate as Dona Isabel let fall from her gesticulating hands. I slept after we left the hotel's shelves of plaster religious statues and pickles behind, and when I woke, stiffnecked but refreshed, it was morning and we had come to a new land.

If this was still Brazil, and I could hardly believe that it was, if it was still the Germanic regions, then it was certainly a world of *Jugendstil*, with trees designed by Aubrey Beardsley to fit the sad misty landscape. The sweeping, exaggerated forms of those araucaria pines stood about the fields, straight and bare-trunked. But at the top they carried curved ribs like a many-branched Jewish candelabra. At the end of each curious branch was a dark-green knob of pine needles. The effect produced was strangely Canadian, like British Columbia, where the great pine forests also rise out of mists. Yet with the golden-rod and pampas grass that bordered the road it could not be Canada, nor with the inverted umbrella of the araucaria, which was more akin to the monkey-puzzle than Canadian pines.

For most of the day we ran through country with whole forests of araucaria. I had seen the trees previously in the gardens of Anapolis. But they had been isolated like monkey-puzzles in English gardens of the last century. But now we passed square miles of them at a time. There were lumber settings and mountains of sawdust where the trees were felled. These pines of Parana were not inexhaustible, however, and already there were areas of reafforestation. After only ten years the trees could be used for paper pulp, and as timber after thirty years of growth. The best quality went mostly to Germany, a country so much like Parana itself that it seemed the timber *ought* to go there. The farther south we went the more Teutonic the landscape and its settlements became. I was not to leave the pines, however, simply by leaving Parana, or even by leaving Brazil, for the *Rubens* had a load of the timber in its holds for delivery in Cork when we stopped on the homeward voyage.

If earlier I had a fleeting impression of Canada, now there was one of Scotland, not only from the forests, but because the countryside between was hedged with stone dykes, doubtless built by slaves and not crofters' debts. Here, too, more hay had been won, giving a suggestion of autumn. The ricks were dressed and topped into odd shapes like Russian church steeples. Then all this changed, too, and became a landscape of vineyards which accompanied us to Caxias do Sul, our last sizeable town before Porto Alegre.

The *gauchos* had come into Caxias for Sunday afternoon. They wore their cowboy outfits—wide brimming hats, baggy trousers with buttons and pleats down the sides caught in the top of their boots, and blankets slung over their shoulders against the night cold. *Gauchos* belonged to the colourful Brazil which hid itself in the interior and which normally was never seen in the cities. Beyond the reach of modern life, traditional Brazil survived. Those cowboys lived as their grandfathers had done, and were the same tough, proud Rio Grandenses. They broke wild colts, and still cooked their meat on spits over wood fires, the *churrasco* that city restaurants imitated all over Brazil. Cowboys they were, proud of their strength in the fields and of their celebrated herds. They also had a monopoly of Brazil's sheep. Rio Grande do Sul produced the country's best wheat and root crops and the finest wines. These people often began their life on horseback, almost from the cradle. Besides many youths trotting along the roads, I saw a boy of ten on horseback rounding up cattle with all the skill of a man three times his age.

In the late afternoon, through a gap in the mountains, we caught a glimpse of Porto Alegre. It appeared as a white blur on a distant plain and in less clear weather would not have been visible. But it had been a fine afternoon through the ranges, where high waterfalls threaded down gorges to the valley floors patterned by vineyards. Neat fields gave place to jagged rocks outcropping on the mountainsides, thick hanging forests swept down and then relented where patchwork paddy-fields began. Once we went down a long, snaking road, crossed a high bridge over a river that rushed wildly down its gorge, and climbed up the other side again to new perspectives.

Perhaps because of its mountains or because of its neat, well-ordered husbandry, this area was known as the 'Brazilian Switzerland'. But it was as much like Switzerland as São Paulo was like Chicago, which is to say, hardly like it at all, though it was a useful label for use in guide-books.

Dona Isabel missed seeing the last mile of our drive through the flat quasi-industrial suburb of Porto Alegre, because she had her nose in the mirror of her powder compact. She reminded me of the toucan in the Brazilian legend who sat one day admiring his splendid beak in a pool. Because of it, he considered himself worthy to be king of the birds. He hopped into a hollow tree and with his beautiful beak protruding announced this to all the passing birds. The great and colourful beak impressed them and all agreed, even the great spoonbills of the northern marshes, that the toucan should indeed be king. Only the blackbird disagreed. He wanted to see the body which went with the beak. When the poor toucan came out of the tree and showed his insignificant body, the blackbird cried 'Why you are nothing but beak' and all the other birds so shrieked with laughter that the toucan flew away in shame.

The only birds I had seen sitting on the farm fences that afternoon had been a type of blackbird. I would have loved to hear their comment as we got out at Porto Alegre, with Dona Isabel at least two tones brighter with powder and lipstick, her beak a little too noticeable.

12

Port Wines

The old man was arguing, first in German then in Portuguese. He was so drunk that he used both languages even in one sentence. His younger companion said nothing but solemnly absorbed the old man's pronouncements. In fact, his only contribution was to make the older one take out his wallet and search among its bare compartments to see if enough money remained for one more beer.

Except for the fluorescent lights and walls tiled like a public lavatory, the café could have been a French bistro. There were tables with none-too-white cloths and shelf after shelf lined with bottles of local wine. I had a bottle of claret and it cost me less than a pint of best beer would have done in London. The regulars arrived and sat at their usual tables. A fat Spanish type of man came in with a beret and a fat woman. A *gaucho* lugubriously ate three platefuls of soup. Four noisy youngsters in the tight Italian suits and winkle-picker shoes you could see any night in the Edgware Road sat over glasses of beer arguing about football and swopping photographs of girls. There were two or three seamen, for the bar was near the docks. They were intrigued by a destitute character who smeared the black dust of some drug on the palms of their hands and showed them how to inhale it together with cigarette smoke, but the seamen would buy none. There were also unshaven, throat-slitting characters who, it turned out, were perfectly harmless stall-keepers from the vegetable market outside.

But the old man took notice of nobody and carried on endless eulogies of his son, though what the son had done to deserve them I could not hear. When the wallet was at last empty and the contents of the old man's big brief-case restored after a search for possible further lurking cruzeiros, he and his silent friend got up to go. Because I had spoken to none of them I said *auf wiedersehen* as they passed.

'*Ach! ein deutcher,*' he exclaimed, and promptly sat down at my table. So did the friend. They had two more bottles of beer each, during which the old man discovered that I was not German, and I discovered that he praised his son because the boy had passed his examinations top of the class, and because now, at twenty-one years old, he was going to start his course as a civil engineer, which, as the fond father said, was more than *he* had ever done, though he had constructed some of Porto Alegre's tallest buildings, including the latest one of twenty-five storeys. He had, moreover, spent a good number of years before the war building in Hamburg, but although both his parents had been German he was born in Porto Alegre and had no wish for me to think that he was anything other than Brazilian. After this, the point of incoherence was reached and the solemn, silent friend tactfully suggested a withdrawal, promising to be there the following night. The old man, however, insisted on paying for the drinks by pawning his pocket watch to the bar owner. The watch had obviously been in and out on numerous previous occasions, so that all was well.

I finished my second bottle of wine and went into the sea-tang of Porto Alegre's night air, more than pleased with my first day in that oddest, yet most captivating, of Brazilian ports. It was not late; trams still rumbled across the square, and cars bumped over the cobbles. But there was a going-home atmosphere nevertheless. Somewhere, just near at hand along the quay, some sailors were singing as they went back to ship or after the girls who lurked in warehouse doorways. I did not stray far and sat under the trees in the Praça 15 de Novembro. It was a small square, and in the day-time was an island of calm in a sea of traffic and trams. On three sides of it the town's towers soared, the new twenty-storey cloud-scrapers (they were not high enough to be real skyscrapers), for Porto Alegre was not only up but coming. Five years previously few, if any, of the modern office and apartment blocks had reached above the older streets. Now, besides the completed blocks, the Porto Alegre skyline was a chessboard, squared by the frames of still-newer and even higher buildings. On some sites the sun glistened through an aerial web of steel, and at night welders' arc torches flashed like the aurora borealis.

In spite of being the up-and-coming capital of Rio Grande do Sul, a state larger than England and Holland together, Porto Alegre was as salty as a plate of whelks. Its jauntiness was like the jauntiness of an Irish air. There was a tingle in the tune of it, and a lightness in the beat of it that would set your feet a-flying in the gayest of jigs. And Porto Alegre's was a different music from that of any place in Brazil.

Porto Alegre's flame was not the same as that which burnt São Paulo. The two kinds of vitality were very different. And because Porto Alegre hugged the coast and the feet of hills behind it, and also had an outlying Terezopolis and a Petropolis, a Leblon and an Ipanema, and surprisingly even a Niteroi, the town was more than just a miniature Rio de Janeiro. The place was not even typically Brazilian, for, of course, as I had discovered, no place was. For me, Brazil was a collection of highly individual, unique people and places which always contradicted preconceived images, and nearly always for the better.

So during my first day I tasted the jaunty, salty air of Porto Alegre. Also, everywhere I went I found that it was odd, like surrealist paintings. The town's recent sudden development seemed to have taken it by surprise. The last word in modernity made a strange bed-fellow with the older way of life. The bold flanks of cloudscrapers rose above the still-narrow streets and balconied houses of the old town. The riveters' hammers on new steel structures rang together with the delicate clatter of pony-traps on the cobbled streets below. Some of Brazil's most beautifully dressed women and up-from-the-country *gauchos* rubbed shoulders in the coffee bars.

The centre's main streets were the oddest and certainly the most wonderful of all, for there the human being had the upper hand over the motor car. A number of streets were closed altogether to cars.

In others, any driver so impudent as to intrude on the groups of people had to wait until they chose to let him pass. Mostly, however, drivers knew their place. It was strictly a man's affair, this late afternoon to early evening lounging, talking, arguing, telling of jokes all over the roads and pavements. Groups and knots of students and business men and those with nothing to do filled the streets from end to end. The noise of voices was louder than the noise of cars and trams in neighbouring streets and almost too loud for conversation to be heard. This classical forum in modern dress showed that the motor-car need not, after all, destroy civilization.

Sixty families from the Azores settled in Porto Alegre two centuries ago. But however markedly Portuguese the original town might have been, other influences had heavily overlaid it since. Perhaps the town lay too near the Uruguayan, Paraguayan and Argentinian borders, and was too early the scene of German immigration, to keep any early character from the Azores. The mixture of races may not have been as rich as São Paulo's, but Porto Alegre always had one quality which São Paulo could never have— a direct link with the sea and ships.

The Atlantic lay more than sixty miles away, overland as the crow flies. But ships approached it down the length of the Lake of Ducks. This was a narrow freshwater lagoon, stretching for more than a hundred and fifty miles from its outlet in the sea to the town's quays at its head. But the docks were not extensive, and so the town itself crowded almost to the water's edge. Some of the tallest buildings looked as though a high wind would topple them into the water.

Two of the main squares gave on to the quays. Except for dock buildings, they would have had a view across to a jigsaw of islands. Here the five rivers feeding the lake emptied themselves through tortuous waterways. Small tankers threaded their way gingerly up the river channels to refineries beyond the town. But from the two squares, funnels and masts could be seen over the dock shed roofs and the occasional noise of ships' sirens drowned the trams' clanking and the noise of talkers in the non-traffic streets. The comings and goings of the sea were intimately part of the town itself and, indeed, were a factor in its present spurt of prosperity.

Even the market flanked the quayside as though the hundred
different fruits and vegetables had been caught like fish in the
lagoon. By nine o'clock at night the market got under way. The
baskets and boxes laid in neat rows in the market square held an
astonishing variety of produce not only of tropical fruits but every
European kind, too. With meticulous care, everything for sale was
sorted and graded to size and quality. There was precision in the
pattern of rows and boxes and of round, shining fruit or leafy
lettuces or cabbages or strange roots which I had never seen before. The whole was laid out like a jeweller's window display. Some
of the things gleaming in the lamplight were not unlike precious
stones. The stall-holders had their own music of voices, singing,
piping, making an orchestration with the customers' background
murmur.

During the day, no trace of the night market remained, though
under the trees in the square next to the market-place there were
basket-women selling freshly cut roses. Roses bloomed, too, in the
square and in all the town's *praças*, adding touches of brighter
colour to the heavy green of palms and plane-trees and to the sombre
tones of bronze statues. The basket-women's limpid, Cupid-lipped
roses could be bought for a song. There were so many women I
could not see how any of them could sell enough to make their
business pay. But then the square, which was quite small, supported
no less than fourteen photographers each with a comic music-hall
camera on a tripod and a black hood. I only once saw one of them
buried under his hood while a woman sat stiffly, gazing mute with
terror at the lens as though it had the evil eye.

In contrast to the rose-women and the fourteen photographers,
shoeshine boys did a roaring trade, for Porto Alegre was as conscious
of its feet as of its hands. Both were well cultivated. To wear
unpolished, or poorly polished shoes on those immaculate, tessellated pavements was worse than to wear no shoes at all, like the
many labourers and streetboys who did not. The hordes of shoeshine boys were kept constantly busy. Most were mobile with their
own home-made footrest-cum-seat and a range of rags and tins of
polish to cope with any kind of shoe. The shine they produced

would have warmed the heart of a Guards regimental sergeant-major. To stand and have your shoes cleaned while chatting to your friends was a kind of social tic, as were those endless tiny cups of coffee everybody drank all through the day.

The Porto Alegrenses were equally proud of their hands, and manicurists and manicure equipment were as vital to the well-dressed man as the shoeshine boys. Many men had varnished finger-nails. And here, as elsewhere in Brazil, was another curious habit which was popular in the Middle East years ago, that of allowing the nail of the little finger to grow long, sometimes up to an inch. This, I supposed, was to show that the wearer never did manual work, and was therefore a social cut above the labourer. So much for the dignity of work!

The waiter at my table in the hotel had these long nails, and I once saw him in a barber's shop which opened to the street, being given a shave, manicure, and a shoe-polish all at once by three different people. He was most anxious to learn English, he said, because it would help him to get a better job. He also said that he liked England very much, not that he had ever been there, but he knew all about the Royal Family and Mr. Armstrong-Jones. Then he asked in what part of the U.S.A. *was* England, and how long did it take to go by car from New York to London. For the rest of my stay I tried to improve his sense of geography. He was grateful. I drew maps on paper napkins. One morning at breakfast I drew on an egg making it into a globe. He was fascinated. On the morning of my departure he wished me *bon voyage*, thanked me again for giving him so many new English words, and it was right, wasn't it, that London was not actually *in* New York but just outside.

The hotel was itself an instance of Porto Alegre's odd variance between new and old. The neon sign in a narrow street off the photographers' square announced that it was 'modern', but the bathrooms all had German-looking wood-burning stoves in the corner which heated the water and behind them were stacks of logs. The bedrooms were about fifteen feet high with circular ventilation holes at the top; a good idea, since Porto Alegre's summer temperature was often over the hundred degree mark. But the place

was scrupulously clean and the food excellent, though—odd again—
the dining-room was lined with white tiles and lit with fluorescent
lamps which seemed to be the town's sole idea for the decoration of
dining-rooms, as I had observed in the bar by the market. But the
hotel was not without its moments, such as when I caught a glimpse
down a corridor of the beautiful Russian maid bent over her sewing
and looking exactly like the famous Dutch painting.

Although the street map of Porto Alegre promised a dull town
visually, the opposite proved to be true. For each street, though
part of a fairly regular grid arrangement, had unique character,
particularly in the town's waterside centre. Here the new buildings
were tallest, and the shops were the smartest and consequently
most expensive. Their neon signs almost touched across the narrow
streets in the brightest reds and blues and yellows, like the banners
of a Chinese festival. Near the hotel an arcade was almost completed, with small shops to cater for the tourist and sailor ashore.
One of these had a fantastic display of Japanese bric-à-brac, with
two Japanese girls as assistants. They were just right with the
beautifully-made dolls of geishas, except that the girls were Brazilians
and only spoke Portuguese. Their parents perhaps had been
Japanese-born, like so many of the market gardeners I had seen in the
market-place.

When evening came on the shops stayed open, keeping the streets
alive after dark. Music filled them as it had done all day, music from
the record-shop loudspeakers which boomed here as they did in all
Brazilian cities. But Porto Alegre also had a special music—from
the street corner accordionists. One man sat on the corner near the
hotel. He was old and blind and seemed to know only one tune which
he played continuously for hours on end, sometimes fitting in
snatches of words. This was a perfect arrangement for passers-by,
who caught only a phrase or two of the melody, dropped a few
cruzeiros into the old man's hat and then went about their business.

But whenever I was in my first-floor room, which faced the street
and looked down to the tram roofs from a balcony, the dreary tune
went on all day. But sometimes it did change, and that was when a
twelve-year-old boy took the old man's accordion and played it

himself. The boy had fine blond hair and could easily have been German—as could the beer-garden sort of music they played. At other street corners, Porto Alegre also had other accordionists, also playing similar German beer-music, though most of the others seemed to have a larger repertoire than my old man. No doubt the songs originated in Germany and had been handed down perhaps for more than a century, becoming Brazilianized on the way by acquiring Portuguese words. There was not, I thought, any influence of the *fado* from Portugal, nor of Brazil's own African music of the north. Perhaps they were *gaucho* songs.

That's what streets are for—music, and standing about with your friends, or wandering about from shops to cafés without fear of being run down by motor-cars, and also perhaps especially for processions. I was in Porto Alegre on 21st April, the day when Tiradentes was martyred in 1792 on the Rio de Janeiro gallows. The Brazilians did not forget him, or lose sight of their freedom. During my whole journey through Brazil talk always turned to the subject of independence, not political, for that was old history, but to economic. And in that sphere there was as much fierce determination as ever possessed Tiradentes and his fellow fighters.

So processions, though loved for their own sake, served a still deeper purpose for Brazilians, a purpose beyond the brilliance of the cavalry parade I saw on Tiradentes Day. It passed through the squares with the sun catching the white of uniforms and the polished brass of helmets and accoutrements. There were lances, too, and among the horses' decorations a curious tattooed checkerboard pattern on their rumps. For Tiradentes, the town turned out everything on feet or wheels it could muster and the procession ended, after the white and gold of the cavalry, with the fire brigade's bright red. This was a fine blaze of colour and of sound too, for the fire-engines' sirens were going all at once in an eerie but penetrating fanfare.

Another occasion for Porto Alegre was the first-year university students' procession. This was a wild, fancy-dress affair with tableaux and floats from which rice straw was showered over the spectators, particularly over the women. I had wondered why the prettiest and youngest girls had made sure of getting good places in front of the crowds. Their screams were the loudest under the showers of straw, and the students made sure they got more than anybody else. Wit is brevity, not to say briefs, even in Porto Alegre. Amongst the public figures lampooned by dressed-up or undressed students was the typical Englishman. He carried a notice which said 'The British Look', and wore nothing but a pair of Y-fronted pants.

Normally, however, the students were as seemly as students ever can be, and haunted the tree-lined avenues near the various faculty buildings and the broad walks of the Parque Farroupilha—a large triangle of parkland wedged into the town. It was a green, clean park, beautifully kept and crammed with a multitude of different tropical plants. The grass could be walked upon and the water of its pools was fresh. Rowing-boats moved calmly over its lake and on a Sunday afternoon hundreds of people went to look at the free zoo. The water birds were the zoo's main splendour. Their plumage had a soft sheen and a whole range of subtle colours that made the brilliance of macaws and toucans crude by comparison. Nine sleepy alligators occupied a pen, lying on their stretch of sand like potential handbags and pairs of shoes. Perhaps to them Porto Alegre's park was really no different from the basking banks of great rivers like the Araguaia at Bananal. Certainly to look at them you would think alligators had no brains at all.

Outside the town's centre, beyond the reach of the smarter shops and bars, the docks and dubious dolly-dives stretched along the shore opposite the river mouths and islands. A new highway, sweeping across the rivers and marshes on concrete stilts, was partially completed. It swung away from the town, high above tree-tops and house-tops, and doubling back on the farther side of the channel, turned to the south. This was the road down to Monte-video, which lay only twelve hours' driving away, and the last stretch of main road leading out of Brazil. A section of the road over the water was made as a lift bridge so that the tankers could go upriver to the refinery.

The town approach to this highway was along the nondescript dock road which alternated between sudden, guilty areas of squalor

and others of the trim neatness which I had come to expect in Porto
Alegre. But the down-and-outs hung about the bars here hoping
for the price of a drink from loitering seamen. From among the
flotsam and jetsam of scrapyards and small factories, gypsies and
poverty-stricken women tried to scavenge things which could be
used in their tents or shacks. They shambled by on their drum-
stick legs with two bundles, the first in front and the second behind,
tied together and slung over their shoulders.

On one Saturday morning they were able to fill their bags with
cat-fish which were shovelled out of the local power station's sewers
along with swarms of sardines. Perhaps Saturday was a regular
sewer-day, so that the women and their tired-looking children could
always be sure of a large and free dinner. The fish must have invaded
the sewers by way of the lagoon and have blocked the pipes. Great
wheelbarrow loads of wriggling fish were taken away, and thousands
of sardines lay taking their last gasps in the gutters.

The railway line also ran by the docks and along the main dock
road, so that the trains were mixed up with trams and tramps and
pony-traps. The engines had cow-catchers in front. But it was not
likely that anybody would get in the way, for the engine was like
those early American ones covered with hooters and funnels and
pipes from which screams of steam escaped. The engines let off
dismal wails from their whistles as they puffed along the dock road.
And the driver tolled a great bell on the boiler, as if the train were
a reminder of the Ouro Preto bells which rang for Tiradentes'
death.

No less a period piece than the engines was the railway station
itself, an essay in Victorian architectural obesity, utterly incongruous
in its setting. However, I was not looking for the station, but for a
bar on the corner opposite. The *Rubens* had docked at Porto Alegre
and some of my friends from the crew were waiting for me at the
marble-topped tables. A cold wind bringing rain blew from the
lagoon when I walked by the deserted station, lit at night by sinister
lamps. I followed the railway track on the road, a pattern identical
with that of Swansea docks. This was a strange link, for the two ports
were the extremities of my journey. Porto Alegre's railway station

could have fitted without so much as a blush into the Swansea dockland and so could the corner bar, for the voices that came out into the wet street were English and Welsh.

Not many of the old crew remained, for seamen are restless. Some think no more of changing ship than they do of changing their shirt—a change that sometimes takes place for both ship and shirt at the end of each voyage. The ship's carpenter had not left, of course, for without Chippy, she would just not have been the *Rubens* any more. He was the ship's *doppelgänger*. But even Chippy had not always been on her. When he lost his ship at the beginning of the war he spent five years as a prisoner in Germany, and it was on another ship afterwards that heavy seas smashed him against the gunwale, leaving him with his slow walk.

My friends in the bar were already looking forward to the next ports of call up the coast. And for several weeks I would enjoy their company before returning to Rio de Janeiro and later to England. The crew knew these coastal towns as a series of bars with names which sounded as romantic as ships' names—Denmark, Texas, Oasis, Big Ben, Heart Break Hotel. In the principal port of Santos on the island of São Vicente, there was Hellfire Corner, a district of dives outside the docks, and at the further end of Santos' curving, fashionable beach, another but slightly more respectable district called by seamen Blue Star Village—for a reason that nobody seemed to know.

By stopping along this chain of little ports, I had a strong impression of the way that early settlements in Brazil had clung tenaciously to the coast. Some of those towns seemed to be copies of identical sea villages along the coast of Portugal, as though the Atlantic, which separated them, was no more than a lake. Yet that was only a first impression. The difference, in reality, was as great as that between Brazil's cities today and the same cities depicted in graceful eighteenth-century prints. For as the *Rubens* worked its way up the coast, taking on araucaria pines here, coffee beans there, tapioca or oranges, dried hides (inoffensive), wet hides (most offensive), soya meal, cotton, cotton, cotton (enough you would have thought to keep the mills of Lancashire busy for a year), I saw the special Brazilian genius for being happy. The air sparkled, the sea sparkled, and the eyes and smiles and laughter sparkled, for the Brazilian's happiness was the exuberance of being alive.

Joie de vivre is the first and simplest of the arts, more highly developed in Romance countries than elsewhere, and perhaps most of all in Brazil. That was one reason why I liked São Francisco do Sul. The little town also pleased me because I was reminded of Ouro Preto. In some ways it excelled the goldmining town five hundred miles away up in the mountains of Minas Gerais. Ouro Preto's many churches stood on their hill-tops as perfect as Greek temples and in a light no less clear or golden. But they lacked the sea to add its blueness to the sky's, and to throw that sparkle into the air. The walls of coastal buildings have that added brightness to catch and transmute into vibrant colour, glowing like molten gold.

Ouro Preto saw molten gold often enough, but never the sea light which radiated from the neat, balconied, cool-roomed little houses along São Francisco's bay. Nor were the mining town's churches, for all their gilding inside, as golden as the walls of the little port's church. It had two blue-tiled domes on its twin towers, and was saturated with the glare from the *praça* surrounding it. Somebody, at some time, had been wise enough to make a formal garden at one side of the square and set shady trees in it. In the hottest part of the day, life moved to this shade, or into the shade of open shop doorways round the square, while the door of the church itself was shut until a more reasonable and cooler hour.

Behind the church was a hill and houses hiding behind bougainvillaea and Cape jasmine. But higher up—where one could look across these gardens and the tops of the trees in the square, across the speckled pantiled roofs of church and town, and even over those two blue domes—the sea itself came into view, with its distant rim of blue mountains receding in layers. The scene was classical. There should have been some mythology of gods concerning the place, and perhaps in a way there was, in the proper place, too— the church. Before the statue of Our Lady of Seafarers, lifebuoys were hung. They bore the names of ships, and the names of all the crews and the dates when the lifebuoys were put in the church. But

PORT WINES

I would not have been surprised to have seen Aphrodite rising from the bay.

São Francisco's bay was more beautiful, though not so spectacular as Rio de Janeiro's. It was more lyrical than the stark drama of Rio, softer yet more radiant in its colour. To enhance the splendour, glistening white gulls sailed over the ships and the little town. These were lesser black-backed gulls, bearing on their upper wings a deep charcoal hue. The cry of gulls is a sad sound anywhere in the world, and was no less so in São Francisco do Sul. Although most of the houses, particularly those facing across the bay, were Portuguese in character with their wrought iron and *azulejos* and ornate plasterwork, not all were so. Some were curiously Danish: low, singled-storeyed, yellow-washed houses which might have been in a Jutland fishing village or the Odense of Hans Andersen's childhood. Yet another part, a narrow street between rows of warehouses, was strikingly French, like a courtyard from Versailles.

While I was wandering dreamily about the town, or swimming from one of the white sandy beaches, the crew, of course, was working. So were the stevedores loading the odd, odourless araucaria pine into the *Rubens's* holds. But the evenings (which extended into the night and usually ended long after daylight) belonged to everybody. São Francisco do Sul was so small that you could be certain to find friends in each of the pleasant bars; those by the waterfront or those on the higher road leading into the town square. The town was not tourist-conscious and existed for ships and sailors. Just as the church had been given the lifebuoys, so the bars had been given mess-room plates from hundreds of different ships which had called at the little port. Like the lifebuoys, each plate bore the name of the ship it came from and the date. They hung precariously on the tiered shelves of bottles. Each plate also bore a picture crudely painted—a tropical island maybe, or a fantastic sunset, or a moonlight scene with silhouetted palms.

These pictures were not up to the standard of Aert van der Neer, of course, but then the Dutch moon-master himself could hardly have improved upon the silver-drenched nights which fell over the sea town and its wide bay. Perhaps the Spanish silversmiths, whose

249

style was borrowed for Plateresque architecture, got ideas for their craft from the intricate pattern of such moonlight on such water as São Francisco's bay. But in thinking this perhaps I was fashioning nature after art again. I wondered if the pines being loaded on to the *Rubens* had been cut when the moon was waning. There was a widespread superstition about this in Brazil. Even architects told me, apparently in earnest, that timber cut in the waning of the moon would consequently warp and twist. That woodwork *did* warp I knew well from many ill-fitting doors and drawers.

We did not stay more than four days in São Francisco. I left it reluctantly, dreaming equally of its heaped platefuls of fried prawns and of the town and the bay. The prawns, served like potato-crisps in bars, were enormous, sweet creatures that quite put to shame the embryo-like things that went by the same name in England. The best place for them was the Jacara Bar, a small place next to the town's cinema and a hundred yards from the quay and the *praça*. The Jacara's principal glory, apart from the prawns and the hot pine-nuts (tastier than chestnuts) sold by little boys who went in all the bars, was the patio completely canopied by purple bougainvillaea. Orchids sprouted all over the twisting branches. Beautiful flowers of another sort—those on two legs—attracted the sailors to the place, and to the clinking of glasses and bottles there was added a babbling in many tongues, not quite drowned by music from a loudspeaker hidden in the bougainvillaea. But old tales of the sea and new ones of love were the same in any language.

We had to leave São Francisco, and the *Rubens* put out to sea, heavier than before with tons of timber, and heavier, too, with another load of memories. For since sailors are restless, they never know when they have seen a place, or a face, for the last time. The gulls followed us out, their deep-toned mewing echoing from the quay, their strident laughter coming after us in mockery. Then the birds wheeled away, soared over the yellow-walled warehouse standing in the water on stone arches where we had berthed. Still crying and mocking, they swept over the local fishing-boats, which were strange craft hollowed from a single tree trunk and fitted with a square Oriental-looking sail. When we left them behind, the gulls' mocking laughter seemed no longer aimed at us, but at the coming and going of all ships. In a few hours, a few days, they would swoop over the other ships at São Francisco, and laugh as they, too, weighed anchor, broke the perfect reflection in that placid blue bay and headed away to sea.

I had a lot of explaining to do at my hotel in Rio de Janeiro. The negress maid on the fourteenth floor who looked after my old room would not rest content until I told her every detail of my southern journey. Her eyes grew wide with wonder and sympathy as the list of towns and cities and rivers and mountains and plains grew. I had, she said, seen the whole world—except Belem. I blushed and had to admit that I had not yet been to her native Belem. Ah! she said triumphantly, you have *not* seen Brazil then. Now in Belem, she went on, blazing with enthusiasm, there is the Ver-o-Peso (See the Weight) market with all the fruits and wonder of the Amazon delta. Just you wait until you get to Belem, really to see Brazil!

But I did not have to wait, in order to see Brazil.

If I simply shut my eyes, wherever I might be, a thousand images cavalcaded before my inner eye, the sun to dazzle and shine from huge skies where piles of cloud sailed over wide rivers. I could see endless forests and empty uplands. And I could conjure up the small villages and the many-towered coastal cities, and that mirage (had it ever been real?) on the great plateau—Brasilia, and the splendour of gilded carving and rococo stone at Ouro Preto. And when these passed there came before my secret eye the moving forms of strong, bronzed bodies, and the smiling black eyes and gleaming teeth of the negro, and the Indian and the lighter-skinned ones, and all the loved faces of my Brazilian friends, and the unknown faces I had passed in the street or saw in the buses or glimpsed as they went by on horseback, the faces of children from the angel bands of the Resurrection Morning's procession, and the faces of luckless, happy shoeshines curled asleep in midnight doorways.

And deaf to less happy sounds, my inner ear could hear laughter in the shade of palms and the fever-in-the-blood of endless sambas. . . .

No, never in my life would I have to wait to see Brazil. It would always be with me.

251

Index

253

INDEX

INDEX

INDEX